What's Coming Next

A CHANNELED GUIDE TO NAVIGATING THE GREATEST SHIFT OF OUR TIME

Anne Tucker

Published by Anne Tucker Healing and Training, LLC.

ISBN: 979-8-218-52741-9

Contents

"

Thus, we say for yourselves to be in attention. To quell your wondering, but to hold this knowledge at a distance from the self. To let it be an apparition to contemplate, to become aware of, and to release. To let the Self imbue and harness the reality of this instant with that future cadence which you know is coming, but resist the temptation to be always in attendance of that next offering. To be wanting, waiting. For in that state of harkening what is not here, you are resisting - relinquishing the gift that is ready.

"

— The Angels, 11.16.22

Introduction

This book is both a story and a reference book. It is a selected compilation of messages I've received over the past four years from the Angels about the collective shift in consciousness we are currently experiencing.

The messages are sorted into topic areas, and then listed chronologically within each topic area. Being able to read all the Angels' messages about a specific topic area at once will give you a much deeper understanding of these important times that we are in. You can read the book all the way through, or browse and read what interests you.

There is an overall summary at the start of each topic area, and a short summary at the start of each message. Most of the messages have a QR code which links to an associated video on YouTube where you can hear my analysis of the message. In some videos, you can also hear the original channeling.

Many people have asked how they can talk to their family about the shift. In the summary of Part 1, I give an overview of what the shift is and why it's happening now. Sharing this summary would be an easy way to sum up and explain the shift to others.

Anne Tucker
Seattle
October 17, 2024

Where We Are Headed:
A Vision of Our Future

If you dared to dream about a utopian world, what would it be like? I think if we all compared notes on our utopian visions, there would be certain themes and ideas that would be consistent for all of us. World peace, a clean and healthy Earth, a deeper sense of connection, respect and love between people, the end of suffering, freedom of time and personal expression, and living in harmony with all life on Earth. And stretching just a bit further, maybe we would be traveling beyond our world as citizens of an immense galaxy that is waiting to be discovered.

What if that shared dream isn't a dream at all? What if that is your intuitive understanding of where we are going?

The main obstacle that rises between us and our shared dream is that humanity isn't capable of world peace. We aren't ready. Something huge would have to happen to change us before we could get past our anger, hatred, selfishness, jealousy and separation. If you ever listen to the news, it often feels like there is more darkness in the world than there is light.

But that is why this time we live in is so incredible. Something big is coming, and it will change us. In fact, our transformation has already begun.

We are in the midst of a grand shift in consciousness. To better understand what this might be like, imagine that you are embroiled in an angry argument. You are barely hearing what the other person says, because you are focused on what you will say next. You are filled with emotion and aren't thinking clearly. You aren't seeing or hearing the other person's perspective, and you may even be reading into their actions and words because you are lost in your own words, thoughts, stories and emotions.

This is the general state of consciousness we all share today. We walk through our lives lost in our own thoughts, seeing things from our own isolated perspective which is crafted from our personal curated collection of wounds and limiting beliefs.

Then imagine, in the middle of that argument, you are struck with a sudden realization that you are seeing the entire argument through an old wound. You realize that the hurt you are blaming on this person and this moment actually lived in your heart from a childhood experience. There were just enough parallels between this argument and your childhood pain that it brought your old wound to the surface.

You suddenly see yourself, and you can now hear the other person. You begin to listen to their words and feel what they are trying to communicate. You see things as they actually are, as opposed to seeing them through the filter of your own wounds.

This is a fair example of a sudden awakening in one moment for one person. Now imagine that this type of awakening happens all at once, for many people at the same time, because of a sudden and massive influx of light that hits the planet.

The timing of this shift isn't random, and it isn't some sort of judgment against humankind. The shift is part of a much larger cycle that occurs approximately every 24,000 years, during which our solar system orbits around a sister star that some believe to be the star Sirius. As we orbit closer to that star, we experience more light, and consequently, a higher state of conscious awareness.

This 24,000-year cycle appears in the wisdom of many different traditions. It is known as the Yuga cycle in Hinduism, and it is also seen in astrology as the progression of ages through the 12 astrological signs, each age lasting 2,000 years.

For the past 12,000 years, we have been orbiting away from the sister star, going further and further into the darkness. This has looked like imbalance and polarity.

Everything on Earth is meant to live in a balance between two opposing and interdependent energies. These are referred to as yin and yang energies, or masculine and feminine energy (which has nothing to do with being a man or a woman). You can also think of it as the positive and negative poles of a battery. The top of our heads would be like the positive end of the battery, and our feet are the negative pole.

Everything in our world dances between these two energies, and it is the balance of these energies that allows us to create. We experience this energy with every breath, expanding into our masculine or yang energy as we inhale, and relaxing into our feminine or yin energy as we exhale.

The gradual building of our masculine, or yang, energy over the past 12,000 years has been enormously helpful to humankind, like a great, big inhale. Because of the expression of this energy, we developed the technologies and structures of society that have enabled our civilizations to grow and flourish. Technology and structure are aspects of masculine energy.

Traveling along our 24,000-year orbit, moving farther and farther away from our sister star and into increasing darkness, has caused us to fall out of balance and over-express our masculine or yang energy. We have become an exaggerated version of ourselves, and this has increased the separation or polarization between people, as well as concentrating wealth and resources into the hands of the few. It's like being at the peak of an inhale, and we are now in the process of turning in our orbit to begin our slow voyage back into balance and into the light. We are ready to exhale.

The utopia of our dreams is emerging from within us. We are being freed from the inside out. And what an amazing world we are going to create!

UPDATE ON THE AWAKENING FROM THE ANGELS!
January 31, 2021

In this message, the Angels tell us that our traditional institutions and power structures will fall, and we will be replaced with enlightened methods of self-governance which will give us much more freedom. We won't have to dedicate our lives to just getting by and making a living. Instead, our lives will become fuller, and we will perceive more of the richness of our experience. They tell us that this period of polarization and separation has been helpful because we've gotten to know ourselves much better, opening the doorway to connect to our higher selves. There will still be many who stay in separation and resist these changes, but the Angels say their fear will subside, and over time we will see that they recognize the light you carry.

Channeled Message

We are now beginning. We speak today about the scene happening here upon your shores; the opening of our instigation of meaningful transformation. You may wonder how we will proceed. It is for the benefit of mankind, this is all. We wish to be in service to your benefit and we are helping with this unfoldment to instigate change within your being, to allow your transformation and enable you to have connection to each other and beyond.

This change, fortuitous in nature, happens with the withdrawal from seated traditions, from contemporary situations of oppression and structure not welcome to your beneficent nature. These patterns of being restrictive will be replaced with more enlightened methods of self-governance.

You will find it simpler to connect among yourselves and won't need the formal patterns of structure that have enabled your peacekeeping and alignment within connected communities.

We are helping to lift that which burdens you all; those patterns beholden to another man, to he who wields the power and control, not distributed to many as should become in this next context. You will be enabled to be more central to your own self-governance, creating more freedom of expression in how you will be on Earth.

You will connect more easily to one another and find those who are following your same directives, who have within themselves the same call to be free and one, separate from the whole of continuity created within this passing era.

You can have much to be excited about in this new unfolding. You will be present to witness more of your life, less ensconced in the trivialities of endurance, of being instructed in life's ways of doing and having and survival of your basic needs.

These are still prevalent - you are continuing to require all the sustenance and happenings of humanity as it has always been. But you will now find yourselves open more pleasant experiences of your existence here. You will find how we may be helping to assist you with this up-leveling of your awareness. You can become more attuned to your own desires. Your own experience becomes richer and fuller.

You see more through the same aperture. Your vision expands to include more subtle gifts brought through tender appreciation of your own self and acknowledging the gifts of your surroundings. Of seeing these with eyes unfettered by difficulty, by the pain of your suffering. These eyes renewed can view the same vista before them and incorporate the knowing of their own dignity, of their view to surrender into each moment and reflect upon its brilliance, it's overwhelming potency of life. Tranquility descends upon yourself in new ways yet unknown by many.

This separation from the busyness of your existence will become habitual and permeate your awareness more regularly to inform how you view your surroundings. Yourself surrendered to this night of temperate joy and breathe in the perfume of love of compassion, of helping and serving, but always remaining present to this awareness of self as one part of this masterful, beautiful Vista.

It has become temperate and calm within yourselves with this due time of separation from one another. Your energies have calmed and pooled within yourselves and allow for clarity of knowing, of curiosity expelled, and central integration informed by your own sweet self.

You have become more enlightened in this process and unveiled the portal for your own becoming, that through-put where you will focus your mind to find your deeper self. This place of wonder internal, of daydreaming and finding yourself amiss, of centering your thoughts in the clouds, firmly battened but not described by yourself, not understood in the same manner. These thoughts have pulled you away from the moment, from the cares and trials of your lives. They have drawn you in and up into the realm of imagination, of clarity, of self-awareness. They have opened the portal for your connection to self-mastery.

You are welcome to join yourself, your "self" above, your masterful expression of all integrity, of all time and being, of all oneness. This "self" resides in this place of imagination, of self-exploration, of conversations internal had quietly in the recess of your minds. These conversations about happenings, puzzling (the) nature of your happiness, the realm of your thoughts most explorative and curious - they are all welcomed here.

You are wondering how we might startle this ongoing experiment of being to incorporate this great advancement. We say have faith in our plan. The unfolding appears most readily. You will find the occurrence of your fearful experiences is not far off and will be jolting for many. This residual fear you may carry must be dispelled. Do not allow yourself to worry that you will be carried away in some fearful flood of your own undoing. It is not for your fearful intention that we wish to explain this happening. We wish to absolve all your fears, to relax your being into peaceful extrapolation, to extend your tranquility into the surround, into those happenings which appear on the horizon.

You see the indications the struggle begins among those intent on separating themselves from one another. They fight this upliftment. They want self-indulgence and fear the connection we seek to provide. It is once forsaken by themselves, and we will persevere to attempt to reunite them with this obstacle that they avoid. We see their fear. Separation feels like safety, and we say not to have fear of their reaction. To understand, they will subside, and you will find this eternal gift becoming more frequently unveiled in those to whom you connect.

You will see how we are present, causing their eyes to drift into focus, to see your truth and admire your reflection of self-expression. They will become capable of absorbing your meaning more fully and find within themselves the portal of understanding each other. This is how we envision your future to come. It will be another invention of spirit within yourselves, to be enjoyed and enabled by our constant provision of love and caring. We have said much, rest now.

UPLIFTING CHANNELED MESSAGE ABOUT WHAT'S COMING
June 10, 2021

In this message, the Angels tell us that we will be living without the same challenges we've experienced. It will be much easier to create our experience consciously, and there will be much more peace and harmony on Earth. But because we are co-creating this new reality, it is essential that we focus on our healing now so that we are creating from a higher vibration.

At the end of this passage is something you don't want to miss. I'm including part of the message that wasn't in the YouTube video because I channeled it a little earlier and it came through awkwardly, as if words were out of order. I was still strengthening my connection and was probably just a little tired. But the message is intriguing! I think as we move through this shift in consciousness, humanity may eventually create a new civilization that feels very different from how we live today. We may find ourselves intuitively drawn to specific areas on the planet that are "hallowed ground", to create a new kind of city where we will live simply but beautifully in "tiny alcoves of warmth and cleanliness".

Channeled Message

You say you have begun speaking as to how this unfolds, the great turning of our template for humanity. How will all resolve to remain here? What will it be like upon completion of this great upending and resolution of forces therein being sanctified ceremoniously to appeal all to this highest outcome and vibration? We are enthralled with the progress you are seeing. More of you are awakening than ever before. More have attuned their vibrations upward, seeing and feeling our presence and their own upliftment.

The upheaval - yes it will be great. Hold on not to one another but to ourselves. Find in your own heart the portal for upliftment, this is the passage through. You wonder, will it have some semblance of order? We say it will not. Chaos ensues - it will be disruptive. But find in your hearts the will to help one another. Be guided by our own voices in your ear, but find your heart willing to aid another.

You can be saved from turmoil. It will be localized, not global in its aftereffect. There will be regions of causality where greater disturbance is viewed and cannot be avoided. We do not indicate with specificity, for you are brethren to those who may suffer some and do not have the capacity to carry this worry, not as you would believe yourself to be prepared for it. You cannot imagine the scale of the chaos, and we say do not attempt it. Remain internal to your own experience.

Have at your ready the supplies you will need;
food and water, cleansing and purification.
These are necessary items, and will be had
now rather easily, but not in times to come
that will pass forward. We say have these and
be ready. Do not fear that which comes, but be
ready with these means of self-preservation.

You can exist as you are. Contemplate your future kindly, without worry.
Consider yourself above the fray. Imagine your world and it will be. Chaos of
the mind creates disorder. Center your heart and mind in celebration of him
we call God ourselves and instill in your mind the presence of divine light.
You will be safely held. Do not fear the catastrophe. We say it will be, it will
pass on and be over. Then there will rise a new way of being, a new central
focus to humanity which perceives itself as limited in focus and now arrives
at the truth of its being: That it has encompassed only part of itself and will
rise to meet more of its being to become greater than before.

It will be better than now. There are greater
opportunities yet ahead in this world as it
becomes. Chances to do and be as you have
not explored yet on Earth. Chances to have
our help in reaffirming your place, to develop
a society based on love and consideration for
one another, to be in harmony and have place
of mind over matter. Indeed, creation becomes
more fertile.

You are living within a greater envelope of potential outcomes and may
enervate that which you wish to partake. You cannot foresee this now. It is
not as it has been, for you are living within patterns expiring. Indeed, they
are not going forward, they are behind you now even as we speak and the
great unfolding begins.

No more will dwell within this space the separation you have experienced.
No more will there be unkindness as it has happened. Consternation, indeed,
it happens. Frustration, yes, of course. For you will be in creation-minded

circumstances and will have the challenge renewed to create a life and living beyond the pale of what came before, to re-create yourselves in his image. But further than before, with more access to detail regarding your full capacity, more understanding of what you are and have been. Still within the constraints of this life, having been birthed into this fold, but having less consternation overall, more peace and harmony.

Still, you must fight within the self to overcome those patterns behind. They do hold yourself back, prevent this upliftment. They must be purged. Do your work. See yourselves. Understand your being. There is no more important topic than this one, for all depend upon this upliftment and you are primary in the cause of it occurring. You must be freed of more energy, troubles forgotten, released. You can do this now with more facility. There is a help here for you now, more than before. Forces converge to prevent the loss of this trajectory of existence.

Light aligns for your benefit and upliftment. Ride it well. Feel the power of these times of energetic persuasion - for you are a pawn while being also the master, the creator and created at once together in your own mind - and control your readiness for this great embrace. We are holding the space, allowing your unfoldment, and preventing obstruction from happening. Your role, you know it well in your heart.

We say this new time will be coming where you can dwell more in coherence. Life will be physical in this generation still. You remain in bodies as you have been, not as light just yet. You will become as a species more luminous with time. It will happen, but now you have tissue and bones and must remain as so.

Energy upliftment is happening now as we speak. You are less dense than you were, and this is necessary for our accomplishment of this upheaval. You cannot ascertain the changes within very easily. Perhaps you notice yourself more vibrant, less transfixed by becoming human. Your brightness elevates.

You'll see the necessary modifications occurring slowly to the self. Color brightens, you may see this already in moments. Feelings of upliftment are more prevalent and become organic. You feel enlightened, joyous, vibrant, happy without provocation.

The following section was not included in the YouTube video.

The effect on humanity will be profound. There are places where you can now go that will be preventable, that are hallowed ground and not subject to the turmoil of which we speak. These are central to our nation of readiness. They are having within themselves the happening of much goodness. There are lakes having water, there are streams and people having jubilation to become more perpetual incarnation. You can relieve their worry from now having only understood the meaning of our placating abandon. But know we are present and have instilled in your heart the willingness to begin another civilization. There are places that will be forlorn and those in readiness, not however proximate to yourselves. You can open your hearts and know the location to be taken there by ourselves. You will inhabit tiny alcoves of warmth and cleanliness, not however grand.

A VISION OF OUR FUTURE
February 11, 2023

In this message, the Angels describe what our new state of awareness will be as a unified consciousness. Humanity will be seen as cooperative, collaborative, and communicative, and we will begin to cherish one another's potential. The methods of communication will be different with the rise of intuition and telepathy. We begin to understand another's experience as if our own, so identity and separation are less important to us. This leads to the dissolution of distinct nations. Instead, we focus on finding ways of being of service to one another and to the Earth.

Channeled Message

We are now supplying a picture in your mind of how things are forming, of where you are conforming to, the now-treasured aspects of your coming to align. We wish to inspire yourselves, to open the veil a bit. Not much, enough to suffice – to tell you where you are. To let you feel the divide yet to be overcome.

You are inspired within the confines of an understanding that is formed by breathing within these times surrounding. You sense yourselves opening now and rising. There is, within these times, a bridging that beckons you on, lifting yourselves to what is known to us: a heavenly-imposed surface, a new statement of yourselves. A new weight, a lightness, a sense of yourselves as aligned more fully.

Completed in this understanding will be your own homecoming, where you are supplied and endowed with the perfection that is nearer than you know. You hold it within yourselves. It announces now its own potency and strength.

We wish you to envision a time before now, before this time, when all was chaos and you were inspired. When all was chaos, and you were apart from here. Before you did arrive. There was a time when you felt this place on the horizon and wondered of it and of this time and felt to the self it was far off… the never-now, the time to arrive that is not yet come. The sense of yourself as inspired, as wanting, as wishing, as leaning toward but not knowing.

And in that time before you came here, you were surveying the circumstances of this place without knowing how it would be and become. You sensed yourself in alignment with this place but did not know your time, could not fathom the distinction of how this place would be.

And yet here you are, thriving in your insistence that this is all you ever were: beings tied to this place. Beings who harmonize with the Earth. When, in fact, this newly formed blessing is but an encounter on a journey that has many tides and breaks, many feelings and knowing, and this is but one of them - this time, this life, this journey, this Earth, this realm, this becoming.

We wish now to inspire yourselves to remember that time before coming, to sense where you are now is not much different.

> You stand at the peak of the horizon and
> watch it form before yourselves without
> knowing exactly where you are and where
> you are headed, but feeling the call of what is
> coming.

You sense that you are on a journey to arrive, that it is inevitable. It is calling forward from now, and you are moving on to meet it, but there is yet the discovery to be had of what it will be like.

We hold you now in this endeavor to inspire, to let you feel yourselves as solid, as you are. As pleasant as these visions are to hold, remember now who you are on this continent, in this separation, at this time. How you are alive: the sense of heartbeat, the endeavor to breathe, to be. In search of greater harmony, but always within what and who you are.

And as you stretch farther, this longing, as you know it, creates the divide between where you are and where you're going. The sense of what you are disperses. The sense of knowing your own self individuated becomes lessened. You are stretched. From this vantage point where you are seeing it, we can only just describe the sensation of it. But in this new way of being, your sentiment toward one another changes. The feelings you have align toward the greater dignity of humanity.

We would speak farther, beyond this knowing into the next surmising of humanity. Of understanding what you are as a collective. To feel the herald of the heavens tumble down to you, to let it draw forward your understanding in formation with one another's knowledge. The separation thus found so easily where you are is dispersed and pleasantly discarded, and you become one Earthly sentient, one Earth organism.

A sense of who you are, embodied now in flesh and blood, but containing all of you inside. The sense of this compatriot-ship, of one another at your side. The sense of this, always. Not as an injury, not at all. Not in the sense of loss of separation, but a loss of the potent forces of your own distinguishing loneliness.

> From this collective state of awareness, all
> things rise to the complexity of one mind and
> fall back down again for equal sharing and
> knowing.

There has not, in the state on the horizon, been the forces to pull your tide farther. There has not yet been the cascade of events that would draw you there. This is yet coming. These instigations have already begun, but there is yet time unfolding, and the drawing onward has yet to come.

For the collective of one mind, how is it felt? How is it molded? And we say, for yourselves to exist in the space of awareness that is shared becomes a gradual acceptance that all knowledge is available to the self. That all the self has experienced, the knowing of what you are, informs the collective. That you are seen deeply. You are known and felt. You are understanding one another in truth, for their purpose, for their originality, for their union with the whole.

You see yourselves as cooperative, collaborative, communicative, as sharing space of equality. An equal cherishing of one another's purpose and potential. And the methods by which you communicate are different. There is within yourselves the knowledge of how thoughts are forming, and the ability to communicate without words.

There is within the self a rising of knowingness as you approach one another. A sense of what you are unfolding before you, and of they to whom you are speaking. The reception of this knowledge, and of you receiving what they are, full and intact; a collaborative gesture of knowing, a sensing, a feeling in the body. A having-been, as though you are remembering what you've always known. A sense of this rising to the awareness, coming from somewhere in your depths that you cannot identify. A resurfacing as though this was someone from your past, though you may not have known them.

And this takes you far, this connection. The sense of what they are, the knowingness provides between you a complexity of endeavor in which the collaboration of your species - the collective - is endowed with more potential. The greater divide between the whole, the astounding measures now taken to create identity and separateness, are dissolved. These nations which you hold dear and important become less so. They do not rise. They find their passage ineffectual and become an old instantiation of control to which you will no longer abide.

You find in the self a way and method of finding your place in the world. A way of being of service to one another. A sense of yourself as part of a collective energy that works upon the Earth to grow her potential. The Earth, she will rise and fall and become more. And you are her thoughts, her vibrations, her senses, her feelings - all of these. You become aware and can attune to her and find your patterns within her embrace. And the collaboration between the human species and the Earth becomes fundamental to your existence.

This is the pathway that is emerging, that you have no sense of, which cannot be elaborated more fully until you reach that point of understanding - of immersion into the new state of being. It is as you were within the chaos before entering this field. In the unknowing, the effervescent glow of opportunity beckons you onward, nearer to Earth, always nearer to Earth.

YOU WILL BE LIVING IN A TIME OF GREAT LOVE AND PROSPERITY
December 9, 2023

Seeing Angels

Susan was walking with a friend and saw a gust of wind swirling up the autumn leaves, which fell around her like rain. She said aloud with a laugh, "Maybe that's the Angels!" It made her wistful to see the Angels with her own eyes, so when she had a zoom session with me later that afternoon and I brought in the Angels, she asked them:

Susan: "Will there ever come a time when I can see you? "

Angels: "We are in presence with you always. You know this - we made ourselves apparent in the dancing leaves of your experience. This was us, was us. You have already seen us."

Susan gasped: "Yes!!"

Angels: "Yes, we enjoyed that, that we enjoy. We will do it again. We will do it again in playful remembrance of our conversation and you will laugh aloud, and we will celebrate and make rain on you."

Susan: "Thank you!"

Angels: "You are welcome, Susan. We are funny in how we make rain on you."

In this beautiful message from the Angels they get specific about some of the wonderful ways that humanity will change in this shift of consciousness, including experiencing Angels, meeting ETs, and world peace. This is a good one!

Channeled Message

There is the sense of all things moving from here in a particular direction, and fear among some does percolate. And we say, and we summon from you your attention, willingly given, to focus upon not what comes next, but what is beginning.

We ask for the bounds of what is remaining in this world to feel gentle, to feel as something that envelopes you in loving endeavor. Feel within yourself, within your soul, as you herald the times to come, that you are made for the memory of this experience. You are made for the purpose of belonging and having the experience of upheaval and re-acclimation; of claiming this world again in the new time frame and making it home, of making within it a settling of humanity, where it comes to know itself more formed, more full.

The inner knowing that develops between you, and among you, is life-affirming. To find within the time frames of what will be known, there is not the same longing that we have spoken of. There is not the absence of friendship, the drawing close of heart form. There is instead the desire to continue between and among you a friendship formed through trouble, through anxiety, through all that does signify great change in your environment. But it instills within you the desire to fight against what is thought of as hardship, and to draw toward one another and rekindle the light and fire of belonging.

It is a time of truth among you. It is a time of bereavement for many. But this does inspire humanity to grow and unfold one another, to draw into you, the friendship of all nations; to make in and among the many you herald as distant, true friends.

There is this time in formation that cannot be avoided, and you are curious as to when and how you shall experience it. You are furious, we have not said it. And we say to yourselves in calming voice, in loving connection, that there is not the predeterminant timing to which all must orchestrate, but it is as it unfolds; and in its unfoldment, all will develop. There is this acute root to understanding this terminology. How can we claim this knowing, to have seen it, and not have in its grounding a concept of when it is happening? And we say that this space of knowledge occurs in rapidity, and it reveals itself piece by piece, overlapping, and there are still potential outcomes by which the occurrence is manipulated and transferred. But having seen it, all outcomes reveal this: that the opportunity will reveal itself. It is coming.

It arrives in all instantiations of time that we see. There is not an outcome that reveals itself without this occurrence. Thus, we are saying that it is coming, that it is happening, and we see this soon on the horizon. The formation of timing ripples incessantly. It creates within itself many disturbances, and these overlap and create and unfurl as they are willing. And thus, we see the waves of time coming, but all carry this outcome and great growth for humanity.

In the times coming, what will it be to belong to humanity? What will it be to be alive on this Earth? What will be the life laid out before you? And we say, do not enshroud yourself against this. Do not fear what opportunities will lay.

In acceptance of the change and its passing, you will find for yourself that all is as it was in some ways, that there will be fragments of life that are much undisturbed. It will feel as though life continues to a certain tune and song of memory. but then become aware that the capacity for the Earth to continue as it was, that the capacity of life to expand as it has been, is disjointed and does not continue. that there will be, beyond the borders of your own experience, the potential for great undoing; and these create within them opportunities for uprising, disjointed efforting.

There will be among and within humanity a great unraveling. But this happens in separateness, here and there. There are pockets - there are places among this great Earth that are as yet untouched by these experiences. And there are some places which are only knowing what is past, based on what is heard.

There is a great movement of peoples. There is the transfer of wealth between nations, the sharing of what is unearthed. There is the desire to maintain for the purpose of living and being among all peoples. A shifting of purpose and focus emerges.

Powerful structures, which emerged in these past decades, find themselves uprooted and unable to continue. But not all such instantiations are wounded. Some find themselves truer to their purpose and more able to experience growth in a time of unfurling. Thus, the world takes new hold, a new capacity.

There is, in this time frame, an expansion of horizons and borders beyond this world. The expansion of travel, new ways of being aloft, and outlying reaches become closer. And this expands yourselves exponentially.

> There is a greater peace among nations, dissolving borders. There is the connection between peoples, and the enablement of this capacity opens the heavens to all races of beings, and there comes to yourselves great aid and guardianship.

In and amongst ourselves who are angels, you become perceptive to us. You become sensitive to our presence. Not all will see us, but some will. Not all will conceive of our presence, but many shall have the experience. And this endowment of grace shifts them purposefully into a direction of communal understanding that we are of this place and of yourselves. And there exists within the hearts of many, a great pull to greater understanding. And you will find yourselves replete, with the many who desire greater depth and greater tutelage, who are in need of service from yourselves, and the many who have come to be of service in this time.

These times you are undertaking have been waylaid, shortened, and the fulfillment of these experiences must be concentrated. There is amongst us who are engaged in the design and fulfillment of your fruition, a commitment to the resolution of these Earthly purges. We are certain it will absolve humanity of many pressures of what has been difficult - hardship, suffering - where there has been the expansion of negativity and frustration; and much dialog has occurred between the darkness and the lost souls of your many races. In the great purge, all that has been stolen from yourselves will be returned again. And this we celebrate.

We say that the aspects of life that are tumultuous, that you experience through the frustration of the orchestration of what you desire, a great shifting occurs that is positive. You find yourselves in a liquefied realm of objects, where all things are transmutable; and that which has been difficult is moldable by you. There is the formation of reality, which is an undertaking you can handle differently. The formation of life stems from you unguarded, and you find your heart, the directive. It becomes a time of greater folly and fruition, more fun for the having, greater ease in life, a greater capacity for joy, a release of beliefs that have been durable and limiting.

It is a time and space in which you feel yourselves delivered from a realm of misunderstanding, misconstrued action, and underdeveloped senses. And in the new space of friendship between humans and all peoples, you become that self you envisioned before coming. You become that self who rises to an experience of life that feels like ease and purpose, married in one expression. You become that self who rises to the tide of need, who dances in the expression of their own beliefs, who stands ashore in the waves of spirit, and holds within them the light of the divine.

We speak to this now in reassurance, in understanding that the dialog we are having cannot supplant the fear. We have the knowing that to be human is to feel decomposed at the prospect of enormous change and fragmentation. But we say to trust in self and other, to trust in humanity, in what is your purpose, in what you have felt, in what you have known, and to be aware that though you have felt the great ripples of these experiences building around yourselves, though you have known the torment of many peoples occurring even as we are speaking, that you are yet held in a pose of relaxation and enjoyment. Through this process and undertaking, to lift humanity from its depths of confusion to the lofty precipice of its evolution we must have suffering. And for this, we are sorry. Through this process, our guardianship is promised. Your safety in our compassion is held as a trusted contract.

We provide for yourselves a suggestion, in the conveyance of your wishes for what shall occur. We speak to this most poignantly. To speak to yourself often, and only, of the desire for the evolution of humanity. To speak to yourself only, and often, of the sense of yourself as part of this great change. To speak to yourself only, and often, that you will be living in a time of great love and prosperity. And this is all. And to wish for nothing more.

For what is to be expected, cannot conform to your knowing; and your concern bedevils all you create. Thus, stand confronted with reality, and receive what is, and be of the perspective that you live in grace and graceful opportunity, and see in all things the blessings; for your race, your peoples, yourself, your family. See the blessings in all things arriving.

CREATING HEAVEN ON EARTH
April 12, 2024

Through this shift, we humans are helping to create a new heaven on Earth.

The Angels have explained that this is the only time that
we have incarnated with two aspects of our soul in one
body, and during this shift, we will be changing from one
to the other while incarnated. Both are still you, but it
is "you" expressed in two different frequencies, kind of
like how the same musical note can be played in two
different octaves. As we go through the events of the shift,
they understand our tendency to feel fear, but they reassure us that we
shouldn't because we are powerful creators, and our ability to form our own
experiences of reality will be increasingly powerful. We are meant to change
the world through our individual actions, thoughts and feelings of love for
ourselves and each other.

Channeled Message

Bring yourselves to the forefront of anticipation and readiness. Bring
yourselves in the following of all that is good and heralded as divine. Have
the understanding of all that comes as presence - as divine awareness settled
upon yourselves - and the watching and caretaking of the eternal spark that
you are.

We succumb to the powers of awareness that carry us all in the river of
awareness that readies you now. We are carried here by the power of the
divine to transport us and how we thrive. It carries us to the prow of your
vessel to instigate a turn from where you are going. A change of habitation
and beingness.

We are instrumental, divinely guided, brought to you now to aid, to assist,
to be there through all that is occurring. To stay with you internal as you
undergo this great transformation. To have the understanding of all that is
readiness for what transpires, and to draw this to you, to the forefront of your
awareness, to help you feel yourselves being blessed in this transformation.
To sense within yourself what you are, what you carry, how you have shown
yourself to be divine.

We instigate what is proprietary to yourselves alone. A great shift underway
amongst your own inhabitation while living. To change within the body
of one incarnation. To experience and follow through upon the wish and

desire that you held before coming. To come into form. To know you are undergoing this change, and you are ready.

There's no fear to be had within the hands of the blessed. There's no fear to draw your hearts too close. There's only light in this passage. There is only love to be shown internal.

Externally, there are challenges yet to come. Externally, all will be housed within the timeframe of this lifetime as it is unfolding. The carrying through of what was begun is unfolding around you gently and increasingly. Formidably, it will appear upon the horizon as though it would unseat humanity. As though it would draw to a close this era of fortune and bring you forward into an experience of life that is aching with subsistence.

We say this will not appear for yourselves. This will not be how you experience your own formation. In these times that are coming, the internal vibration that you house becomes louder. Takes on new meaning. Speaks to you with more force. The energy of your own bodies is changing under the influence of what is transported here. How we have brought you full-circle to the place of opportunity where all can unfold internal, within.

The experience of life is drawn from here, and you are becoming something more of your divinity. This shall radiate from within. Your spirit shall prevail. You shall not succumb to the experience of suffering and degradation. You shall not succumb, should you only fear nothing. Draw yourself into the spirit of your own divinity. Sense yourself being transported into the illumination as it is provided. Know you are rising with the times, not left behind.

Know you are coming forward. You are being drawn into the energy that transports you even now, unfolding around. Shall you experience hardship for some duration? You shall. Shall you know the world in its gyrations of self-discovery? Yes. You shall see unfolding a great, new, powerful dynamic of interdependence and reliance upon each other. A powerful new experience of being human within which all shall find one another well, and this forms the foundation of your own well-being.

It is a new time, and in the unraveling there's much to share and be revealed. We say you shall find these changings to be self-directed, from within your own self. The choices that you make. The friendships, the bonds that tie you there. These become the way showers. The ways you herald as bringing about your own internal transformation. The love that binds you together as one species. As one generative aspect of this world that creates the divine in all that you share between you.

Do not fear, we say. It shall not prevent you from aligning with this new frequency. But it is not necessary to be afraid. There is nothing to fear but the sensation of limitation inspired by fear. For you are endless. You are all things divine, brought into form. The world that surrounds you now speaks to your purpose in its own unfolding. You are the creator in the physical.

Fear settles upon your brow and constrains your vision. It limits you where limitation does no good. It limits you and forges into form what you would rather not see. Thus, we say fear, fear can be left behind. Know yourselves held in the palms of surrender to a God of love who cherishes your existence. Know you are held as sacred, and sacred beings.

Know you are brought into form for purpose. For love to transpire between and among you. And this you shall forge through your choices and your actions, through your thoughts and emotions. You create divinity within the bonds of strength between you. The love that transpires, the hearts that shall grow; this is where we settle our touch and celebration. Blessings.

DETAILS ABOUT OUR FUTURE AND HOW TO GET THERE!
July 26, 2024

The Angels describe some aspects of what our future world and experience of life will be like. They also offer a practice we can use right now that will help us through the shift. It is a walking meditation that will develop muscle memory in the body we can call on during the flash of light. To better understand this practice, read the second section of Part 6 of this book, about our transformation in the flash of light that will change everything.

Channeled Message

We wish to speak upon the transcendent variety of your nature, of your many ways of being, of the all-ways of consciousness that envelop you. You are a substantial incarnation of truth. An endowment of reality exists within your heart that has not been yet seen. We wish to elucidate for you today an incorporating method by which you can draw down and further gather toward yourself the full endowment of what you are. This is a process by which you are enabled to feel your capacity broaden to speculate upon the distancing between you now and the shape and horizon of what will come.

We wish to aid you, guide you through a separation of what is possible in the now - into a foray, an endowment of grace that comes to you more easily. In the space of this suggestion, we supply you with an encumbrance, a heavier weight than what is endowed in your natural walking. A state of self in more gravity. A heightened state and capacity within which to endow yourself with a broadening reach into the foreground of the new reality.

It comes to you in the distance of a walk. In the distance of the transfer of your balance between 2 feet, in the space of your own awareness, in the process, in the perambulation of the body. We wish to draw you into this comprehending of this process now. Do not speculate on what it will endow, on how you will transform. Simply be in the gathering state of acknowledging your presence as you begin.

Stand with feet apart as it is necessary to weigh yourself equally. To be in a state of surrendered readiness you must wait, halting, hesitating, stopping the now moment. The time being. The becoming state of hesitation. I wait. I wait to begin. I wait. Hesitate. Stand at the start. Wait.

Walking begins with the pendulum swing of the body's force forward. The pendulum nature of the walk, the drawing forward into a horizon not yet met. Contemplate this. As you stand, feet separated, walking instigates from here, but not easily. It is a starting mechanism that draws you onward. It is the contemplation of your desire to move from here that begins the catapult of your leg forward.

Become aware as you draw and gather the resources into the body to begin this motion. Become aware of the disturbance of your muscles. Of the torrent of energy that must flow in the direction from hesitation to halting motion. It is a becoming, a becomingness of tomorrow.

Gather yourself and thrust a foot, a pendulum swing forward, and anchor one foot upon the next horizon. And pause for a moment to reflect on where you come from. From the endowed state of stasis to the beginnings of motion. And as you move, do not hesitate now. Allow the next swing to come into play. And movement, one upon another, has begun.

The movement, the gentle swaying of the body, the rhythmic motion of the arms and the legs, the movement toward a destination you shall meet, for it is endowed with presence. Thus, as you are walking within a space, within a place of reality, you can become the conduit of self to encounter any horizon.

The walking space of 10 feet must be gathered, drawn to you now. In halting preparation, you step forward and, gathering the space of readiness, you walk 10 paces. 10 movements. Five on the left, five on the right. In this processing of behavior, the body recognizes the pendulum swing, the reality that comes to meet you. The processing of arrival, the instigation of stopping, and the commencement of a new now.

In this process you have met with the bridging from one nature to the beyond next. In this endowment of movement within the reality where you are, you have instigated an accumulating of experience which will draw and gather to you what shall happen in the instigation of the new reality. It is a beginning met with stasis. A pendulum swing must instigate to draw you into the foray, into the gap of opportunity, into the space, the distance between two measures, through which you must swing, fall forward.

Not pounce! Not leap! The movement supple, balanced, even harmonious. A conjoining of the left and right has draws you into the fluidity of repetitive motion. And through this flow, reality joins you. You come, you halt at your destination, and all is prepared again.

We wish to remind the self that, in the opportunity of this practice, presence is most important. The conceptual understanding of the halting behavior in physicality, the hesitation, the ambulation and the resulting arrival, and again the pause that it necessitates. That this experience can be met with a reality that is not yet transformed. You are within it. You are within a space within which distance is interpreted as it is met by the opportunity for movement. And we wish to explain to the self that the horizon which shall be met cannot be interpreted in the same manner. It is not a distancing that separates you in the same way as this one does.

However, the physicalization of the journey does incorporate into the tendencies for comprehension a new method by which you can transmit yourself through. It is a readiness of behavior. It is a method by which you instigate movement. A sense of self as "I am moving forthwith." The will to be done. The will to move beyond. The sensation of "I will."

Become aware that, in the process of walking you are freely falling forward, capitulating into the next positioning of a foot which must be gathered and thrust before you to catch the interception, yes, of a precipitous tumble. And should the foot not be met with solid ground you shall fall into a position less comfortable. Thus, it is indeed the leap into the nature of what will become.

We asked the self to place this processing behavior, a motioning, a consort through which you can become more ready. A way in which to physicalize the nature of a journey which cannot yet be understood. To take the step, the opportunity, to move through the bridging in your imagination. To stand at the doorstep in halting hesitation. To imagine the self walking through. To imagine the self moving freely in rhythmic steps, rhythmic movement, as if you are graced with ease. As if nothing separates you from your destiny on the other side. And within 10 steps of arrival, the penultimate of completion, you pause, you wait, you rest, you allow the self to become.

In the new state of being, all that shall move freely from your heart must be understood in the new now. It must be contemplated as the richness of a new field of imaginings. In this new beginning time, there shall be met with so many changes you cannot yet conceive of.

There will be and become many places of richness, a variety of energetic pulsation that will draw you to them as if you hear a loudspeaker calling in your slumber. Calling to you, come hither. It will be as if in the new reality there are placements of focus which can calm you, can soothe the soul, the body. They speak to you, and you shall be drawn from your places of privacy, of settled nature, and called into presence with one another.

This shall yet become. Not immediately - no, not as you are settled into the new becoming - but as time moves through you. As the creative power of your new imaginations builds a reality that is worth exploring. These shall become into the free form of personification.

These placements of gathering, these spacious starships of human ideology which shall be as concrete as your own natures, as your own physical bodies, but not transferable in all ways to all beings. These placements of energetic focus shall become a harbor of entry within which you shall arrive and absolve all prior ways of living.

It shall come, not immediately, as we have said. Not as available to all persons. But only as they who are found within the reach of these frequencies within freedom, who find themselves in ease and comfort in grace. Where opportunity can find within yourself for the entrance of such an apparition. Where there is allowing, where there is a spaciousness to your demeanor. These frequencies will be felt. This shall not happen immediately. It shall take some time.

Time, though fleeting, does come in waves differently in the new reality you will seek. It comes as you seek it. Time arrives and is spent more in ease with your own gathering. How shall this minute take place? Shall it be longer or shorter? Shall it meet my need? Shall I take this time and condense or replay it? Shall I make it taller, stouter, more full?

There is timing that governs your nature now as if it is solid; a solidly felt template for all ways of beginning. But even now, within the reality of focus that you currently exchange amongst yourself, time is felt differently depending on how you occupy yourselves. Therefore, it is not such a stretch to imagine the time of your future as becoming highly individuated.

> There will be an experience of light in the new beginnings that will come to your irises in frequencies you have not yet known in this incarnation, as if the very surface of things vibrates in attunement with frequencies you do not yet see.

And they will come alive, seemingly as if they carry information upon their surface. As if there is noise that has not translated to your ears. It will seem as if the solidity of things cannot be counted upon, as if there is a membrane of solidity that can be pierced.

This is how you perceive things as you integrate into a new reality of becoming. Not immediately, as we are saying, but as time comes. As time separates you from what was; from your old expectations and endowments of reality. These we express and explain for your own joyful transfer. To transmit into your perception a concept of what may be.

The excitement may lay, may dawn moment by moment, each to be anticipated in joyful reflection of the changes at hand.

We say within your new capacity that you will gain, you will find yourself stepping upon a threshold much like this exercise through which we guide you. You will find yourself in a position to halt, to wait, or to move. And the first step is most important. And we do guide you, ask you, suggest that should you merely lean forward, your feet will catch you. We say blessings. Blessings. Goodbye.

SUFFERING WILL END! HERE'S HOW
September 27, 2024

In this message, the Angels explain how we will soon have the opportunity to live without suffering! It's a message that ties together so much of the wisdom from so many traditions and teachings, but into a clear and practical understanding of where we are headed right now with our shift in consciousness. They explain that in our heightened state of consciousness our wants and needs will change because we will be attuned to the thoughts and feelings of those around us and of the Earth. We will create things that are in alignment with everyone's highest and best good.

Channeled Message

Be with us now, for we herald the times. They are short. They are shortening. We wish to bring you the sound of your own peace, the sound of your own surrender to what is.

There is a fragrance of what is lost that lingers on the horizon, that beckons you on and forward into the dimensional recreation of what has been. And we would speak to you now of your longing, of the gestures of your own goodwill to re-create, to live again what has been before.

And we would speak to you now in the offering of what has become. And speak to you from the perspective we have of where you are going. And we wish to share that all is not lost, though surrendered. All need not be gone, though you must release it.

There will be within the new beginnings much which has been shared before. There will be the makings of a time that speaks to your own knowledge and your own points of reference. There will be the sensation of what you have known, though it will reveal itself differently.

You will understand yourself to have foregone some things, lived without what has previously been revealed as necessary. There will be the sense of yourselves as no longer wanting some things. But in the new tomorrow that comes, that which you find necessary shall be. That which you find inherent to your own happiness shall be afforded.

You will discover within your own heart that you have the makings of creation. You will discover that you have, within your own abilities, a reference point which can come into preparation and realization. You will discover yourselves within an ancient memory which has lain dormant within which you knew yourselves to be able to draw forward into presence that what you require. This shall come again.

There shall be, amongst yourselves, the many memories of what once was shared as if recalled upon a sudden moment. There shall be these shared points of reference where you shall call upon one another to embody those souls you have been before, to draw forward into the then-now moment what you shall require.

There are many skills which you are lacking and needing. There are many thought points which have not occurred before to yourselves, and these shall be formed anew. They shall come into presence. You shall have what you require, what is needed.

How will it be determined what is lacking, what is needed, what you have want of? It shall come through in the form of decision points. It shall come through in the sensation of your own desire for something. Not as in a relaxation into the energies of what has been, for your selves will be changed. You shall no longer be desirous of those things which are toxic and against the human condition. Shall no longer frame your reference point from among the societal constraints which you have become accustomed to.

You shall form your knowledge of what is from the perspective of hearts that feel gladness. From the perspective of life and love that intermixes within one another's own sense of yourselves as together, as one. And within this perspective what shall rise to your awareness is what shall serve the all. What shall come to serve all of humanity and Earth herself. What shall come to service us all? And within this perspective, all you want and desire shall be made.

It shall feel as if you have disturbed something within your own hearts. As if there is a longing that can be shared amongst yourselves. As if all have agreed upon a desire for something that is not there, and it shall then materialize. Not all at once. Not as if you can press upon a desire and have it made.

It shall come into the foundation of your own experience. It shall come as if you have created something and it is the want that you are needing. You shall find yourselves available, and have available to yourselves the tools that are necessary, the means that shall be provided, the structures that are needed to create what is wanted. It will be as if you are a part of the apparatus of creation.

And you shall have want of nothing. You shall find yourselves well equipped in the desires which are easily fulfilled by what is surrounding yourselves. It shall be as if all that is was made for the purpose of satisfying that which you want. And what you want is made for the purpose of being satisfied.

All that is occurring now is in dissimilarity to that experience which you will have. The world you are in is created for the opportunity of seeing what you lack. Of experiencing suffering. It is as if the current moment of now polarizes itself against your own want and need so that you may experience the absence of that which you desire, and can focus upon it and experience your polarity in juxtaposition to that which you would create. It is a process by which you have been given the opportunity to confront your own disharmonies from within.

But in the new times that are forming, all that you are has changed. All that you are going forth shall not be in seek or want of contrast to the same measure. You shall not search for that which you are in want of. You shall instead find harmony and live harmoniously within a realm that is created from your own desire to want nothing. And thus, you shall have exactly what is needed.

There shall be provided to yourselves shelter. Home, as it shall be found, is made with one another and amongst the ease of a world that needs no second guessing. That has no doubt within itself. That does not need to prove its worth to anyone. You shall find yourselves found again in the center of your own love and friendship.

And this shall form the foundations of a world that is filled with plenty. There shall not be a need for that legacy of striving. You shall find yourselves pulled into creative endeavor and shall discover, amongst yourselves, great swirls of opportunity to form into reality that which you have thought of. And this shall delight and amaze you and your friends. You shall find yourselves in a creative purpose, abundantly expressive in all ways.

For some it shall be through the arts of healing one another. For some it shall be through the thought of creative expression in words and stories. For some it shall be artistic endeavor. Some shall wish to create through architecture.

There are many forays that can be made, all of which are formed within the concept of self as adequate, enough. Of having been met with abundance at every turn. And there shall not be a sense of yourselves as in contrast with one another or anything. There shall not be the need to strive against another's comparative force.

The magnanimous behavior of humanity shines in the new generative focus of your own consciousness. You shall find yourselves not needing, not behaving against what is offered, but enjoying what is, and finding prosperity because of it. You shall not suffer any longer.

PART 2

Who Is Coming Along:
The Shift Is for Everyone

Many of our global religions teach that there are consequences for not following a specific belief system. Often those consequences are about being left behind, excluded from heaven or sent to a not-nice place after death. The Angels tell us that this is not the case! They say that the shift in consciousness is equally available to everyone. However, our free will is always respected, so we need to affirmatively choose to shift. We have the capacity to resist it if we want to.

Resisting the shift simply means trying to hold on to the way things used to be. In order to lean into the shift, we need to let go of our fears, expectations and desire for control, and allow it to happen. It's the ultimate trust fall.

The idea that some people would deliberately be excluded from the shift makes no sense, because the Angels tell us that we are one. All of humanity is one collective consciousness. For this reason, we are not in competition with each other to achieve this higher state of being. No individual is valued more or less than any other. We want to raise all boats in a rising tide and bring everyone with us!

However, there will be some souls who choose not to shift. There's absolutely nothing wrong with that decision. Some souls may feel like they can make faster progress by staying in a karmic construct, learning through the challenges and the pain we've been experiencing. The Angels have said that those souls will live out their natural life spans on Earth but won't reincarnate here because they will no longer be in alignment with Earth's higher frequency. Instead, they will leave the Earth school and reincarnate in another, karmic world where they will be able to continue the growth they've been working on.

The choice to shift or not is made by our higher selves, although we can change that choice at any time while here on Earth. Our free will is always respected. Regardless of which choice we make, the Angels support us at every step and will guide us toward the fulfillment of the plan we made for ourselves for this incarnation, and our current desires.

There will be many souls who leave the planet during the events of the shift. However, they will not experience the physical trauma of that transition and will be lifted from their bodies before death. I believe this is the source of the "rapture" teachings found in some religions. These souls will experience the shift in their frequency as part of that transition. They will then be free to reincarnate on Earth into the new, higher state of being.

Those that remain on Earth after the events of the shift will work to help one another through the transition process, building a new world and a new way of living together. Some souls that remain will be open to the shift when the expected flash of light occurs (You can read more about the flash of light in Part 6). Others will have the remainder of their natural lives on the planet to discover themselves and experience the transition. Many lightworkers are here on the planet now to help guide these souls as they become ready.

NO ONE FORGOTTEN IN THE ASCENSION
September 7, 2020

In this message, the Angels explain that the Earth herself is raising her vibration, and we need to match that vibration to remain here on Earth. However, the choice is ours to make, and the Angels will support us either way. They say there are some people who may pass during the Earth events they have told us about, but that they will achieve a higher level of awareness in the process, potentially breaking free from stubborn karmic patterns. No one is forgotten in this great shift, and the Angels are protecting and guiding us all.

Channeled Message

An opening is what develops, an opening in possibility. A chance for ascension. We must take this opportunity for humanity. It rises up within each person like a wave of possibility for them, to ride or pass, to join or fall. They will determine their own path. They may choose. It will be a choice for them to be lifted with the rest or left behind. It's OK.

We are equally in service to either opportunity, but we wish for as many as possible to join and rise, to be more of what is possible, to experience a greater reality than what they have known. It can be achieved now with our help. We assist to make this happen. We want all to have the chance.

You wish for all to be saved. Not all will ascend. It will be, as we said, their choice. You can wish, it is kind. But know that they are sovereign. You must respect their destiny as chosen by themselves. It will be all it is meant to be. Have not the trouble of taking on worries, trauma, not your own. Be not the savior of every being. Help those who help themselves. Who wish to follow. Who want to ascend.

You must be nearer to source so that you can continue to breathe the air of this Earth because, as you are aware, it evolves into being higher than it has been. Therefore, you may not remain within its toxic embrace for those who have not achieved enlightenment. You have tried many times to achieve this for others, however they are unwilling and will be removed because they cannot stay in their vibration any longer here. Therefore, we assist with their removal.

We have acknowledged their pattern of growth. They are enumerated by receipt of their occurrence each and every lifetime, and we know this habit has endured for many lifetimes. We have taken care to sustain their pattern to another level of their being so that they can transfer their parade to yet another location where they will be sustained - but not here.

You have identified the way in which we have decided it is best to remove so many. This is going to be happening within the envelope of your experience. It happens. Now you have understood that we will be overseeing this process so that all are protected and ensnared in this vacuum that will ensure their delivery to their new location. They will be protected.

Enlightenment is achieved in part through the process of their removal. They will achieve a higher level of awareness when they access this new dimension. Therefore, they are willing to go to this place. They have not yet experienced what it can be. They are experiencing some ambiguity, which is natural given what they are going to do. They have not succeeded in receiving the energies of awareness.

You may continue with your existence here because you are lightened enough to be able to stay. You have received the vibrations we have transmitted for all. But not many are receptive to these energies because they have not achieved the level that is needed in order for them to stay. So, we will help them relocate.

Do not fear for their happiness or their recent struggle. We know it's hard to imagine that they will perish so heatedly, but they are in agreement with this process because they have the chance to uplift their vibration.

WHO WILL ASCEND
October 24, 2020

The Angels are here to support and guide us through our shift in consciousness.

They have given us the choice at the superconscious level whether each person wants to evolve to the higher frequency of the new Earth, or not. Some people may feel incomplete or feel that they can make better progress in a karmic construct, so they may not choose to shift into the higher frequency of the new Earth. They would live their natural lifespan on Earth, but they won't reincarnate on Earth.

Everyone can choose to shift. They just need to be open to it. The Angels remind us that we are precious to them, and they will be with us and look after us regardless of whether someone chooses to ascend or not.

Channeled Message

We have much to say, you are ready to receive. We are delighted to have this opportunity to explore with you the beacon of hope that you are moving toward. Ascend and find how you are going to be. You are curious, worried, fretting about what will occur, what will happen. We are clearing your fears as they arise, if you are allowing.

We have now instructed our regents to be ready for your being to experience this arrival. For your own self to be lifted as it once was before in our embrace. You are now surrounded by our people and we are guiding your expatriation into a new hollow, a new way of being now ready for your occupation.

You may find this process slow. It will occur within the period of your two lives, within your own hyper-drawn torment you will find our experts there. And again, when exalted, you are yet in our kiss. We have landed to fortify you so that you may be at either pole and find this path.

However, do not try to find us when all is asunder. It must be after the cloud has passed. After all has become equal, and one field is open to another.

You are going to experience some disturbance as we are heading into this fracas. It will elevate the Earth, and you will find that all are not capable of remaining. However, more have become open. More are listening to our call. We have asked you each at the superconscious level to assume this new valence, and not all have responded. Some have asked to remain within this period of sulta. To be themselves tried anew to bring about their greatest healing. They are yet consumed with fear and loathing. With pride, bereft of good omen. We are sure they will be cared for and led to another venture.

You are wondering about how you can be sure all are not lost. How you are sure to ascend. You are certain if you are aware of the question, that is all it takes. Are you open to the energies? Are you willing to climb our tower of trust and be enveloped in our arms once again? Will you proceed with your unwilling avoidance or open to our call? Heed our energy, beckoning you at all times, asking permission to mingle with your own. And we will, through to you, be clear always. You can rest assured we are here. We are worthy of your leap. Be well within our touch and feel the purchase of our embrace. It is all happening for your internal upliftment. To improve your own feeling. To experience oneness once again.

You have asked us, am I forsaken? Am I forgotten? Never. You are precious to all Angels and above. You are watched and guarded. We have lingered over your efforts and added our enchantment to improve your divine outcome. We are here in constant observation of your benefit. We are yours in all meaning. Do not fear the possibility of being forsaken. No, it is unfathomable.

TIDAL PROCESS OF LEAVING THE PLANET
October 14, 2022

This message brings peace and calm from Archangel Azrael. It gives more details about the souls who have chosen to leave the planet to continue to work on their Karma elsewhere. It tells us what we need to do to weather the shift most easily. Azreal is the archangel who delivers souls from their bodies as they transition at death, but he is also the benevolent transformer of mental and emotional anxiety. As we think about large numbers of people leaving the planet, it can bring peace to know the Angels have told us that people will be delivered from their bodies prior to experiencing the trauma of death. It will be like the peaceful and loving "rapture" that many religions have described.

Channeled Message

In harmony we speak, all as one. We introduce to you another whose claims will weather. The introduction proceeds from here. Welcome to you.

We introduce he who has been near but never through. To you who have seen his appearance, it is felt more often than seen. But know him to be good. You may feel as if one should acknowledge, in his presence, their own mastery of spiritual giving. He is inspirited with the calm, the peace from on high. He gives through his own light and illumination, singing into life the calm he brings. He wishes to give you peace. To give you reflection in these times coming. To strengthen your heart in speaking the verse of the heavens. The shrill noise of efforting cannot drown out the light of his being. He enters you now in peace. Accept this blessing.

I am within. I carry the rod, the staff, to bring the light down to your people. The ones who are suffering, who leave their last breath now, we raise them to be freed of this destiny and leave you in peace. Without shadow, without the calm rising to separate you from and create distance between. We take them, those who are rising, into this opening. Relieve them of their turmoil, their pain, and let them journey longer in the direction of their choosing.

None shall remain here but they who prosper in these times. These strengths that you carry, the love you are speaking from your own heart, guards you well. And we raise those who are done here. Who no longer wish to be Earthly. Who pass the tide of their suffering to exchange for new life. To live on beyond this realm, continuing.

They leave now. We enfold them with our beings. We guard them restlessly, watching. Unrelenting tide of exchange is coming. The tidal process of leaving. Release what does not serve this version of Earth. Release what must be done and move on living. They go beyond this time. They are moving. We have them well, surrounded in light, in love, in opportunity. For what comes to them, we are offering new realms of situation and schooling. New beginnings for them as well.

For yourselves who go on through, who remain, who wish to be here, who stay and take on the reins of this new day, we beseech you to pattern your heart on our opening. To leave your comeuppance and empty your throat of all utterances that no longer set within this grace you are seeking. Release your grudge you are bearing, the hatred that follows. Let down your guard against one another and enter the throws of compassionate living. Be within one another's calm. Be each other's peace.

Be now ready for what follows. What is coming. The tidal shift, it rises, and a rift is formed in new Earth beginning. And you are seeking the opening. Live taller in your aspect. Reach with your energy. Be no longer in strife with one another. Hold the light we offer of peace. A light, an energy you can feel. We bring to you now an offering. A touch, a lifting. An access point to forgive your turmoil. What ought to cause you hardship, release it. Let yourselves be freed.

In death and in life, we love equally. All who have risen are here to feel, to hold the breach to allow your passage through the opening to what is revealed within your own persons. What you seek is within your bearing, your heart's tuning. Allow this. We seek to offer our blessing of calm, of peace for your entry to this dark night of passage. You are rising from underneath. Take care, your heart's joy, let yourself be seen.

THE TIMING OF THE SHIFT IS OUR OWN
April 19, 2024

While all of us will be lifted and changed significantly by the flash of light, shifting is a gradual, cumulative process that has been building within us for some time. Many people will continue to shift after the flash of light occurs. The exact timing of each person's complete transition will be on our own schedule and will be a combination of the rapidly increasing frequencies from waves of light hitting the planet as well as our own internal growth and self-acceptance. In other words, no one misses the boat! We all have the time we need to make this transition, if we are open to it.

Channeled Message

Blessings. We bring to you a message from the unknown. A message by which you can surmise tomorrow. When it will arrive, how far it will come to take you down into the acceptance of all that is unfolding. Into the letting go. Into the forging of the next instantiation of who you are.

Today's suffering will not be allowed. Will not be felt as though it is an eternal method by which you are incorporated in this Earth. Suffering, as it has been known - a blanketed perception of all things that tear at you in separation, isolation. Forging, instead of a bond between you, creating within you anxiety and tendencies to separate further from who you are.

We wish to draw your attention to the nexus of the whole. To the incorporation thus far completed. To what you are becoming. To the centrally held focal point of the All-that-is. You are nearer to this now than ever before. There is a rising sensation from within that you are being called to come forward, to draw closer, to come nearer to this joining with each other.

What shall it be like? How shall you come forward? When shall this time of separation begin? When shall the current that undoes, (as seen in) the great disasters of this past century, run through and demolish what has been in need of relinquishing? And we say the timing of this governs what is withholding within your own understanding. The timing of this is a point of connection. A point, an umbrella, which envelops you all, taking down now what has been harbored within your understanding - the context and the solutioning by which you endeavor to live your lives as they are, in a frequency of avoidance.

But the timing, as such, does draw you together into the now, into a placement of yourself where it cannot be avoided. Where all things come to center, as though you are drawn by magnetic point. As though you are pulled from within. The inner longings for one another, toward one another, you are drawn to the great center of the whole of what you are.

To perceive it thus, as a central sun that you are part of. As a magnetic point of reference that can draw you forward. You need only lean in now and feel it calling.

The temerity of the times adjacent which draw you backward, which pull you against this flow, they are stronger yet still. They are stronger than the pull to come forward. They draw you into hesitation, limitation, suspicion, and judgment. But they are faltering. They are crumbling now. Even as we speak, they are drawing into their own close and finding themselves ricocheted from within by the violence and indeterminate malevolence which is found there.

You will find yourselves repelled by this, increasingly, and drawn to the center.

The center of what? The center of who and how? It is yourselves, dears. It is the truth of who you are. It is the unity that lives within each and, combined, you all together. It is the sense of who you are as one and one another. It is the sense of yourself as rising into a new timeframe.

And poignant, yes, we hold aloft the barrier to your knowledge - when. When shall it arrive for us? When shall we come full-term? When shall we reach the pinnacle of our own expression? And we say the timing holds you thus, still assembled. Ready and accumulating what is needed within your hearts, within your energy. The forces must conspire between you.

The timing, gently known, must beat to a rhythm of your own congruence. It must come through you, for you, it must rise within you. It cannot be done in a solitary manner. It must come from around, within and through you.

And the timing will happen as you are supplied the energy of your own focus. It will come to and through you as you are ready to allow it. As your own nature becomes freed. As your self-reliance increases, and your sense of otherhood is developed.

In the unknown, the template of love will change. And who you are and have suffered to become will not be as you are currently known. You will feel yourself as one another, with one another, for one another. It is not as it has been.

The timing, the time frame will change now as you incorporate more of what is energy. More of what is allowing, what is graceful within your own heart. As you open within to receive the blanketing tendrils of energy that weave their way through this plane of existence. They are moving across the surface even now as we are speaking - finding, holding, relieving you of the pressures that you've known. Lifting you as though you alone have been selected.

But to know within your heart that oneness pervades all in this instantiation of humanity. That all move forward who care to. All are drawn into the rhythm of this ascension, should they only release their attachment to what is and allow the new, the unknown to take hold into fruition.

The timing, therefore, is driven partly by what is within you. By what is held in your own hearts. There will be moments of ascension between you. There will be shared experiences, ungovernable, which shall come and lift you into a celebratory pose of having risen. Moments upon which you can dwell and remind one another you are cared for. There are times in the near now which shall rise in between and lift you.

Ascension in your own frequency is driven partly by these external forces, and partly by the rhythms within. By your own heart beating into the new. Thus the timing for each of you shall be governed by your own choices. By your own dignity of expression. By your own willingness to allow it there.

We say have no fear of being left behind. Of losing focus. Of being left below in some other choice. For you are with us. You are with us in every moment, in every day, in every second. And in the thoughts that pass, in the sufferings that are felt, you may be drawn into a temporary, regretful feeling. But this we know and can allow.

Know within your choices, within the source of your own divine aspirations, there is wisdom that speaks you here. That draws you to this change. That draws you to this surrendering. And you will make this voyage with us.

We bring you peace and the suggestion to raise your own vibration. To draw into your own hearts what can be light. What can be tolerated. Even higher now, your perception may climb. More of yourself is waiting for discovery. You may simply open your hearts to what you are. Allow yourself to be and become your fullest. To see what you are - a blessing, through and through.

All parts, all aspects, all memories of you must be held as sacred. And in this process, you alleviate from yourself the resistance that draws you from us. For we are what you are, and as you callously reject the tender parts of your own soul, we are rejected with you. We draw you to us in the gentlest of embraces, and whisper our prayers of ascension.

PART 3

We've Already Begun:
Raising and Releasing Separation

We've already started our process of shifting. Think of this time as the early labor pains that will gradually increase as we get closer to the flash of light. We are already being inundated with solar energy, which is helping to bring our individual and societal wounds to the surface. That is why the world seems to be getting crazier as opposed to calmer. We are being pushed into increasing polarity and extremism, surfacing all the pain that separation has created between and within us. It must be felt in order to be released.

It can be hard to imagine a new world of peace and harmony when we are seeing so much conflict and suffering in our world. In these messages, the Angels ask us to let go of the need to understand the process, let go of our attachment to our material world and to focus on love. We want to be open to what moves through us. They understand that we are still torn between the new freedom we want to embrace and the aching of our souls that can't yet let go of the pain we've experienced. But we have the power to create a better experience for ourselves, even during these times. The frequency of the planet is rising around us already.

ASCENDANCE \ WE'RE ALREADY SEPARATING FROM THIS REALITY
July 31, 2021

In this message, the Angels are acknowledging our tendency to pull away from our difficult experience of being on Earth. Before we incarnated, we were passionate about coming to Earth because we wanted to learn about ourselves. The Angels understand that it's difficult to be caught between those lofty ideals and the reality of our existence here. As the Earth begins to shift, they ask us to lean into those memories of passion from before we came. The Angels see us in our future, and we've already made it to our new state of being. They say not to worry about our lack of passion for this reality. Instead, see it as a sign of the change that is happening around us. Our passion will rise with the changing times.

Channeled Message

We wish to begin with our understanding of your breakage of your passion, of the lack of meaning that entices you forward. There is reluctance among many to belong to this life. Withdrawal is persistent. You do feel it difficult to be here. Many surmise that all will be as was done before, that all will still live in surrender to the circumstances that you knew. It is not so.

There are circumstances of arrival at comportment and delivery upon Earth that you are reimagining, now that you have embedded in the self, that draw you asunder, that pull you from here. There is not the same capture of passion and belonging that you did once perceive from whence you came.

You imagined your sojourn upon the Earth as one instructive, but of great interest and good fortune. You did wish to come, did plead and ask. We now instruct the self to remind you that these times before the fall are precious, to be believed, an opportunity for self-exploration and understanding.

We understand it is hard to be captured between the sensation of your own uprising. Your spirit soars, your awareness develops, you have more capacity for source light, and yet remain here ensconced in subsiding passion. Longing for clarity, for belonging, for substance in the self, for the sense of wonderment that drew you here. But, in its place, you experience your own divergence from this place.

You recognize a separation of yourself from that which surrounds. You feel disengagement on some level, the awareness that you are not like all that surrounding yourself. Not all feel what you have, beginning to press forward, and belonging becomes harder still.

The Earth does tremor. It shakes, it awakens. But not all feel it. You do. You know that circumstances are not forever. That you are facing a transition and fear not. The separation you are in, that leaves such sense of withdrawal in the self, is not long-lived. You do not need to dwell in the soul place of abandonment, of misunderstanding, of leaving and separating from what was. This passion plays back into your mind. You remember a time forlorn, of being less than experienced, feeling separate, and now you begin to rise. You feel ourselves nearby and we begin.

How you begin to feel recommends the passage forward of what comes - your beginning of aspiration toward a new destination. It is a symptom of pull, a disenchantment with what is, that pulls you onward and into the becoming of what will lie beyond.

We know this well, the symptom and arrival. It does hearken to a future we know exists. Trouble yourself not that this becoming arrives not how we see it, how we perceive. Its up-ending reconstitution of yourselves and this life you live has already been done.

> You are peeling from the layers of what
> has been to resonate more in tune with the
> coming truth of where you are become.

You are arrived here now in our view of things. We see it now; it exists in reality and will permeate the layers of your becoming to instill its effects upon the plane of your awareness.

Your feeling of separation, of unity perhaps with a limited community of fellow beings who are united in their truth of form, the separation from what is, occurs in many ways. You feel it in how you seek ourselves and each other on planes higher than this one. You begin to find one another above the fray and folly of life, in existence of mind temporal, to astral time, to connect in meaningful ways. You find one another and remark upon the existence of your united selves in other dimension. You rise unknowingly. You feel ourselves more urgently. You feel your place in community with selves sharing your journey upward and divorce yourself from those circumstances dragging you downward.

This passage, it happens to yourself, your individual self, in harmony with all that is and becomes. You arrive as well. Fear not your passion subsiding. Feel instead the birth of a new way of being, and feel it rise with passion newly found in the self.

THE SHIFT IS RISING FROM WITHIN
August 5, 2021

In this message, the Angels tell us that we are already experiencing moments of heightened frequency, but we can't hold it yet. We can make the transition more easily by letting go of our need for clarity and let the change evolve from within our hearts. The Angels say the Earth will change and not everyone will accept those changes easily. Those that don't will move on to another realm. But you can find calm within the chaos by aligning your mind to the new reality, as well as helping and embracing others. We can let go of materialism and focus on being more present with one another. The Angels ask us to recognize the privilege of being here now, and to feel the saturation of love that is here surrounding us, helping us through this experience. They say that this sort of evolution is a first for humanity, and we are worthy of it.

Channeled Message

We would like to continue our conversation with you all regarding what is coming. The ascension draws near. Break your mind of all patterns of longing for what has been. Withdraw from your habits of pursuing that which draws you away from your centered course. Pursue not those actions which held yourself in arrears, which held you down no higher than that which dwells in the mind of others.

You have let go of much, and now we proceed. You are ready to begin the great unveiling of what will become. We say how your ascending is not far from the experience you have achieved in times past. You have known, been, within the vibration of which we speak. You have endured the shifting upward only to find yourselves drawn back to this reality now.

You can enliven this new becoming with your own imaginings. You can exhume your instinct for clarity and let it evolve on its own. Let it arrive, let it be what it will become. You have knelt in its powerful storm of magnetic illusion and limited your perception therein. You have held this reality so close and yet resisted its force upon your mind. Now it rises within and lets yourself become. It becomes that which dwells in your own heart.

The up leveling has begun. Internally you rise from within, your own mind, your own participation in this frequency of elevation does begin to bring it round, for you do feel it now.

The Earth will change, torn asunder. Not all will devolve, but some - many will feel the effects. Not all will have done. You will rise as beginning to feel the same, to feel this frequency within your own resonance changing, shifting mightily.

Not all can subsume their identity with this realm, and they shall pass on to another realm. But those who choose to stay, yourselves to be included, should you wish it, will remain through the chaos and then pursue the calm within. You'll find respite from external chaos in the alignment of your own mind. Your helpful deed, your kind embrace of another draws you further into the fold.

However, as we spoke of times present, let go of need and having. Let go of self-worthy speculation. Let your heart go to one another. Let your mind find peace in heaven internal, the realm of your own thinking that rises as we speak. You are not far from this event and must guard your opportunity to become more present, more abundantly present with the Self and others, attuned to the well-being of all.

This frequency must rise in humanity. The passage indeterminate forms as we speak, as each decides their own passage internal. Each one becomes at their own pace. You have held in your hearts one another before, and again this rise does become the pattern of your evolution. Embrace it well.

We encourage, nay, entreat you all to enjoy your elevation. To feel the privilege of your existence and the saturation of love on your plane of awareness - the degree to which each of you are held by ourselves and all in attendance. We watch and wait and guide and assist as we may.

We entreat you to enjoy this spectacle of self. This great evolution of your kind becomes the breadth of knowledge we carry of this sort of evolution. It has not occurred before. You are worthy and willing and will rise into what lies beyond. You will become more of what you are; becoming more spirit, less astral; more conjoined, less separate; more feeling, less thinking; more understanding, less knowing. We know this field, this happening, this circumstance of evolution, broad and unchained in this existence, will become what it will be.

> We support you now with ecstatic joy to see you rise into becoming, to see you all choosing your paths, awakening by force of your own experience, and having the resources within to drive your own healing. You are empowered to become, and we enjoy the spectacle of your light.

We thank you.

THE RULES ARE CHANGING!
August 27, 2021

The polarity of our times is all around us and hard to ignore. The Angels tell us there is a method to this madness! They say that the rules of our experience here on Earth have changed so that we are more separated into our own experience than ever before, "into realities perceived by you alone". This is helping us to become increasingly aware of ourselves. As we go deeper into our own perspectives, we find more and more contrast and friction with each other. This helps to trigger our wounding, bringing it to the surface for healing so that we can come into internal harmony with ourselves. This will then allow us to come into external harmony with each other.

Channeled Message

We are with you. We say we would have some time to share our thoughts. Have new beginnings underfoot, new ways of beginning. The tide that follows will be renewing, reconciling yourselves with what has been. You are becoming more fluid in form and willing to understand what will be coming now into reality, what will be in store for humanity, the coming passage of great things beyond.

The veil thins. Your selves become uplifted. You are renown in knowing yourselves. You have this passage clear, to make your own selves embodied. You have encountered much less friction in existence there, you are all unpacked to awaken. You are all beginning this arrival, you are all welcome.

We have begun an opening, of sorting your reality into concealing drifts of awareness, into the passage of what seems real for each person. We separate your experience from one another, exaggerating the form you feel and encounter. This provides the maximum contact for yourselves to encounter yourself with more rapidity, to encourage your enlightenment, to bring you hither more quickly in time before all heavens are opened upon the selves and chances are not for upliftment. Now is the time you bother, you move, you change within this friction you feel.

It energizes the planet for enrichment. It is a passage separate for each self.

> Normally all experience the draft of life as a wind that is shared, but no longer does it appear in this fashion. Now you are apart in your awareness of daily ritual, and perspective does shift and polarize into truths unknown to each other, into realities perceived by you alone.

This transference, subtle to your awareness, has occurred, and you are adrift in the reality of your own choosing. It houses other beings within who share not your trajectory. This is not how it seems. You are aware of them and they of yourself, but life moves in different directions.

This experience is required for this time of separation of the selves, many selves, requiring upliftment. Many more opportunities will be had in this manner. Many chances form as polarized beings encounter one another, as your life more richly portrays your own internal mind into fruition. You see and encounter yourself more fully than before.

This is necessary, for how can we make greater strides toward unity but through polarity? We must first expand and then contract. We pull, then release. It is done fluidly, in tempo with the Earth's rising. You rise as well into internal harmony with the self, and then external harmony with each other. Hard won it will be. You achieve it though, you get there. We see it now as it will be, your reality as it becomes. Beauty emanates from each inhabitant. Each soul of humanity is enlivened and enjoyed, separate and intertwined.

But now, feel the enrichment of this time, of this infusion of yourself in now. Inhabit fully your own being. Allow your mind to comprehend that which you see as yourself. Let this richness impact your being and extract those dark sores. Remorse, guilty feelings, sadness, and shame, let them rise. Anger, together with friction, it will be felt. Let it! Fear, it comes and wanes. Let it! See yourself. See the richness of your real expression into reality and embrace who you are in depth and profound feeling.

Embrace your hardship and trouble. It all serves, it all comes into being to aid in this time of ascendance. Extract yourself from your hidden corners. Let yourself be seen and loved by your own mind, your own being in full truth. Let it be. You are rising through this tumultuous time. You are feeling the precursor to all that dwells in humanity. Let it rise and be seen. Love it now. Love with a compassionate heart as you love yourself. Be willing, be open. It comes, this greater now, in the distance, on the horizon, it comes. Be well.

WE'RE READY! STEPS TO FEEL ASCENSION ENERGY (AN EXERCISE TO PRACTICE)
September 16, 2021

In this message, the Angels talk about the impact of solar rays and extreme influx on your energy levels, which may have caused fatigue and stress. But the Angels tell us that these energies are helping us to embrace more power and abilities. Here the Angels offer us a process to help us take full advantage of these energies. They are aligned with your heart, and ready to lift you up to experience a higher plane of existence. To start this exercise, the Angels ask you to trust them and to visualize reaching up as high as you can to reach them. Once you perceive them on their "lofty precipice", they will reach down to gather you up.

Be open to perceive this process in any way that suits you. "You can perceive the wind of our wing, or feel the shift in vibration. You can see in your mind's eye. You can hear the sound of our pitch changing as we rise." Simply ask the Angels, and trust. It will help you to move out of fear and to experience the joy of being loved and cared for by the Angels. While you won't be able to stay in that vibration all the time, you can move in and out of it as you wish. Doing this now will help to prepare you for an even greater shift in our vibrations that is yet to come.

Channeled Message

We feel you have begun to seek more potential. You are all housing, embodying your essential selves. You have, within, the connection you seek. How we are transcribing your desire for connection raises you higher still, to embody yet more of who you are to be, to become. You are readying, becoming still within, quiet.

It has now the repercussion of enlargement. You are processing the energies we have spoken of; the solar rays and influx extreme which modulates your frequency beyond where it has been. These advances have caused some to feel external fatigue - tired, sore, weary, stressed.

A haven appears, not far from here. You will receive more power within. Enlargement of your faculties, your abilities transform within this light you have received. You are integrating, understanding your own progression, and now the feelings change. You can rise within, advancement profound. Your longing, still for upward connection, is fulfilled. You feel more aligned as we are advancing you higher within the fold of our embrace.

We use this trajectory acquired not far long ago, just now you have felt the becoming. Your own enrichment was occurring, and, now saturated, you are become and prepared for more elevation.

We speak now of this, for we are within you, each and every one. We are nearby. We are aligned with your heart and ready to lift you up more than you have been, more advancement. You are ready. We beseech you now, hear us. We are close by. We will assist, should you let us.

Lift us in your mind's eye. Lift us higher, a higher plane of existence. See it now, rising higher. We are there. Once you perceive in your awareness our lofty precipice, we reach down and gather you to us. We bring you up. We lift you here. See us now.

Your perception is essential. You can feel our rising experientially. You can perceive the wind of our wing or feel the shift in vibration. You can see in your mind's eye. You can hear the sound of our pitch changing as we rise.

All are okay. All will work. You must only work to perceive and let it come into your awareness as it may.

Be ready. Perceive now, we rise. You will do this if you choose. Ask us now, and when you feel prepared.

> Ask us to lift you higher. Be engaged with our vibration. You can move up now, this moment is here. Not the ascension you seek in all its entirety, but an aspect of rising vibration.

An element of trust you must develop. An experience is necessary to instruct the self that here is worthy of achievement and you are ready to perform the upliftment. Trust in self, trust in our part and process, in our power to aid and help you all.

This experience, should you choose to avail yourself of it, will lift, will rise and confirm your tears of happy joy, your love of God Creator, your readiness to perceive more of who you are becoming. This now will rise you beyond that inquiet, beyond the fray of the becoming, lift you higher than your fear of lack and abundance gone. You will feel your self supported, cared for, held by ourselves, seen in the greater context of your eternal being.

You cannot hold this sphere ongoing. It will not depart, but you can modulate your frequency up and beneath, rise and fall.

You can have all time to prepare oneself, to live a sheltered being, to be provided and saved and protected.

> This time is sharp, glowing with abundant reality, with extremes of faction and disturbance of weather, and you have chosen to be here now in this chaotic circus. And we say here is the revered, forthcoming rise.

We begin. We rise up. Not all at once, no indeed. A step, a progression, an abundance in your field of opportunity for glowing brightly as ourselves, for taking on the feeling of joy. This process of allowing and trusting readies the self for what may come in time, the arrival of greater frequency still, another level higher and beyond.

You can do this now. We'd like to invite, to request, to ask you, each and every one, to rise, to lift as we express, to do this now as we ask and feel your own accomplishment, to feel the temporary suspension in this higher bridge of aliveness, to feel our light penetrating where you are, to feel our love more clearly, more fully than you have done.

> Rise with us fully. Be in our light. Simply ask and visualize or feel as we have said. Let yourself rise and we will do the rest. We seek you now. We say delay not this joy, it waits.

We love you.

AUTHORITARIANISM NEEDS TO BURN ITSELF OUT
February 25, 2022

In this message, the Angels describe an energy we are experiencing which is forcing things to the surface and into polarity with each other. We are experiencing this internally, for example, by wanting things to stay familiar and comfortable but also wanting change. Externally, we have been experiencing the over-expression of our divine masculine energy, and this is now being brought into polarity as feminine energy - is re-emerging in our world so that the two energies can be brought into balance. The Angels encourage us to embrace this change and find peace within ourselves, as this will help to bring about a more unified and peaceful world.

Channeled Message

You begin to see the horizons not far coming. This energy that spends itself recklessly, the forcing of the planet into dichotomy. Fear now broils in the belly of many. This opening trajectory beckons into now, a forcing period in which the unveiling of tensions in the self come forward for reckoning.

Your own housing is split among desires for what is known and comfortable, and what is now and ready. You wish to have peace within, peace external.

But as your planet enfolds and becomes its twin of opposition, a movement rises, bold to express the feminine mind of itself, that energy dormant for so long in this past expression.

The turmoil for so many, that masculine desire to control and affect, to make the world how you wish it. This is spending its darkest expression to make room for the feminine mind to carry onward. There is in harmony a blending of these forces, but now we reach a pinnacle point of expression for the masculine power.

The time of this passing we have endured a reign of male mind, of timing and building and forming and projecting. Most productive for the race of all beings it has become. But now we shift and those energies darkest that come from the male mind inglorious, where it descends into depths of immaturity, these must fire and purge in a great expression of undoing. And in its path, as fire lays waste, blossom blooms and feminine mind we seek again. Brotherhood with one another. Peace. Allowing. Being within the frame of existence that expands and grows the spirit.

The sequence of these comings, these expression of one done as sequential parts, does illuminate to the human mind your own inner turmoil. Your own forcing of these energies to bind the self in your judgments of wrongdoing, of lack. You find yourself moving between these fields, wishing, reaching for the balance that enables you to bloom.

Here we have the example, writ large upon this plane, of one passage into another. As this moment, this shift is upon us, the energy will rise in its darkest hour. The desire and expression of control and elimination, intolerance of divergence, this is upon you now. It grows in its expression. It becomes a plague upon the mind of this plane of existence and burrows deeply to find those pockets of ready fuel for its expression.

Fear not this rising. Yes, it grows. Inferno building, this large expression of divergence, separation, leads eventually into the fold of entrance to bind these two together. Harmony is practiced. It comes. It will emerge. But now, the rise, this power extreme in its action and woe, it spreads and does its harm. It must burn its fuel. All expression is of God. All light empowers life. Understanding even this, the art of warring.

Peace will come. It brings a level of dictation not in keeping with this hour. It will be a time of opening. Be ready in your understanding. Be ready to see, to feel and understand what is novel and untried.

> But in this time of darkness, we see you through. More will be spreading. It is dark times upon us, but these wash away the spirit of separation to allow for unification. It must purge and bind you now so release may bring its welcome vision.

We invite you now to feel at peace in your own being. To hold this now, this energy of love for self in all your incarnations. Of loving light for your infractions, mistakes and misgivings. To be in peace with your own self brings these horizons of possibility nearer, brings peace for all in having.

THE SEPARATION OF ALL THINGS
July 29, 2022

 Here the Angels are asking us not to take on the problems in the world. They say the current reality feels like compression, as things become fractalized and separated. They say we can elevate our frequency and escape the negativity of this time by focusing on positive things, working on our healing and maintaining good energy hygiene.

Channeled Message

We wish to begin speaking on this. We share our perspective of watching yourselves, of being aware of your internal transfiguration. You're bringing to mind a beginning, a swansong and ending. Yes, a transition point, time. Things are changing internally for yourselves. You're watching your happenings, observing them, feeling all things as real. They are not. They're only happenings. They are things that occur outside of the self.

Be aware of this now as you're watching all things unwinding. They are not yourself. You are not of them, of those things. You're in separation from this. You're moving into a direction to transpose where you've been onto a new template of rising, to bring in your whole essence. It is separation, yes, it is, but not as you are thinking.

What you are experiencing now is compression. A compression against what was. There was the portal of entry to which you have become inured. The lifelong habit of living within this stream has made it feel familiar, welcoming. But it is now harboring an energy of catastrophe. It is feeling as though all things diminish and magnify in complexity. This is how you're feeling when you are ensconced in the current reality. It feels like compression of the mind, of the spirit, of the whole being. A sense of the self as diminished.

A fractalization of society, a separation of all things from one another. A separation of things from where they have been harbored. Emotions freeing, yes, this as well. A separation from what was felt and resolved inside your being. But also, in worldly goods and dwellings. People separated from one another, things separated from where they were destined. All things fractalized, turned into a discordant choir of energetic pulsation and mixing.

This energy mixture is one with the selves when you are longing for dwelling in what was. You become mired in the chaos, the chaotic frequency of what is happening all around yourselves in all ways, large and small.

> Information is not what it was, it cannot be counted upon. It has separation within its very vowels. There is separation in all things, a coming apart at the seams.

Yes, this is happening in all ways. Energetically, and you are feeling it in your very bones as compression to the being, to the spirit, to the wandering of yourselves in this realm.

You are now sensing within us the possibility of some other sensation, and this is true. We invite yourselves to go on rising. You must prepare the self and leaven your being to escape this sensory mixture. You must elevate your own frequency and take part in the leaving of this agony. You can do this by choice. It is a leavening now to love.

> You are wondering how to do this, to raise your frequency. It can be simple, it need not be complicated to raise your spirit, your energy through feeling good things. Focusing where you are grateful. Resuming your healing. Yes, orchestrating regular clearing and healing of your own field.

Finding this in preparation for all things changing, maintaining yourself in good health energetically. Clearing your field, maintaining your thought forms, maintaining your focus on what comes. Lifting yourself deliberately is a focus point you are engaging.

You can lift the self. Focus positively, not allowing the negativity of these times to seek into the minds you're carrying. To bring upward toward your own self, your higher being, your entire body. Allowing yourself to fill up with divinity and to let this carry you through these happenings.

It is the portal on offer, the passageway of which we are speaking. To be enmired in this escapes what is happening in large degree. It allows yourself to circumvent the chaos and restructuring. It allows the self to remain on Earth in pleasant remembering. To stay within the self, to maintain your perspective of all things. To see things as they are happening and understanding the spiritual wisdom contained in each breach. To see how Earth is shifting and understand the meaning to the self and all humanity, and to feel within the own self how you are affecting all beings by harnessing God's light within thee.

It is a passageway, yes. The opening you are invited into. This energy you're feeling. Chaos ensues momentarily. A compression you are feeling. Allow this and move freely by your own design into this higher state of feeling. It is lifting. You may ask us each for assistance. You may ask us, we are ready. We are ready. We are willing. We are helping.

THE NEW NOW IS MORE POTENT
November 18, 2023

We are preparing to birth a long-foretold but unfathomable reality from

within us. But it will be a rocky road to get there, and it might be hard for us to imagine that a beautiful new reality could arrive in the midst of so much turmoil. There will be waves of contraction and release which will help us to move through the personal and societal healing that needs to happen. But despite the chaos in the world, the Angels tell us that we will have the power to create our own experience. They say that there is more power in our current now than

before, and they tell us how to embody the new state of being so that we can consciously create with it.

Channeled Message

Beginnings are upon you now. We celebrate the time to surrender. We celebrate you now. We invite you to become more of what you are. We invite yourselves to relinquish your hold on what was, to surrender to the now and to embrace yourselves.

This next second, the next second arriving, becomes more soulful, more ready, more potent. The next second you're experiencing is evolving. It is holding more power, more potency. It is ready for your greater understanding of divinity and yourself. It is holding the power and the potency of your ready expression.

What is now is a beginning in time. An expression of humanity not yet brought into being. In these times coming, in the next moment, your surrendering heart will yield for itself an open stance that invites a journey long foretold but never experienced. A second hopeful embrace of life in this instantiation, a new birth. An awareness of yourselves as being driven from home into a fold of what is now unfathomable. A new reality.

What are these times on your horizon? How will they arrive? How will you experience them? They are openings before you now. A sense of yourself as having been loved forever. An empowering stance in dialogue with your circumstances, where all things in your purview are an unfoldment of feelings drawn from awareness. Where you feel yourself at length and in dialogue with all things surrounding yourself. That this life is an embrace worth undertaking.

These new expressions of how you are begin to come to mind, begin to expand and extend. The feelings of "I am suffering", lack, and poverty, seem to feel a distant shadow of overwhelm you can no longer recall. There is within your housing a readiness to embrace and surrender to this new light. To dialogue into this new frame.

But your hesitancy to surrender to this freedom and its calling, you are not this. It feels as though the self cannot be and become what it is. In these points of transition overwhelming, as the spirit does soar back into the soul that is aching, we speak to you lovingly and coax you onward into the unfoldment, the new beginning.

You ask us, is it near? This potency, this new formation? And we say, have no fear, it is opening around yourselves already. The instigation of this life and new way of being is accessible. The ways and means of becoming more of what is are surrounding you now. Simply open your hearts more full, more ready to be of yourself.

Lengthen the time in between the moments. Focus upon the next second and feel in your soul and your depth what shall unfold. The unfoldment which you bring into reality is an extension of self, as always. But in this new time now forming, the context you are in is more suggestive. The reality forms more readily. It comes as a dialogue of expression between yourself and your awareness, not just a subconscious gesture. It is the self that is wholly in the power of now. All soul's context and reframing comes into expression.

For this you are ready. You are ready for the circumstance of your own unfolding. There is doubt amongst you. Doubt that this freedom will bring you harmony. Doubt that you won't be perturbed by such extremism as you've been feeling. That all things around yourself will percolate and be as they are and have always been.

We say, in the time frames of your own experience, there will be an abundance of conflict remaining. There will be circumstances unfolding to which you would rather not belong. These we are well aware. As you are experiencing these hardships, how will it be that the next instantiation of self can become? Where does it become to? In what context or reality can you make way for what is peaceful, melodic and harmonic in your own expression?

We say make way, for the sun shines in all contexts. There is always light upon the Earth, and you are this. The substance of what you are makes way from and through this Earth. In this context, you are spinning your own freedom from the substance of what is drawn to you.

This may differ from person to person. But feel that even in the context where suffering is present, your own energetic pulse creates a different tone of freedom. Sense that what is within you will pervade your own experience. See that, within this Earth, many blessings can run concurrently. Your own field may diverge from the person next to you. Feel this difference in the knowing that all persons are met equally with the opportunity to view themselves and their experience. See this not as injustice or inequality but as a readiness to engage themselves in the context they are in.

We wish to move from the context of suffering, from lack, from subservience. But in these times that are coming, this transfer of power from the few to the many is drawn out and lengthy. It takes place in the surges of contraction and release, and the great Earth tumult will aid thee. There will be abundance. There will be those mired in it who shall have and hold onto more than their share. We say the times that are coming will let loose the dialogues of understanding where many shall come to partake, and shall take on in their hardship a more endearing position.

> The transfer has begun. The sensation of "all are for each other" and "all beget into one another." A truth of no separation. And in this context, none shall remain in the hardship of suffering.

However, stillness does calm the pulse of your own body, the context of your heart and its contents. And thus, even while you carry one another through this journey, there is among yourselves differentiation. There is hardship in its distilled form. A sense of yourself as being encountered.

These variations amongst yourselves will be allowed as an expression of harmonious interplay. Of understanding within friendship with yourself. It is a conversation that has been lacking and often misunderstood, and here you have unfolding a greater dialogue and opportunity to be as one with each other in the unfoldment of humanity's graceful expression on Earth.

PART 4

How We Will Change:
We Rise From Within

It's hard for us to fathom how different we will be after the shift. Our perceptive abilities will change. It will be like we've been peering at the world through a peephole, and now we will finally get to open the door and see what's out there. The way we see our world, ourselves and each other will change dramatically.

We will begin to live in a much more spiritual way. We will be freed from our karma. (By karma, I mean the learning experiences we planned for ourselves in this life, both positive and negative. Many of the most difficult patterns or challenges in our lives are karmic.) We will exist in the present moment, and time will become bendable and flexible. We will have new sensory abilities that will allow us to connect with one another at a much deeper level than we have ever imagined, and that will make many of our assumptions and expectations about how we get along irrelevant. When people care about others as much as they care about themselves, many of the structures, values and ideals we accept in our world stop making sense. Today our laws, institutions, and borders define what is mine and what is yours. But what happens when we are one? How could I sit by and watch you suffer if I have more than my share to give?

People often worry about safety and security for themselves, their loved ones and their pets amidst all the events we are expecting. It's natural to feel that way, since some of the events the Angels tell us about in these messages sound terrible and frightening. We are accustomed to a world where people suffer, so we can't currently understand how these events won't cause us to suffer.

But in the future, we will become very aware of ourselves as energetic beings who can manifest what we need and change the world around us with our intention. If your needs are always met, you no longer worry about safety or security. Instead of seeking comfort, we would be seeking connection. The material things we currently can't imagine being without won't matter to us that much anymore. I don't know if we will be able to embody this change in ourselves right away, or over time. It will be hard for us to understand what living in this way is like until we achieve it, but it sounds pretty amazing.

Section 1.
From Karma to Dharma

HOW WE WILL GROW WITHOUT KARMA
February 12, 2022

In this message, the Angels tell us that after the shift, we will be living on Earth without karma. So, the question is, if there's no karma, is Earth still a school? And how will we continue to grow? They explain that our new reality will allow for growth and learning without the need for difficult choices. We will choose our challenges as opportunities and have confidence in our ability to face them, which will create more joy and happiness in our lives.

Channeled Message

We are opening through time an avenue for your development. A freeway by which you can bypass what has been historically offered for your transformation. The freeway of which we speak is made up of an energetic construct. A lessening of your obligation to what has formed this life's causalities, what has made your journey of complexity. An opening in between.

The chance to eliminate some or all of these happenings, the difficulties you would release. This pathway of which we speak is now beginning. It starts happening, there is an avenue to it. Your awakening, your pathway becomes clear. The entrance just beyond where you dwell, where you are limited.

Your opening mind, it halves the reality of this time into two measures; that which you understand and comprehend and that which you do not. You feel your way through these openings, having only understanding of some things and leaving to serendipity that which befalls your choices. This current understanding allows yourselves the freedom of self-direction while imposing the limits to your freedom that will entertain your being in bringing you forward. Those conundrums and difficulties, the surprises you offered yourself, the planning of moments, serendipity as you would feel. But these absences of mind permit within your field the chance to operate on Earth as divinely planned. To control and be led simultaneously.

This planning heretofore has been the pathway forward. This is how it has been. But now we offer a new opening in which you are sounding the transition of self for your own being. Where your awakening is more complete, your understanding more ready. You can feel your being and understand its meaning, and feel your prosperous pathway. More attuned to your being, this way informs yourself of other avenues, of new directions, of methods of growth and learning that do not involve the difficult choices.

No more blindly will you feel yourself maneuvering. Instead, your field opens to choice made with more certainty. You choose to feel a certain obligation or opportunity, to play a role, a part for humanity. And this you do without the piece that has been meaning your lack of observance, a veil to understanding.

You were in the dark. Now you'll be able to perceive for yourself and navigate more freely. Your vision holds all directions and understanding. Your body feels the wisdom of choices made through understanding these passages in time. Your living and being becomes a lesson in itself, fabricated through joyful experience and pleasantry.

No longer needed is the harsh, cruel world of karmic blossoming, now replaced with a more complex understanding, where you can feel your growth nearing. Where you understand how you are becoming and what is needed to improve your comprehension - how to grow, how to feel, what to move, how to deal with your internal resistance. These complexities no more left to the circumstantial arrival of incidents. Instead, you embrace your ability to perceive.

You arrange your life for your own happiness, and joy comes from doing what was perceived difficulty. To moving in the direction of what feels hard and challenging by choice. To feel the pleasure of arriving. To know yourself capable. Yes, to choose your opportunity.

This pathway opens, reveals for some who are ready - for yourself, should you arrive to claim it. It is here just beyond the nearness, just into the next moment. It is a pathway of understanding we are building for yourselves, to let you feel your own proximity to what is happening within. To anchor your woes here, to be left behind. To grow, to loosen the hold of self-doubt and injury and live more full to your capacity. But no longer bled by circumstances of arrival, what comes. Instead offering your own mind the perception you are needing to know what comes. To answer your own bedevilment. To solve your own awakening.

Yes, awareness, it comes. You will feel its passage. This place, this trail, this pathway, it invites you now. It is opening. Feel for it now. Feel your rhythm changing. Feel as your awakening heart senses its own beat. So shall you understand your meaning. You are awakening. We invite you onward.

HOW YOUR ENERGY IS CHANGING (BECOMING EMPTY OF ALL THINGS)

This message has not been shared on YouTube.

May 19, 2022

The Angels hold the energy of self-love within us, and now we are ready to open to this energy more fully. We are slowly letting go of our karma. Transformation is near for those who are actively healing their energy and working to understand themselves. We will be able to hold this way of being for longer and longer periods, where everything will become easier. The transformation starts from within, when we accept ourselves.

Channeled Message

You are striving to become one with ourselves and we invite this opportunity. We beckon you in. We start to calibrate ourselves differently. We are in the instance of our inhabitation that is within you now. The presence of our light and living, it breathes grace into your being. It is the instigation of loving energy, the feeling of being found and honored by ourselves. This you have now, an illumination of yourselves to keep, and prosper with it.

But now all things change, and you are arriving differently. You open yourselves to us more fully. You are becoming empty of all things that transpired in your mind's energy. You are slowly dropping those objectives which you were born across. The dilution of your harmony is being resolved. Feel at this point in time your temperature is rising. All the same, for humanity does dwell within this period together, and all arc into this position, a fixation with yourselves and your journey.

Those who are willing to acknowledge our presence, who are working to better understand themselves, they are altering their journey and transformation is near. All things become easier. There is an entry in times passing that opens to yourselves and you begin to process life differently. There is no storm and bother necessary. All does conquer those ills that define them and make themselves in new image. A separation and release of what was and is departing.

This option to renew your light with our blessing, it takes its form upon your willing moment the instant you acknowledge this path in your being. It is an entry that possesses you now in an instant, for a moment, a fraction of your being. You feel it as opportunity, ease, collated for your highest expression.

But there is more yet coming. These instances, they reflect the time elongating. What fun you shall have in begetting the reality you are choosing! It lengthens to become periods where you assume this nature of being, and it elongates until you are ready to withdraw completely from how it has been. An unwinding takes place in your energy, a release of dirt and earth and solvent dynasty, the temperance of will that holds your energy and makes you small.

This new way of being requires a feeling about yourselves that you are complete. You are all your meaning. You are an energy of wisdom come through. A peace in your being. This emanates outward and envelops your existence.

It is a separation for you from how things have been. You are an instrument now of your own will, subject to the influence of untoward measures in your own energy. Life projects through you now into the field of creating. And in future times, when you are ready, you become the creation point of fixed and ready consequence.

The meaning of what you are is an energy that takes its place on Earth and projects from within. It is a method of being that now instructs your energy through means unnecessary, when all is done against you. It is a new way of unfolding reality.

But start now with the thought and thinking that all are new and consequential beings. That you are to be you. To feel your own energy and understand yourself through this passage.

> All comes clear when you accept your energy
> and stand in witness of your own perfection.
> When no longer held are the methods by
> which you denigrate your existence, and
> instead a calm does fill you.

A peace that separates you from then and leaves you tranquil in now. It is a presence. Stay here now. An effort can be made, an instant of rejoicing who you are. An effort to be made to stay in present. Do this now and know you are longer in the vision of what is coming.

OUR PATH HAS CHANGED
July 22, 2022

This is a unique time of healing, where we are being supported in bringing our wounding to the surface for expression. We are meant to relax our resistance to these wounds and open more fully to our own light within. "Each culmination, passage point is a relief, is a relaxing, is a letting go. And in this process become lighter."

The Angels ask us to be present and aware of our healing. We want to use our healing process to better understand ourselves. They ask us to be very gentle with ourselves and others, because many people won't understand the purpose of this time. It may feel like tragedy for no reason. But if we can hold on to the vision and the knowledge of where we are headed and understand this difficult time as a passageway to get there, we will feel more peace in the process.

Channeled Message

We are one, done thinking about ourselves as separate beings. We are all things and one, individually. We are heaven's opening, the gateway, the entrance for yourselves. We are offering in this time a passageway, an entrance to believe.

You are receiving light energy blanketing the Earth now. It is coming to fruition, resolving what has plagued your past. You're experiencing a quandary, conundrum, difficulties, all things culminating in what was, an entrance to the new way of being.

You are harnessing the power of this now. All things gravitate to you now. Time for resolving; it is a time for coalescing what you have been. Of bringing forward that which needed clearing, which was empty, void of yourself, an absence of spirit. Those aspects of self which are dragging you down, which are related to past substance of self, of memory, of habit.

We offer you now this passage, an entrance to the new becoming. It is opening like a walkway. You must pass through it. It is a thoroughfare, not a byway. It is for everyone. It is for all beings. It is possible now to pass through it, to receive now what is being offered. The leaving behind of the tragedy, the turmoil, the difficulty, and lifting up into a passage.

From now on all things culminate within the self. You bring forward for healing that which troubled your past. Not this one only. The pasts of many selves that you accumulate and bring now, all ready to reenact, call into now, to place your centered self within them and to arbitrate your reason and longevity as spirit to make yourself glow more brightly. You have done this, you are doing this now. You are in the process.

There is much difficulty compounding around you now. All peoples feel this. There's anger being lifted. There is justification and bifurcation of peoples. There is endemic difficulty inbred within families. There is this, your feeling as you think on your own passage; worry, fear, suffering, expectation of this. All of this nears to your expression. For feeling and expression, limitation must be released. You are in the process of feeling, allowing this passage, opening to be felt more. To become tangible to yourselves.

It is like a light through which you must walk. A passageway. It is unfolding. It is not now, in an instant, a moment, but long. It is a long passage. It is a passage through which you will move gently. Sometimes in peace, occasionally in turmoil. But it is the moving that is necessary. The embracing what is coming. Embracing what is coming for the self, for your own journey. The embracing of this through the walkway. Understanding your purpose in this passage is to release what has held you down.

Understanding circumstances are different. This is not how it has been. It is not how it has been. It is not how it was, even recently. It is now a change. You're expecting things to be different. You know not how. This is how. You are embracing this passage you are moving through. You must recognize within the self each culmination, passage point, is a relief, is a relaxing, is a letting go. And in this process become lighter.

The acceptance of the illumination, the saturation of your skin, of your soul self; the gravity must form in your being. The gravity in the body of your soul self, your soul spirit. The embracing more of self. The allowing in more access to your own flame, letting this settle with the body. The bearing continues on.

You may move forward through the passage as you attain more gravity. As you attain more centeredness within the self, you continue on through the passage. Your gravity draws you down, through, beyond what was. It is an access point, a passage through, beyond.

The limitations of yore do not pull you now in the same direction. There are elements of fruition which are culminating now. There's an energy of support all around you now to aid you in the disbursement, displacement of these energies you bear. There's movement among the lineage of your own genealogy. There's movement there which accumulates within your own bones. The bread you seek, the food you eat; all of this contains now the illumination of which we speak. The light comes through and soaks the Earth. It moves through every being.

You're all encouraged to write. To encompass the life with meaning. To understand the self through this passage, to comprehend what is happening to your own being. To spend the time in conscious alignment. To comprehend all that you are doing as you work upon the self. To take into your own harbor the truth of this, that you are marching onward in a gradual alignment of self and dispersing that which plagued you.

There have been times in forming, prior to this, in which you have concentrated on the disbursement of life energy that was not in alignment with your higher being. However, in those times of passage there was not the alignment available now. It was not the same fruition.

> The concourse has changed. It was before a circuitous passage. A placement of things to drive you now and then in a winding loop of recreation. An experimental time of trying things. Of experiencing life in new ways. It is not this that you are in at this time. Is now different. It is now a passage of lengthening, of changing the self, of altering the being. It is not how it has been.

In this time coming that you are in, that is happening now, we beseech you to spend your time comforting your own being. To be in sympathy with your own self. To be understanding of what you are needing. To let this time be a passage of gentle formation for the self and for others who know less what you are about and what is happening. To be with gentleness with all things. To understand the difficulty of these culminating times.

To feel in each raindrop the measure of life, and to feel it cascading down. To know within this substance the Earth rides to its passage into the light. To know that you are bearing this liquid form in your own body. That it cannot be ignored. That you are absorbing it as we speak. That it moves into you.

That you are carried on in a form not recognized by your prior self. And it must be comprehended, be understood to be relished as a journey, a passage of greatness. For otherwise it may feel as though this topsy-turvy life has no meaning, is not welcoming, is not an embrace but rather a rejection from how things have been. We wish to accompany yourself in the mind and the placement of your thoughts, and to offer you this. We are there always. You are moving in a direction most kind to your being, most kind to all humans. Most kind.

THE PATH IS OPENED
July 29. 2022

We started our lives with a karmic blueprint or template for our journey. It may have been a hard way to live, but it was at least familiar! Now we are transforming our lives into a more dharmic, undefined journey where we can create as we like. It's hard not to doubt our ability to live in this way because we have known self-doubt for so long. But we are learning to let go of the wounds, patterns and self-doubt that we've been drowning in. We just need to accept that the new, dharmic journey is possible for us. Each step we take, each limiting belief or wound we let go of will help us in this gradual process. This new freedom might feel scary, but the Angels are telling us that we are ready for it.

Channeled Message

We can begin. We are sharing some information for you. We wish to sing the announcement that you are entering a new phase of beginning. Yes, you have brought yourselves to this point of entering. The substance of what you are is shifting. Now you transform. Everything moves from here. From now on you are beginning anew.

You have within you a blueprint, a template for who you are. How you were born, what you will move through in your life's journey. You have this started already. An agreed-upon orchestration, a journey. But now you are moving through to what is undefined. A new journey upon which you can create as you like. A firmer settlement of yourself in this life. An institutional shift for your beginning. This life changes from here on as you are moving toward this new instigation of life.

This new beginning we herald in is like a transfer of living from that which was to this new instance in which you are creating just as it was occurring in your mind's recesses. It is now a thought process, a shifting in your own vibration, and the emanation of what will unfold. It becomes instant manifestation as you have been hearing. Yes, there is this. But you are missing the more important part of this explanation.

There is, within the self, an alteration of how you've been. Your life journey, incomplete though it may seem, is shifting to a new template. And this will be beginning. It is instantaneous for some, this transfer. Others will find and seek it with time coming.

> It is an effortful movement, not easy, for you must conquer your own desires for life-giving familiarity. You must release what was and move into the new beginning. You must unfold yourself more fully into your own body. You must allow the beginning.

It is not easy, for there are hurdles and obstacles that feel as though they linger because you feel unworthy. There is the sense of the self of being unable, incapable, that it's not possible. All things dwindle back to this sense of self, undermined. Undermining self, and in this disempowered state you seek for control to adapt your surroundings. To entertain what was for security in fearful living.

Within that state you cannot adhere to the new steps being broken into. You cannot feel the movement around you. You cannot lift yourselves as you must do. It is a statement to your own truth that we require for you, that we enlist your help with, that we wish for, that we help with.

It is a statement of the purity of your spirit within you. A template reformed. Absented is the lingering sentiment that came from before - the sense of the self as broken, as needing patches, and remembering all you went through before this time. These can be discarded. These elements of the self that drowned you.

And in this statement that we are making we are announcing the possibility to entrance the self with what is new. To lift into the next beyond, we are saying is possible now. We are asking to please enshroud your being in an essence of new. A new journey is possible.

And you are living as you have been, as you have done, always. Never before was this opportunity before you. It has not been offered on this plane. A new existence before you. It must be stepped into. And the after-effects will unfold gradually, with ease, with grace, for all things along this path must do.

But know in the self that the causal juncture of acceptance comes from within you. An acceptance of what you are, the truth of you. And letting go of what drowns you. Of what drowns - your efforting, your plaguing mind, the heaviness you bear, the orchestrations of the lives that keep you within barred suffocation. All this must purge.

We ask you along this passage, as we have been saying, to begin somewhere. To take on the lingering pose of that last reflection which drew you down, and discard it like lost woes, and lift yourself temporarily to a new effort, and to sense the self beginning. And begin again. And each beginning leads you on. Each next acceptance of change, of difference, moves you into a new frequency of living lighter, easier. And more easily you become.

It is an essence. You are lifting your own fragrance you're keeping. And moving from yourself that which detains you, which boxes you in, which harbors within it grief, intolerance, rejection.

Plainspoken, we ask you to please unveil your new beginning to yourself. To accept this. To move into the passage of what's next. To lift yourself. A journey, each shoe a step toward what is next. Each movement within you, each release, each acceptance, a new beginning. Tolerance of change is necessary. Acceptance that all is new surrounding you and moving with easy heartbeat into that next unfamiliar space.

You will make it. It is a journey. You will make it. Simply trust and follow through. Listen to your own being, it is made for this. This decade, this timeline, this space of living, this next period you're living through. It is a message from us we carry through to ask you to mind your own heartbeat. To accept this. The acceptance, the allowing, the moving, the release. It is about becoming easy with the self within you. Yes, you can do this.

> It sounds heavy, this freedom. It feels
> frightening to be without the chains that bind
> you. It feels unfamiliar. But we ask you to let
> go, longingly though you may do. To let go
> what harms you and to be with us.

This next stage of opening. You have time dears, it is not settled. It must not be thought of as a chance to be missed. It is an option, an opportunity for some and all, always opened, now to infinity, for you. You will have this option to move through. It is opened, this is the announcement. It is opened.

We invite you to come through. Lift yourself freely, lift yourself into the passage. Lift, reflect, move on, allow and receive yourself. We thank you.

STEPPING TO THE DHARMIC PATH
October 28, 2022

We have always understood our reality based on our past. Our perceptions of reality were informed by our wounding, expectations, and history. But as we heal and let go of what was, we will find ourselves in a state of transition where our new reality is undefined. We are creating our new reality from within, so there are no rule books or defined processes that we can turn to. We are the creators, and need to open to loving ourselves so that love will be the organizing principle of our new existence on Earth.

Channeled Message

The knowing ways of your forbearers are dwindling now. And beneath you rises a constituency that is ready for helping. A new branching of you. A destiny pulls your focus, a new unveiling of what you will be. And the resources that are drawn to you in this time forming will be unveiled. It is not as you are or have been. It is not the continuing of your internal state of healing. It is not the bridging and renumeration of the histories that you possess, what is forming the lifeblood of your heritage. These are falling, dwindling in their capacity to inform you. It is the release of this, and the acceptance of a new way, a new method of bearing witness to your own journey.

How is it to process on Earth what it is to be living? How is it to put in context for comprehension and understanding? It has always been done through historical measures. Through the comparison and juxtaposition to what has passed in your own heritage as well as in the full encumbrance of humanity. To see yourselves in the context and fruition of worldly bias. These things lose their tendency to impress. They become less important, less voluble and resounding in their chorus of meaning. They lose their impression on your awareness.

WHAT'S COMING NEXT: A Channeled Guide to Navigating the Greatest Shift of Our Time

> You feel the self, toiling to makeshift some
> new understanding. You feel the self, reaching.
> There is no other context at present. Thus,
> you are standing in the barren mixture of
> the nothingness that needs forming, in the
> histories that digressed from your purpose. We
> say in this liminal state made for journeying,
> in this state of beginning, you are forming
> what is next. You are holding within the self
> the opportunity to grow a context from your
> own being. To be the self that will inform the
> world and its new dawning.

What holds you in this power of understanding? What holds you to draw forward? What will now be present in your mind as the Earth herself is turning? How will you guide your focus for this journey? Bring forward what calls you now from the heart space. Draw into your bodies the truth of who you are, your presence. Make this known to one another. Lean into the fruition of yourselves. Let this be the template that rises to guide humanity.

Be not that one who conspires to level down into the muck of yesteryear. Be instead that one who strives to discern, through their own understanding, a new template that dawns for the yearning of the betterment of humanity. Who reaches into the beyond next moment and distills their own joyful purpose, to bring into each other their heart's pattern of learning.

How to dawn a new civilization for humanity, built upon the spores of love that transfer between one another? Built upon the conveyance of your offering, of your gifting? Of what is given unto you before entering and what you are carrying to share with others. To build this, we wish to bring you into harmony with yourselves as you are opening. To let this liminal state do its business of ridding you of the flavors of what you have become used to. And to let the self feel in this open state the readiness, the preparation, the instilling in your mind space of new potential. To recognize where you are as humanity. To see this state as one of grace, as one of doing, in the action of becoming that which will be.

Let the unwinding happen. Recognize in this friction is created a potent force for up-leveling humanity. There is the action of the undoing which powers the new now. It must present a force of reaction which is then utilized for the conquering of the old self, the dwindling of that old habit, and the instilling in your breast a hopeful state. A loving state, a caring state for one another.

This energy transfer, it is a process we are working. We are watching, we are unearthing for yourselves. This juncture for humanity represents a transfer of your energy from that which was, to which you were beholden, in the bodies, in the histories and the comprehension, the solar plexus of your figure, of all things you have known. The transfer of this energy of pleasing the self by matching and comparing to your history.

And instead, with the unraveling of all this, the creation of a new sort. A new history to unfold forward. A new template for life built upon love. No more strife. Only peaceful transfer of energy from one power to another, from one soul who beckons to another who is receptive.

The emptying of energy and refocusing of yourselves. This is what you are allowing. This potent space that you are in, acknowledge this. It is an emptiness. A sense of floating. A sense of not knowing the next beginning. A new template is unfolding, embrace this. Allow the self your discovery, for there is no instruction. There is no reason given. There is no masterful method by which you must conjoin to the new reality. It is the selves who are dawning from within. It is the selves who are instrumental in the creating. Therefore, be. Be and allow yourselves.

This mastery, this dawning, let it be yourselves who do the defining through the joyful experience of self-loving. It is this we are informing - your own selves, creating harmony within, the balance of your light, the truth of who you are. This you are capturing, to let this transfer onto the next new now that is coming. We love you.

WE SAY YOUR NAME
January 4, 2023

The poet Angels brought us such a beautiful message! It's about how we need to practice being out in the world, holding our vibration as high as we can, not dimming our light to accommodate or fit in with others. They ask us to work on letting go of past wounds and influences so that we can express our true self, which is expressed in our name. They want to "say our name" because our soul is too important to keep quiet, and if we won't express ourselves, they want to help us do it!

Channeled Message

We speak your name aloud each time you refrain from expressing what you are. We speak your name. We call you out among the timbers of the forest that remains. The decades that unfurl, the spot that you embrace, we take you now, your journey onward, and lead you into this next time forming.

We speak your name. We claim it loud. We speak you out and herald the new time coming. We speak you out into the sun dance on the leaves as they settle in the forest. Among the trees. You are welcome, imprint to the soil. Watch the Rain dance. We invite you now to speak your name. To claim the light you share, the reverberation of where you are formed, within the belly, your entrance to this life.

The solace never found again is your own expression. Your felt-throughout-destiny in these times that remain, to be felt out loud in praise. We say your name.

We invite you now to step proud, to be that heightened state. To call yourself into the embrace of the ones who will share. The forest and the trees who know you well. Who speak your tone, who envelop you now in their shade, who welcome you. Solemn retreat into a glade of passing time. A welcome to be felt aloud when we say your name.

You are called here by ourselves to speak aloud the chime of what is important to your mind. To speak aloud the celebration of the centuries past. To say to yourself, "I abound with what was, what is no longer, and it dwells like canker, like a sore within myself. I wish to purge. I wish to blend. I wish to allow what is. I wish to be that self that rises now and answers to my name. I want to be that self that calls you now to come and see me, to see my flame. That enters now to the prism, into the stone of this plane where all are welcomed by their name. Where all are made to feel at home.

Here all are stopped and startled to their day and live on in the remembrance of where they were. We invite you now to take on the legend of what was and drop it down. Let it unfurl. Let it be what was. Take your time. Let it unfurl. Speak the names and rituals of they who danced and remembered their days. Who are gone from this Earth, speak them well. But they who dwelled, who only came to feel this Earth, to see it now as it is different, who came and left, and solidly they played their part in this play. But they do not remain. You are still harboring the energy of what was.

We speak into you the possibilities from whence you came. The ones that blocked your entrance, who laid their way and encumbered yourself, we wish now to dissolve these, to make a place within the space where you are at truce with what you are. Where you embrace this now rising time and feel the self as you are, encumbered no more. Lifting beyond the shadow of that which played in longer days.

Now time is short, its passage marked by the breath of what is sought. Yourself. Yourself, in these passage times, to stay and say your name is what remains. To stay and say your name. To be that self you are and none other.

> To be the one that challenges the known. To be the self with open heart. To be the self that feels their essence and stays within the certainty of what is right to them. To be the self that has knowledge which was gained through experience and self-knowing. To share this in the blanket of your field, and to let it drip and merge between the syllables of each word. To say again your name, from whence you came. To speak this language, to emerge, to let yourself feel the Earth and its purge. To be the self, unconquered.

The daily ritual of life that will emerge, the self, enfolded by daylight. The trees relinquish their claim upon you now. They shade you no more. The instant of this time beckons you onward and you must make ready. The times will change and your life, in its perilous form, must move onward into the space of heady understanding of the self that you are. Unconquered, unrelenting, and yet at ease in their own self. To be that self, intertwined within your spirit, undivided, yearning no more. The blanket of what you are is completed and may be shed like the leaves. No longer bare, but revealed for what you are. Take hold. You are required. We say your name.

THE COMPLETION OF THE PUZZLE (CLEARING ALL PAST LIVES IN THIS ONE)

February 23, 2023

This channeled message from the Angels explains that this life we are living

now is not like our others. It's a culmination of all our lives and gives us the chance to learn from and heal everything that came before. In our past incarnations, we only had access to those lives that were specifically relevant to the karma we were working on. But now, for the first time in human history, all our past lives are accessible in this life.

This is because the nature of the Earth experience is changing in this shift, and it will no longer be a karmic school like it has been. So, we are being given the chance to clear the slate and get as much learning as we can out of the experiences we've had. We want to heal all our past wounds, so that they become benign and no longer influence the life we create for ourselves.

Channeled Message

We begin again to entrain you now, to instigate the new envelope that you are understanding. The housing that you are wearing, your physical senses, the encumbrance of all that is tearing your focus from the heavens - all of these are giving way to the heralding of the new understanding of yourselves.

Be aware, souls, this time is approaching. The heavens are upon us now, with their entrance just beyond the next known encumbrance. You are lifting yourselves with each breath. You are knowing yourselves better. You are anchoring your light into the now, and relenting against the pull, the urge of your undoing.

We wish to bridge to you, in this time coming, the effervescent light of the heavens. To let you feel its summons. To understand you are of it. To never doubt for a moment that you are carrying it within you. That you have this now and forever. To let you feel it while incarnated, yes, this is the journey. To sense in yourself that you are divine. To know you are a part of one thing, shared among many. That you are part of the heavens in your understanding and your knowingness, in all that comes round to your perception. That you are guided. That you are instrumental in the divine understanding of life.

This awakening, the bridge to your homecoming - what seems an arrival is only just returning. Coming back to what you were in some small measure. Allowing the self a greater acceptance of your truth while embodied. There is, for the self, greater heights to be achieved beyond this realm. But to be that self while here on Earth is a new thing that you are uncovering. A new layered understanding of your abilities, of your truth, of your wholeness.

The apparition of this time and this instance of incarnation does bring to you an understanding of your timeline in the full frame of its existence. It lets you feel into the self from whence you came, and the duration of each instance. Of each moment in time. To feel it as present.

> This time in your understanding is different.
> It is the congealing of all of these efforts.
> The coming together into one frame the
> many times of many past lives, of many past
> thoughts and beginnings, all accumulated and
> brought forward into you now.

This time is special. For this awakening time, this opening does not exist for long. The chance to understand what you are in whole, not in part. The sum of your parts. The completion of the puzzle that you are made of. This is a unique time. In this unfolding as you are experiencing it, your body is a catacomb of many beginnings. And in the unfolding, as you delve into its depths, into its points and its placements, you will discover yourself again and again.

The over wrapping, the outer life of this existence, merely contains the measured focus for your current existence. But within that, yes, your whole frame is riddled with connections to all that was and has ever been in your consciousness. And through these alleyways and byways we find the passage to draw forward into now that which you would call into frame. To let them become benign again. To let them infiltrate no more your energetic patterns. To let them fold and follow and not become the presence that you have been mired in.

To become the soul uncluttered, without the dissolution of that self in the midst of your own process of understanding what you are. To bring that fold to a close. To let it die down in your heightened state. To let it become emptied of its influence. To let it fold now. And as it retires and you say goodbye to those familiar focuses, you let them glide and pattern no more.

You find in the self a reverie of delight and tranquility. You sense in yourself that you are as you ever were, an instrumental pilot of God's light. A transient moment in this life in which to elucidate the particular genealogy that you have embodied, infused with this divinity. To let it be and breathe. To let it sing its plight. To be in this life in joyful remembrance of your wholeness and inclusivity to all that is and is becoming.

It is an instant. A night, a day. A heaven sent breath upon the face of this Earth, where you exist and then no more. Not again.

> This soul, this life, this incarnated being
> is not to come again. Not exactly as you
> are. Therefore, give this Earth your fullest
> expression. Give this Earth your fullest
> passion. Your fullest allowing of that light in
> this incarnated expression.

Let it become a fluid illustration of heralding divine at all times, letting yourself breathe and be.

In these times to come, the forces of purging will dwindle and you will see yourselves as you are. But for now, to focus upon the self and all you are come from. To let this rise. There is more yet. There is more yet to find. There are instances of what you are to be learned from. To glean all that resides within. Let this be your life. Let this be your essence, your reason for being created at this time. To understand what you are through the life lessons on offer. Through the experiences of torment to purge. To let the life congeal into now. Become as you were. Let them rise. Let them lift you to the next plane of existence. For each time you purge, you emerge a little brighter. You come closer to the truth.

You are instilling in yourself the habit of reasonable understanding of all that is divine within yourself. Of letting the self admit and agree that you are God's essence on Earth.

LIVING WITHOUT SUFFERING
December 2, 2023

This channeled message from the Angels connects many of the concepts they've shared, explaining what growth without karma will look like in a higher state of consciousness where we are able to experience unity and oneness. In this new dharmic context of living, our trials can be navigated with love and purpose, fostering individual and collective evolution.

Channeled Message

The substance of where you are is changing substantially now. The practice of keeping yourselves in wonder, in acceptance, in the knowing that the ALL forms of and by yourselves, these maintain your fluidity in the times now that are coming.

We speak to you now of the changing circumstances that you are in. The heaviness that bridges your expectations, the falling shadow that heaves your mind into the formation of fear and rigidity, is peeling away the layers of your own soul's injustices. The forms and formations by which you have denigrated the self. Through multiple incarnations you have held rigidity, and the time is now to structure yourselves differently.

There is within yourselves an allowance, a willingness to take on what shall not be compiled of truisms. A sense of self as solely and purposefully at the center of all wrongdoing. The sense of yourself as having been instructive and instrumental, yes, in your own peaceful undertakings, but also as the witness and forebearer of things that have been painful. Of hardships. Of ways in which you have grown.

These substantial iterations of experience have left upon you a wishful desire to be changed. To do differently. To come to this Earth and to play a role in a space that really encounters these hardships. That plays them now into a form for better understanding, for more clarity, to release yourselves from these patternings. To allow yourselves to feel these hardships are done, are through, and you're ready.

We say the time is now for these in your passing to be passed on, to be left in your trajectory. To find in yourselves a willingness to open and re-frame what has happened in the past and past keeping. To feel in yourselves and your hearts an opening toward yourself. To feel you are whole and each encounter, in each life, in each blessing.

The knowledge of who you are, what you are, is expanding. See your own truth in your capacity for hardship. See how you have been unveiled by these experiences. What is in keeping with your own understanding, your own knowledge of how you would be and perform a life under each circumstance. These hardships are formative to the person you are.

The soul's blessings come in the form of riddles made for the purpose of digestion. Made for the encounter of each self that you are, indeterminate at birth and complex, and its possibilities. And through the process of life, you unravel and unfurl the blossoms within you. These cannot be constructed by simple appreciation, but must be found and unearthed in the process of living.

The process thus far has been one of hardship and formation by trial, but these times coming, the riddle moves differently. It becomes a solving that can be done without the construct of painful separation. It can be done in union and the blessing of community and oneness. Within this new frame of reference, all hardship is seen differently. It becomes a form by which you can join with all that is. It becomes a method by which you experience truth.

It forms you no less purposefully, no less meaningfully, but without the same suffering. For suffering is the absence of self and soul. Separation is what creates hardship. The sense of loss and impermanence of self. What humanity knows of living is an experience formed under the umbrella of suffering and separation from what you are, from oneness, from the capacity to love each other.

In this new context of living, the great trials of life are opened to the self for the enjoyment of loving purposefully what you are. For the ability to see your soul and self as it opens and reveals its many convoluted ways of being. You come to terms with what you are, and through this growth and endowment of living you become brighter. When solitude riddles you no more, the blessings of what you are are, encountered in the wholeness of communal understanding, and you are witnessed in your unfolding.

Section 2.
From separation to Oneness

OUR RISING IS AS ONE
August 19, 2020

We are evolving towards an expanded state of consciousness which is unified and submerged within God. We are seeking enlightenment within the context of this superstructure for humanity, rather than as separate parts. The Angels are encouraging us to evolve towards a greater sense of self that is permeated by oneness, contained within the substance of God's light. Within this new state of being, we will experience more love, joy, satisfaction and meaning. It will feel like our potential is unlimited! We will have to develop our ability to stay in this enlightened awareness. As we do, we are influencing others around us so that everyone can evolve to this new state of being.

Channeled Message

Oneness. You are evolving now. We come through your head, your arms are weightless. Feel us enter your body. You're moving to us, like us, with us now. We are within you. We speak now of many things, sorting through the history of what you are. Through your history, from now until time moves on, you will encounter us.

Degrees of wakefulness impart knowledge. The housing you embody, the shape you are in, calcifies around us now. We are hearing within yourself a movement to begin. A hardening of this outer circumference, that external valence of what is now, is cracking. The circumference you are in. Your housing must reshape itself.

You are wondering, how will this impart knowledge now? How will we learn from this experience? How will it impart to us greater degrees of freedom in thinking, knowing, belonging to one another? The circumference of what is now is becoming larger, beckoning beyond the shell you are in. It is expanded. An expanded state is waiting. Expansion of what you are, of how you've been. How you've arrived. In this expanded state, the knowledge of self conforms to all things.

The sense of self as what you are degrades your own sentencing. The inhabitation for purpose of living alone has imparted a temporary reprieve from the knowledge of soul and self. In this time arriving, you are separating from what was. The housing you are in becomes aligned with your greater soul spirit. And in this process a one-ship develops, a kin ship between beings.

All humanity must unite as one organism, as one being, as one unified consciousness submerged within God himself. God living, God breathing, God knowing. All of humanity unites within this - the sense of self as part of this, the greatness of being. We are merging as one, into one. The conscious effort it takes for living is a sense of oneself as a part of something, a part of one another. A continuum of life on offer through living and being.

Your grace is easy. Temporal structures strain your sense of living within his being. Temporal constraints separate the self from time in now, and these fall away to the structures imposed by the collective unity of one thinking. Attending to the self within this super-structure remains. The self is one thing, one being, but fulfillment contains more meaning. The sense of the self is permeated by oneness, is permeated by the housing you are contained within, which is the substance of God's light and bearing.

Become him, one with him. A super structure for humanity. Yes, this is evolving, but not now. Not yet. Humanity is seeking a position within universal light consciousness. A sense of itself as greater than humanity has previously been seen, as separated parts, as one degraded into many living beings. But once the central Self resumes its place, beckons you now into the Self, into the housing from whence it came, you are reunited with your placement among the stars and feel the Self enjoying every breath, every moment living.

More fulfillment, more joy is on offering.
More satisfaction in what you are, in the
very sense of Self. In your housing you feel
unlimited potential within yourself. A sense of
self as calibrated to find meaning.

A difference, yes, from how things have been. The separation has been part of the exploration of now living. Of being one with self only. Of being within the self alone. A tangential thought, a separated nuance of what was once orchestrated light. And you become this in your housing, and you live it well on purpose.

You transform your being unto the point you feel the self drawn into proportionate relationship with that exalted sensation of oneness.

The self becomes inundated with glorious sensations. A sense of love unbounded. And train the self to remain in this purpose. To stay within this energy, to stay within it. The longing remains, but the ability to stay must be developed. It is a sensation you're seeking, a sense of the self which craves meaning.

A return to the light that you are. There is, within this very fabric of the self, this meaning. This housing of your being contains these energies of the collective form. You understand this in the marrow of your being, in your beginning. You know this well.

How close are we to becoming one with source, and can individual people achieve enlightenment for themselves?

Enlightenment, as you call it, flavors your existence. The nuance of living and breathing within the light flavors you now, instills in yourself a longing for more. A sense of the self as rising, as becoming. More nuanced is this to your eye. You see it now as something of the self, and individuation from the whole, as the self evolves separated from the populace. But we say the true North to which you would arrive is that within the whole, encompassed by all who is and are among yourselves. A sense of self evolving now into the comfort of they, but seen from within a greater lens of embodiment.

They all must rise as yourself has done. One folding, a gesture of humanity. One being arising, yes, it is done. It is a gesture of a human being. One element can refocus the whole. The beings who rise now take part in the rising of all. They lead the compass to the north. They draw forward the focus of all beings, entailing with themselves a pull against humanity. A towing sensation. A sense that all will follow, but in their own time keeping.

They must fall away from what was and release their hold on how they've been. And those who ascend into the pull of God's light, who feel their soul-self enlightened, who tap into and connect with the truth of who they are, of God's purity and alignment with themselves, feel the state within them bridging the gap beyond the veil, living eternal within themselves. Knowledge they seek to contain infuses them, every cell, and they are whole within themselves.

But this tempers the experience of all things until all will rise into the now. There is within the self, yes, the drive to achieve. The desire to rise. And it will be more, but there must be all. All will rise in time. All will feel the draw, the pull as your own sensations permeate the living beings who remain on this plane. Your own sensations are the bridge of meaning to draw them onward. Thus it is known positive that you can evolve and change and find the light individuated, but as a whole you must complete.

HOW TO UNIFY HUMANITY
February 12, 2021

In this channeled message from the Angels, they share how each person can help move us toward unity and "bring humanity back to levels of godliness as yet unseen by one another in these lifetimes" It's about letting go of our separation to find unity and clarity of mind. They say that we all have shared collective memories of past lives lived in judgement of others and polarization, which led to those lives, relationships or societies falling apart. The Angels tell us that forgiveness towards ourselves and others is the key to transforming our lives and society now. They encourage us to focus on love and caring for one another, to let go of vindictiveness, and to work towards a unified existence.

Channeled Message

We are near, we are within. We have to discuss some things. You can begin.

We are transporting your vindication from that which has always held its current progress near. You can assume that this is not the sum-total that we would transfer. It is indeed more. That, we would say.

We have journeyed there and back. We know the vicissitudes of your weary head and heart. We understand how you embark upon your journey, foretold in the books and passages we read together to plan this venture you are on.

We wish to employ your more meaningful indictment. Your judgment of each other, vindictive, must pass, and we would instead employ that care of heart you hold most dear for them and those you cherish dear. We say this may be the method of passage into the great beyond.

You have not circumvented this estrangement between you all. This happened once, not twice, in your past. You upheld the beliefs of one against them all, and held the truth in your own heart to amplify the curse you spread with vindication. But this was firmly held in the awareness of yourselves.

The sinking life you held so dear dissolved itself into nothingness, and now you seek another pass, a moment to return and redo, rewrite that history of separation. You can find within yourselves each a memory of belonging to this history. Unique to few, shared by all in unified consciousness. You all bear the mark of this dissolution and must march to relieve the injustices of that past life memory. The feeling of separation must abate and find in its place the love from your heart, given freely.

Understand that not all participants in this charade know the boundaries and rules we set. There are some who would torment this thoughtful process and would prefer vindictive renumeration for their perceived rejection and offense. We would say to them, behold the life you live of your own creation, and delve within yourselves to correct the injustice you feel.

But they are not here, and you are, so to you we share our song of freedom, our freedom song. It sings like love and emancipation from this torment in the air, this tortuous impregnation that lingers and festers beneath the surface. You all feel the wrath, that lasting durable consequence of defeating another, who (then) perceives injustice. Hatred permeates the skin of this nation, and we would see it dissolve, fall away, to be replaced with kindred spirit, with solace and love for one another.

It starts with one and another. All can transform in the light of your forgiveness of self. Loving them. Loving now - these circumstances, your existence, unpalatable though it may be. To separate as you have been.

You may all find something to forgive, and we say this love transforms. Forgive your life. Forgive that which dissolves and leaves no trace. Forgive your disappointments. You have now opened the chance to forgive and be renewed by our grace and caring.

We have now the possibility of transforming that which you struggle against so mightily. We can find within your heart the forgiving path forward, to forgive that which is not as it should be.

This consequence immense will undo some perpetration of effort. Scold those ties to self, to independence, and create instead this link together. This facet of indigenous creation has been temporarily forgotten. Forgive your individual freedoms and renew your unity to one another.

This releasing of ills will recover that grand united sense of wonder, of calm at its center, of belonging to each other in this space we call Earth. You here can find the release from this tension. Release your need for renewal of self, of one pitted in contrast to each other. Instead, focus on the release of grievance. Find your health in the hands of one another, and be renumeration with a belonging you have forgotten still.

It is release that is required to unify the collective. You must empty your jar of grievance, of separation, for this amplifies the energies causal. Creating the energy of clarity of mind will happen when you do this simple pass. Not so simple, we understand, in feeling, but to know that the result can bring back humanity to levels of godliness as yet unseen by one another in these lifetimes.

You will find the release of your sorrows dictates the surrender of separation, and this unifies the population. It is not the only way, but it is one way through which we advise. For each step of progress made is in total to your benefit, and none are lost. Even if you are not victorious through this method, it is all of consequence, and moves you closer to one another. It is the separation of your state of mind reflected into your environment. Unify your mind (to create a) unified existence. You can see the direct causality we teach. We ask your forgiveness for sharing more news of work to be done by all. These are difficult times we know, and exciting to be sure, for these times are about your possibility as humanity. Your potential is great, and we salute your many leaps of advance. We love you all, in service.

THE FIRST STEP IN HUMANITY'S ASCENDANCE
October 1, 2021

When humanity came into being, there was an electric charge which separated us from spirit, from each other and from global awareness and understanding. We often refer to this as "the veil". It has been helpful to our process of self-exploration, but now we are rising into unifying thought. It won't be a process that happens instantly. We each have a careful plan for our own journey through this shift, that is designed in stages for our best and highest outcome. The challenge for us is to gently get past our natural fear of change - to understand that we embody change. In true form, we are unidentified and unchained, and yet contain all potential and possibility.

Channeled Message

We say, now begins the happenings. You are entrapped in a world of mixed beginnings. A separation of short duration occurred at its instigation. Yes, at the beginning of humanity there was a charge electric that did terminate in the global awareness and understanding was severed from yourselves. A divergence in your comprehension. You came to know yourselves as you are, as separate beings.

Uniform throughout time was this separate alignment within the whole of humanity. Enlarged as it became, en masse as you are today, you are still suffering from this divergence. It does occur to aid the self, but understanding is limited, and you are now experiencing the rise of awareness into unifying thought and comprehension.

We say this knowing that you are seasoned in the ways of being as you are, that you know what it is to become one separate from who you are. You know this now, but we are releasing some understanding that may aid you up higher as you develop toward your new arriving.

You have now wondered often, "what will be the state of humanity? How will we arrive? What does this housing do as we transport our awareness beyond it?" And we say fear not the dispersal of your enlightenment. Do not fear that all is one just yet. There are stages to this arrival. It must happen in a phase, one space at a time, one blanket lifted and then another past. Know that we are entering into the time of this rising, but not all will occur in an instant. It will happen as is laid out in plan, in phase for your best dynamic evolution, for your own understanding to take in and ponder each phase of this rising.

Yes, it is done in an instant, the moment of change - all different thereafter, but it is but a beginning in the phase of this start. It is the motion commenced, and your first instruction divined for the self is to rise into that sensation of change, to accommodate the fixation humanity has currently with static and settled circumstances, and to alleviate the fear that comes with the sensation of movement, adjustment, alteration and the unknown.

It is becoming familiar with a state of incongruency, of self in misstep with what evolves. Never planted, never fixed, always in motion between, stepping from one to the next, in transition, becoming. This fixation of evolution, the desire to stay put as you are, is a plague against humanity and must be carefully calmed, serenaded, cajoled into fruition to reveal the open self, allowing, passing, moving.

This aspect of humanity rising is essential, for it is in coherence with who you are in evolution. Who you become is one who resides in between, who rides the wave of possibility, who is open, revealing, serenading change itself. For this is the avenue of expression, and this opening results in humanity rising to become more whole, less resistant to itself. For in true form you are unidentified, unchained, un-fabricated, and yet possess all things, all potentials. You exist in a state of becoming always, and this alignment is essential to rise into being open, fearless of your arrival, carrying the wisdom of eternity in your being, and knowing that all that proceeds from the self arises from a place of love and understanding of all things.

The release of this terminal lifeforce, the desire, the strong will to remain as you are, will result in your upliftment. This opening comes with the release of fear of what you are. The release of fear of each other and of life circumstances.

Question: What about anger?

Anger yes, it is near. You have it beneath the self, holding down your pattern of evolution, and it must rise. But now we speak of this, of trust, of love, of light that rises with faith in what you become. Of fleeing that thought, that past, and letting a new settle in for the instant, until the next will arrive. For your understanding, your evolution of thought - always present, always allowing, unfolding - this is where the dynamic hand of God enters your being and flows through you.

WE ARE ONE ORGANISM
November 18, 2022

In this channeled message from the Angels, they explain how we will shift our consciousness away from individuation toward a trusting, open unity with one another. We have been experiencing our unique spark of the divine separately to better understand ourselves, and now we are trying to bring that understanding back into the collective. We are meant to be ourselves loudly and triumphantly, while at the same time being one with everyone - understanding that humanity is the embodiment of many different aspects of the same being. We are truly one.

Channeled Message

We are a collective of humanity. Of humanity's presence. Your awareness guides us now. Your conscious dawning of thoughtful remembrance brings us into focus. We are ourselves, and we are what you capitulate into. The breathing you allow, the essence you draw down and in. We are ourselves, and we are what you now call other.

Separateness is a state of opinion, as you would see it. A state of habituated withdrawal from other and from yourselves. It is a state in which you employ your comprehension to diverge more fully. To encapsulate your own essence as one body in the heavens, one being on the planet.

Separating defines the complexity that you are.

Contrast is what you seek. You enable the self to glide more easily toward that fuller renown of self-expression. To allow the self to resonate, full and complete, by announcing your differences. By claiming individuation. It is a tool of happening, of allowing the self to diverge and experience all that is from one vantage point.

You have been here yourselves; defined in this manner, calling ourselves "others", separates, not yourselves. But we are, again, reforming yourselves and what you are habituated to be. You are realigning your awareness toward a frontier you are unfamiliar with. Toward a sense of what you are as being a divergence, and yet the continuity within the whole. It is the self, embedded within the axiom of humanity. The self, the fragrance of your capacity, echoed, remembered, called upon and known for what you have been in understanding of self. And allowing the permanence of this gesture of living to imbue all beings. To share of the self completely. To remove all boundaries. To access the self as one thought within a choir, sung loudly. Triumphantly.

For humanity must evolve as beings into that which we foresee. The evolution of self-knowing, the processing of experience, the comprehension of self against others, this is the crux of your dilemma. To define the self, humanity has evolved to share a common reflection of conscious being. And to illuminate themselves for patterns of understanding through contrast with their neighbor. Separateness has been essential. To be aligned in this vertical state, a triumphant bar in the stream of notes that is your species. To be allowed and heard in density. To be expressed, fully saturated. And now the joining, the union.

The effervescence you acquire through this cohesion and connection will ignite human comprehension to a level of understanding that empowers further light. That lifts you to a presence of enjoyment you cannot yet fathom.

> It is the transfer of the self into this state
> beyond comparing for the sake of knowing,
> into the state of shared evolution and trust of
> each other. To elucidate the whole, not just the
> self. To understand everyone as intimately as
> you comprehend your own beings and doings.

To be of this now, it is a change of magnificence in its impact to your growth and development as a species.

> You are but one organism, depopulated into
> many streams of consciousness.

And will evolve into humanity as expressed in one collision, unification, expression. One shared mind to transfer, to know, to imbue each your perspective. And to share amongst yourselves equally the written pledge of belonging to one self. One whole. One measure. Existence is, of itself, an experience to treasure. To share the knowledge of selves within this whole construct of human formation elevates yourselves to a disposition, a formation much higher than you have ever become.

This next stage of evolution requires the laying down of forms and patterns to which you have become accustomed. Ways of being that feel necessary but aren't. Rules of existence you found as truth now come into examination and are discarded. To allow, to trust, to feel your presence and the presence of others. It all happens within the field you share with one another. It is happening. The trust within which you are bound together must evolve to become this. You are inspired.

A NEW PHASE OF BECOMING
December 16, 2022

The Angels know our future and will share what they know, but warn us against dwelling on it to escape "the gift that is ready", our present moment. They say that we will reach future states of awareness where we will feel much closer and more tender with one another. Not all people will feel this. Some will be in resistance, and we shouldn't judge them or their journey. Feel only your own excitement at what you are experiencing, and the Angels will support your upliftment.

Channeled Message

We are sharing some revelations that you are seeking, an understanding. We have, harbored within ourselves, the knowledge of what is coming. We have an understanding we are willing to share with yourselves. But in knowing such as this comes the effect of longing, of lack and suffering. For there is within this knowing the power of not altering what is coming. Of languishing in the mire of what is today, of feeling the self, stuck in the readiness for the ever escaping tomorrow that never yields what you are expecting.

Thus, we say for yourselves to be in attention. To quell your wondering, but to hold this knowledge at a distance from the self. To let it be an apparition to contemplate, to become aware of, and to release. To let the self imbue and harness the reality of this instant with that future cadence which you know is coming, but resist the temptation to be always in attendance of that next offering. To be wanting, waiting. For in that state of harkening what is not here, you are resisting, relinquishing the gift that is ready.

We speak to yourselves of these times in our awareness. Potential outcomes, what is nearing. There is in offering for yourselves a time of tempest which is nearing, coming on strong. Sought out to harness the awareness of mankind, to let drift into the summer's eve of last year the tranquility and ire which both constricted your awareness. To let loose upon this new formed field a sense of yourselves in contemplation.

This next passing is about the selves contemplative. In understanding the self, in minding the self. To bear witness to one another's selves. To be in the element of trust. To be ready for the acceptance of what is. To be sharing yourselves. This is what is unfolding.

The nearness of this creates pressure upon the egoist structure, the self of separateness. The desire for release from oneness. The contemplative self understands what is nearness, what is the self in contrast, and wishes to offer this. An understanding. A perspective. What is felt, what is offered is the self in truth. Boundless, without separation. This sharing-ness, nearer than is felt, is available to you now in the offering. The sense of what you are, opened, penetrable, accessible to any.

The contemplative self originates in self-understanding. In harnessing what is now pressing, what is passing, what is occurring as a reflection of that internal now-ness, of what "I am".

We are nearing a time in future states of awareness as you elevate the selves in which your access to the selves draws near to others' awareness. That when you access, harness your own nature, when you draw this into awareness, you are accessing the readiness of all who are near. You are drawing this up and into presence so that as you breathe you feel the peace and surrender of being surrounded by nature, oneness, union.

A tenderness evolves within humanity, for one another, for grace. The softening of resistance. Not all will feel this. Not all stand in readiness. Many will bear witness to occurring. Many will feel the pressure of rising and resist. There is anxiety in these times. Fitfulness, frightfulness. There is anguish in these times.

Be not in judgment of those who are barbed and ready to deflect. Be not anxious for the surrender of those who feel nothing. Be not tender for the rejection that may form on their lips. Feel only the joyful exuberance of your own finding. And in this we anchor you to ourselves. We allow you access to our herald in coming. That you feel the resistance of your own time passing, existing no longer within the self. And rising above this, you enter into a new phase of your own becoming.

We wish you to know that these times are rare in their formation. The accelerated energies which circulate among you to support you, to enliven you in this effort, take you anywhere. They may begin with downfall and struggle or lift you into the slumber of denial. But we would herald your awareness to coast into the next epoch with ourselves. To feel the surrender of these times. To let them go and to become what you are. To anchor with us now into the next beyond. We invite you.

WHAT IT WILL BE LIKE
January 14, 2023

The Angels understand that oneness can be scary for us. We are used to  protecting ourselves from one another. Here they are encouraging us to surrender to flow and oneness. As we let in more light, it will help us unearth and release our deepest wounds, which will help us be more receptive to one another. By opening to our collective consciousness and collective history, we broaden our experience of life and can feel accepted, loved and embraced by everyone.

Channeled Message

Into the bliss, the abyss of what you are, we instill in your hearts now a thought of surrender. To release the self from your own understanding. The power of this time unfolding is to be lightened from within. To let the unfolding of this now time draw you further, deeper into what you are. Your own blooming.

The feeling of this as you are turning over, under, rethinking, is to be that self, aligned with source. To be the one you are in quiet times, alone.

To let your source light underneath the
very echoes of your beginnings. To let them
shudder and release, and be that lightning
bolt that's piercing, that removes the unjust
moments from your conscious understanding.

Be the self that encounters what is new, is open and receptive. As your speaking terms allow, see what you are from within you and without, on all sides. Paramount to this understanding, what is new is your perspective unfolding differently. To see how you are now within the harness of your awareness, within that blanket of comprehension ancestral and limiting. And as we pass through the fold of this next generative existence, you will become a newly shaded beginning. A next emptying and re-assigning your awareness. To see it differently. To perceive what is now unfolding from perspectives not your own. To harness the belonging that is available to you now. To enter into the agreement of understanding that is shared.

To be the one that employs their own harness on perspective limits the degree to which they have been instrumental in forming what is about to be encountered. Let the history and knowledge of all that surrounds the self be included. Be inclusive in your design of this life as you do live it. Let this understanding of what you are broaden and extend beyond the limitation of your physical being. See the self as you are, within the harness of love for one another.

Yes, this encountering stretches and permeates your thinking. It encounters what you are now, a hesitant energy. A desire to remain as you are, safe among yourselves within your own helmet for safekeeping. To protect oneself from that external dredge through understanding.

For it is hardship to re-encounter all things
differently. It is painful to the suppositions
upon which your life is made. It takes apart
the conquered notions of what is true and
positive and makes these unfold differently.
And this is challenging.

We wish for the self now to encounter how this happens when fruitful within humanity. When others abound within the time and space of your reality, when you see them as you are, encountered no differently. When their feelings and justifications arrive like the tide with each new day forming, and you see this from the vantage point of all things in understanding. When you see them as they are, the construction of this now moment, you begin to live it fully. To see things as nothing was when you are empty in the silence of your own solitude. Instead, you rise into the beginning of the hive of belonging, and from here the golden moments unfurl.

There is tenderness and longing to be a soul who is fruitful. Who is manipulating time for their own benefit. Who feels the self an instrument, a manager who controls their outcome. These are passages not well serving in these times coming.

What arrives as you rise above these temperamental constructs and begin to focus on the merging of your design with others, you see the life and it's unfurling as one of welcome opportunity. As one of instances of love abounding, where all things may be serving. Where all encounters are now deemed worthy. Where each instant that arrives is full of compassion. Where your eyes no longer seek for a placement for yourself where you are deserving. Instead, you find yourself empty of those thoughts of being unworthy and encounter the self differently. As one who rises among the many and feels their place in perpetuity. A sense of self as connected, as one with everyone.

In this instance and in this space, the arrival of the now comes for the comfort and the freedom of all beings who are present. There is within the flavor of each moment a difference for the ones who are living. There is, in this incarnated state, the positive and negative with which you are learning. But there is also objectivity. There is absence and rejoining.

And from the state above in heavenly surrender, you feel this overture of belonging and wish for no more consequence than to be the one who is enraptured with the positive embrace of everyone.

We wish to inform you now of these essences that surround you. Of the life and times that are unraveling, and how they unfurl differently from what was. How in the times that are coming there are not the same junctures in your mind which are matching, where you can call upon the history. That's paused now. We feel within your hearts the positive embrace of what is happening.

YOU ARE OMNIPRESENT
January 20, 2023

Your higher self is knocking at the door! It is inviting you to peel away your inhibitions and limiting beliefs. Not to eliminate all suffering, because we understand that a little suffering helps us to see ourselves. But as you unwrap and heal your wounds, your inner self is revealed, and this is how you find freedom in this life. Once you embody your higher self, the normal triggers of life won't affect you in the same way. You will be able to move through life with less friction.

Channeled Message

We are bridging you to the concept of your next awakening. We wish you to comply with your own wishes. To tenderly take the ear and the heart of the context that you are in to make the self stable and reckoning.

To be this light now, the essence of what you are, offers yourself one thing, the context to comply with your own divine mind. To be that, start from where you are of all things beneficial to your being. Being in the heart in each moment in the context of your own breathing. Letting the self unwind and settle into the surface of your own second skin.

The self as you know it has come reckoning. Has asked you now for your own compliance. The wellspring it offers in this time coming is to teach you now of where you've been and how you've encountered yourself. To let this rattle and moan within. Let it syncopate to your heartbeat and become renown within the body. Let the self unveil all this within.

See within your heart now the passages of time as you've known it. See it as you are grown and growing. See that all you are now, in the context of this life, is an accumulation of the sort of stuff you would rather not encounter. All that has limited yourself. All that dwells within your habits that you would conquer. And we say, as these peel away, what is revealed is the surface of your skin, without the known inhibitions.

We would unveil what you are more slowly in the context of now. We would let you feel your way to this new beginning. Let you suffer some, though not too much. For to be in this Earthly context does require some conflict and contraction to make yourself aware of where you're bidden. There is within the self a desire to learn. To be that self who conquers all ills within their frequency. Who knows the self deeply and then discards that which is unveiled.

It is like unwrapping a present, a gifting of the self to your own knowledge. For these layers of your understanding are not the self. They are merely the wrapping. And as you delve more deeply through these contextual sufferings, through these envelopes and over wrappings, you will eventually find the self within. And she or he who is present is the one, unconquered knowing of what you are in the context of all things, drawn down into this life to experience this unwrapping.

It is the self that knows what you are at the center. To be the self, unacknowledged, omnipresent, every where at once. To be the self, united in harmony with all things. To be this enterprising substance of conquered notions, of inhibitions left behind, of all things in freedom in the context of this life, in this surface.

It can be a known beginning. You can start this life within these awarenesses as the self unveils its own form. You can live this life as you are, within this context, but be and do differently. To be within the context, coming from the heart of what you are. A restart of this life currently.

It feels as though the self acknowledges what is, and does not taste it. Does not feel it. Does relinquish the sense of form and substance. But is, at the same time, unconquered by it. May dwell within the context of this Earth and feel its chills and surrenders, and be within it but be not of it. To be one with the Earth, yet within her context, to exist more full and fully in the presence of your own compassionate learnings. To sense within your heart that there is no difficulty, no overturning that is relevant to what you are.

There is only now, in this embrace - the sense of this journey and of it being omnipresent to the awareness that you embody. But to feel in your housing a level of detachment and joyful presence that enables your concourse to proceed much differently. To feel as though your presence here is by art and gift. As though your essence and your tuning do not enter fully but stay above the fray, and feel with all the things the context where you are, and suffer none of the substance of the injury.

There is no more passage in this life that can do you harm should you allow the self to find your center point.

There is no more injury that would pave its metal across your road should you only feel yourself relieved of it. You are heightened now, in the state where you are. You are ready. You are ready to relieve yourselves of these burdens Earthly. To be that self, more fully conquered. That self who has made the journey from yourself and back again. Who has transited the starlight and found their way into a new beginning. To be that self that journeys here and comes of mind and presence and feels their path forward without injury.

There is known to the self, yes, there will be difficulty. And some will be felt and heralded as challenge. But in the self, in the center self, there can be no mind of presence that does not accept their own suffering as heralded and informative. And sees it now is something of their own essence. And then regards it once again as something to be envoyed into a new contemplation of what they are. To see the self as what you are - as an omnipresent being. And to sense all this as merely the consequence of your own expulsion of that which has distracted you from the truth of your awareness.

And to let them go and surrender to the flow and tide of that release. And be that self that rises from the midst of the chaos of your own feeling, and sense you are in freedom. Freedom from being subjected to the whims of your own nature and to find, within the conquered life, that you are omnipresent. There is only self within all things, and you may regard it as such to free your thinking.

HOW TO ASCEND
January 26, 2023

In this message the Angels are telling us that this is a new season for humanity, where all things will be different, and there is a separation unfolding from the old way of thinking. We can lean into the center of the storm and into the center of ourselves to find peace and tranquility. The key is to judge nothing, and to resist nothing because those thoughts and feelings push us apart from others. To move into our center, we need to claim all-that-is as one with ourselves.

Channeled Message

We say you are now feeling the justification of where you've been from, of all things hounding your perception. You feel them as a longing to be with the familiar. To be back again to what was known and welcoming, to stay within the shade and shadows of old thinking, for it is comfortable. This we know and understand.

Humanity has entered into a new season. A new statement for their own unfolding. A new method and way of being. In this time you're encountering now, all things will be different. There is not the same circumstance to lead you on in the way of yesteryear. Now you must put aside your yearnings and feel into your potential, into what will unfold. To let yourself not linger against the tide of the oncoming, but to move into the center of the storm and find your peace.

There is peacefulness to be had for yourself. There is tranquility on offer. It can be announced to the self simply and made broader by your undertaking to release yourself from those encounters of fear and justification. To feel within the self that you are able to anchor into what is next for you. To trust: to trust us, to trust yourself, to trust all that has come, that it is for you.

To be with yourself in this new nation unfolding, you will find yourself untethered to what was, and this is disconcerting. A separation is evident. A separation is unfolding. The world is not as it was. All seems regular, and yet it does dishevel. All seems as it was, and yet nothing proceeds in the same manner. All things disentangle.

Prepare yourselves. Lean in. Lean into the center. Feel nothing of what was a pull upon yourselves. Feel only the calm surrender to what comes. Lean in, lean in yourself. Find no resistance to the flow on offer. Sense within it that times of turbulence congeal and become a new reality. All things will bend, not break, but will bend and renew themselves in some new favor.

There is, for yourselves, a great angst in these times to be unveiled. A great angst for the entirety of humankind. And this we are aware of. We know not of the distance and time of its offering, for it comes as you are waiting, as you are hesitant, as you are lifting. It comes in response to your beings. It comes as you are ready. It will be, however. This we are sure of. It will be.

There are amongst you those who are not feeling themselves complete. Who are sensing themselves of a duration not long for this Earth, and that we acknowledge. And they will be taking care of, fear nothing. But for yourselves who are wanting, who are enduring, who will stay and venture on into the next coming, lean in. Lean in, you are beckoned.

Lean into the center, where things are still, and your presence and your knowledge and your resistance seems indefinite. Where you can feel no judgment against the self, or against anything. Where you sense yourself on par and equal with all that is. And in your essence, you find the truth of who you are in your presence with everyone.

> Lean into the center. Judge not. Judge nothing.
> Feel the self neither wrong nor right, only
> essence. Resist nothing. For the judging of
> the mind is an effort to conquer the body. An
> effort to divert your energetic focus away from
> your incarnating. A way of dividing yourself
> apart from things. And in this effort, to move
> toward the center, you must claim all as one
> with yourself.

To be of this Earth and of the light, this tempting offer remains: to stay the course, to be present, to be of mind and matter.

That you are gentle with yourself, that you are centered, that you are ready. Lean into the center. Find your pace and comeuppance to be regular, like breathing, without effort. A sense of yourself as rising, lifting simply by being, by allowing. Resist nothing. This is the method, the way.

Through love at its center, the universe guides you onward. The temptation to swirl and to stir yourself into frenzy is present. Deny this, all of it. Let it be for the self to rise only at the call of the heavens, to feel the stirring of the heart at your center, and to be beloved and one with everything. It is for yourself and yourself alone to acknowledge that you are part of the universe.

YOUR AWARENESS CAN GO ANYWHERE, HAS NO BOUNDARIES.
April 7, 2023

To help us understand our current state of separation, the Angels start this message explaining their own unified state of being, where nothing is apart from them. In contrast, we are experiencing ourselves as an island, which is of value because it gives us the experience of the divine within, rather than outside, of ourselves. We see things from one facet or angle of the divine and are meant to express that facet fully. But the culmination of this experience is to eventually become aware again of the fluidity of our perception, and our connection to everything.

Channeled Message

We are speaking to you from our home. From a place not like where you are. A void of absence. A separation from nothing. A sense of oneness is where we are from. A sense of all things connected. Harboring within, we carry the triumphant noise of everyone jostling at once. We are all things, an energy pervasive. A confluence of energies, separated and yet united. We are all things at once and one with yourselves.

We are in a void of separateness. There is no one and nothing that is apart from us. There is nothing we cannot touch. Therefore, as you triangulate our position, understand nothing as being where it is. See things as being translucent. As being in your presence, with yourself and yet nonexistent. You can see it and it is not there. You can feel it, you can touch it, and yet it is omnipresent. It is everywhere. In its presence with yourself, it is specific, and in general. It is thus both consecrated in your awareness and underneath in the subconscious, ever present. We are this.

You are of an instantiation of separation. One who is contained within energy and frequency expressed as oneself who is in avoidance of other's frequencies. Who feels the self and island of self. You feel only your own thought patterns and frequencies. You sense you are an island for exploration, of discovery, of understanding, and from this place of perspective your voice is shared with us.

In this you trust; that you are, you exist. You feel your own presence. But of us, you are not sure. You cannot feel us, sense us, always. You sense yourself in a void without others. And in this conundrum of difference, we would express this experience of self; that you are one with us, nonetheless. You are intertwined with us. You are filled with us. Your existence culminates with us, beginning and ending and starting again, intertwining to eternity. You're always within us.

And we would separate from you, never. Thus, your sense of yourself as alone is perceptual. A perception of difference among many things that are similar. A perception of one face, one facet, one angle, one indoctrination of living, one method. An instantiation. And this is of value. To feel alone like this gives yourself the presence of the all within the alone self.

You learn to trust what is from the point of reference of one angle. One self, one viewpoint. To see it full and at length. To understand it in its completeness and to express this. To express it as though there is no one else, as though the complete inhabitation of this perception meets no diminishment in its convoluted expression through the many that you actually are.

The force of this life in laughter, in expression, in love given, in the trueness of your own thoughts and furies, is given with the flavor of your own composure. With the full, unbridled heat of this one facet that you are living. It takes what you are and condenses it into a point of expression that has knowledge of only the self and this life and its current. This encounter, much like a wave that travels through a narrow passage, moves faster, quicker, deeper, fuller. It carries with it the blurred vision of all prior interactions. It makes the self aware of no one else upon this planet. To see things from the instantiation of, I am the hereafter.

We would say the culmination of this vision, the expression of this toward the understanding of your solo, uniquely felt expression allows you greater depth of learning. But as you move toward the center of what you are and begin craving a connection with those around you, as you begin reaching across the boundaries of your own perception and feeling beyond your own knowing, beyond your own reflections, tuning into what is around you, become aware, dears, of the fluidity of your perception.

> It can go anywhere, be anywhere, be anyone. The fluidity that is you has no boundary, has no need to be contained within you. It is the reflection of the self outward that expresses limitation. But from within, all is accessible around you.

Everything. Every place, every word, every vision, every mind, every happiness is a place that you can visit. Everywhere you wish to be, you can be there through your vision. Through this understanding of what it is to be an island.

And from within, the inner vision is empowered to express beyond this livelihood. Beyond this living. To take a step inside and through. To let the self dialogue with the fluid of all things, of which you are a part. And to see the self not as you are in this instantiation, but as you are a part of the human form. Of the anatomy of this planet. Of the universe. Of all things. That you belong to the greater tide of coming to the oneness of the above and the expression of the divine.

From this comprehension there is no boundary except self-limitation. The knowledge that you can be a bridge of understanding across nations and boundaries that don't exist beyond this reality. That you can be a someone, anyone, and feel their feelings, read their perceptions, know their habitudes, and know within them, what they are needing. This is available to you.

It can be a calming influence, a guidance pulling you toward a reflection of society built on loving respect for one another. A sense of what you are as blended. As in cohabitation. Not an island, but a perception that is shared with many. That your perception is available as a tool for knowledge. Your way of seeing, of breathing, and being can be accepted and understood by many, should you choose to share it. And they whom you encounter are opening as well to be available as points of reference. To see the self, yes, and each other.

To know the human race, what it is to become someone. What it is to live. To feel this place. This surface is yours to play upon, to learn and graze and influence and be. Accept this as your knowledge, that you are everywhere at once, and you are ready to explore it.

Section 3.
From Telephoning to Telepathic

DEVELOPING TELEPATHY
August 26, 2022

In this channeled message from the Angels, they help us better understand the telepathy we are already experiencing, how it is different from empathy, and how we can continue to develop this important skill that is a steppingstone on our path to oneness. They say our level of telepathic skill will become so developed, we will be able to understand the "absolute entanglement" of others in the context they are living in. However, they say this is not the same as absorbing someone else's perception, and the division between your own opinions and the opinions of others will remain clear. This new form of communication will make some communication technologies obsolete.

Channeled Message

There is, within the world developing, a sensation of oneness of which we have foretold. A sense of yourselves as becoming closer, bonding, connecting. Heretofore unspoken has been the definition of this bonding, closeness.

There has been an understanding of the connection between yourselves as something unbroken. Distilled. Feelings suffice for how it is transferred, but there is more than this that arrives. The sense of yourselves in thought form, speaking with others, the sense of yourselves in connection through good spirited volleys of thought. The sense of yourselves as one mind, one presence. This is evolving.

You are enjoying the instigation of this. The beginnings. The thought forms are compounding. You are developing, in your awareness, greater freedom in the opening of your consciousness. You're finding in the self a comprehension of those thoughts of someone else. You're beginning. You're feeling a sensation, in your own mind, of thoughts to arrive. An awareness, a knowingness of someone else. A sense of them, a presence.

Sometimes this instigation comes to the self as an invitation to begin a conversation, and they will say, "I was just thinking of yourself." And you will know the transfer is complete. Their thoughts arrived thus to your awareness. But as this progresses, the thought forms become complete. Your immersion in their sensory apparatus, in the sensations of living their experience, your awareness of their complete and total framework of understanding, is the ultimate goal. And along this transit, you will find yourself unveiling each and every part of the understanding.

You will find as you begin moving closer to this destiny, that you find your housing more permeable to their sensations. Not as you have been feeling. Not as empathic souls describe when they encounter another's vibration and feel their resonance within their own skin. For this is what is in yourself that vibrates akin to another's feeling.

What we're speaking of builds on this, for your perception is worthy. It builds on this to the extension of the self, to the reception of another's thought form. Not merely their emotional frequency. It is a sense of them; what they are perceiving, their perception, their conclusion which is drawn, their absolute entanglement in the context they are living in. The comprehension of this they're transferring.

It may be a wish they are speaking to see yourself. You receive the context of your own name and being in connection with them, as well as the desire to focus your attention there. You feel this twofold in yourself: as a knowledge of their presence and awareness of their focus, a desire for contact. It is a multi-folded opportunity you're experiencing.

When this occurs, and you encounter such a thing, do not dismiss the lot of your understanding. Do not assume it was infrequent, a mere bias in the self to arrive at this conclusion. Give it full prospect. Understand its meaning as significant, to see it as the trail you are upon - as something of this journey which will conclude with your own passage to a point of such enrapture with your own perceptivity that you are able to encounter another in their frequency, and understanding wherever they may be.

To communicate telepathically is where you are headed, Dears. Not now, not immediately. But to lay the footprints of your beginning, the starting of this adventure. You have all passed some circumstance such as this. Through humanity there exists this tendency, but it is erratic, uncontrolled. A whim, a fancy. Not given its full import. And we wish now to bring it to the forefront - to show yourselves that it is forming within you.

The consciousness rises. You're more capable, more perceptive, more limber in your understanding. The echoes of what is spoken in your honor comes more liberally to your conscious forefront. Let this begin. Allow, receive. Do not template your own understanding. Simply be with that one who transfers their thought. Simply be with their energy. Allow their perception to move through thee.

It is a sensation of other part. It does not feel as though you're experiencing their part as your own. Here is a difference from what you may be perceiving. It is not as though it is of your own sort.

It is a strength of connection, but division of focus. A sense of yourself alone and connected thus. As in two parts. Both lines are strong. The sense of your own, and theirs as well. You are aware of the focus of yourself and of their focus, and can disentangle them at will.

There is not the conundrum faced by many in the present day of a joining or union between your focus and that of another, where one does feel as though you have absorbed the perception of another being. This is not the occurrence into which you are stepping. We wish to make this clear for your journey to prosper. To sense in the self the division, the transfer will be made ready, easy, simple.

The passing of this will include such easy remedy to the now problems in the making. Such simple and supple capability can replace many means of technology.

It will not be easy at first for all beings. It will take time and increasing frequency. An increasing sense of this. An awareness. The juxtaposition of which we spoke takes cultivating. You will arrive, dears. It will arrive more frequently.

It will astound thee, each and every presence of this focus of which we are speaking. It will astound thee. It will reimagine being as humanity. The feeling as one. This communication connects thee in such a strengthening method, it conjures for the self an awareness of your placement within the collective of humanity. It aids you on your journey to oneness.

ABOUT OUR NEW SENSES THAT WILL GUIDE US
February 2, 2024

The power of our 5 senses brings our awareness into the present moment, intensifying our experience of this reality. But as we lift to our higher frequency in the shift, we will open to a sixth sense which will surpass all the others. This new sense will be so much more powerful than the other 5; it will be like evolving from telegraph communication to video conversations on Zoom. It will be an expansion of our hearts that will connect us to all things.

Channeled Message

Still ones, the breath of your heart is awakening. We speak to you now of the coming times.

You are being held in instrumentation, as a method by which you read the surroundings. The feelings you are having guide you now. Sense you are holding, in the position of appointment, the physical body as an encounter to this highly orchestrated unveiling. A new circumstance surrounds you now, and the awareness that it holds, the encounter, the physical stuff of sensibilities, the senses you are endowed with, come into play.

The awarenesses you are having bodily, the physical formulation of reality, does feel, in and of itself, as an encounter with the now-forming day. It fills what you are. Its appearance, smell, the endowment of the senses. But in this interplay between yourselves and what's around you now, you herald a change. A transfer of awareness that blinds you temporarily to what is coming.

On the horizon what forms, what you are sensible of, is the fatiguing memories of encountering what is hardship. The physical sensations of where you are. The memories you have formed based on the physical substance of feelings, separated only by the suggestion of sensation. A physical longing for something of peace and surrender.

The fragrance of now overpowers. The senses of where you are transform yourselves bodily. The empowerment of the physical space is to encounter YOU as an endowment of presence. To draw you into the fever of awareness. To let you encounter it as a suggestive pose. As a formulaic transfer of your own selves into physical presence.

This endowment you have been given, in the appearance of fragrance, of subtle hearing, of sight and sense, it draws you into the feelings of momentary recall and awareness. It traps you within an embrace of intensification. It holds you there, even now, in the surrendering pose of intoxication and lets you be revealed as what you are.

In the now that is coming, you surrender here less. Less imposing becomes the senses where you are. Less aware of fragrance, of the passage as it is measured by what is seen and felt in the eyes.

In the heart, there is no boundary between yourself and what is. There is no awareness that can come to self beyond what is. There is no sensibility that is required or needed to draw you into relationship which comes easily, the easy endowment. The fragility of the communion blossoms into regularity.

The five senses. Though they interplay and reawaken upon suggestive understanding, they are not the guide that is spoken. They are not the figurative meaning of reality as you are perceiving. They are not the sensory organs of your most dedicated awareness. They become the second fiddle.

The feelings of light and laughter linger, and draw you closer to what is feeding your heightening comprehension. The awareness is softening, a lighter prospect drawing you into a stationary reverie where you can absorb a sensory apparatus that attunes you now to the greatness of all things. To the awarenesses that cascade upon you now.

From the perspective of this heightening state, your own bodily apparatus is still needed. It is still a part of sense and feeling. But it is not your primary guide any longer. The awarenesses which cascade and fall, like tendrils and vines that appear to you, these become the sensory pleasure. A sense of further integration with the All. Awarenesses that draw you into the semblance of becoming another thing. Becoming into oneness. An understanding of heart expansion.

A feeling that you are wandering in the jungle of happenings, that happen at a fevered pitch. The awarenesses you attune to begin speaking loudly, and these cascade around your perception, and you become, in the midst of this vibratory column which holds you and endows you, the graceful presence of perception.

It feels to the self like a melding. Like a transfer of perceptual understanding from one organism to the next. These happenings can transfer with them the wisdom of each being. The feelings they contain.

The sensory apparatus as it has been becomes secondary. It no longer contains the same meaningful interaction with your space. It holds within it navigational tools that separate you from what is physical, but they cannot embrace this larger picture which is now available to you. They cannot feel, see, or touch what your awareness can perceive.

Thus, the embodiment as you have been graced becomes a vehicle tangential to what is real. The self as you ARE becomes the operator of a livelihood and way of living that extends far beyond the capacity of the physical being. And this, we say, is your enjoyment to come.

Section 4.
From the Head to the Heart

EMBRACE THE ASCENSION, LEAD WITH THE HEART!
January 13, 2022

In this message the Angels encourage us to let go of logical thinking and  instead use our hearts to guide us. We are accustomed to leading with our head, and now we are transitioning to a way of being that leads with our hearts. We can understand and relate to anything from the perspective of feeling, even inanimate objects such as a bridge.

Channeled Message

You are how we're unfolding this epoch. You're the placement of this new Dawn. Within yourselves, find rising the dew of awe, the settling of thought.

You are holding the key, the patterning for your own rising. You own the placement of your thoughts. Your beginning thought, that new crest of awareness that dawns; its placement is on your horizon. You think to what matters, what arrives, what will be and come towards you now. Your freedom to feel all things reveals your heart's opening. These feelings rise up into calm understanding. Your heart opening reveals to you now your own direction unfolding.

Your heart's message, understood with readiness, your head it bothers. The conundrum it seems, on offer, to breathe the truth of your arrival, to feel what you have brewing within, or leave the passage to another. To make your heart open or last within the frame of makeshift understanding.

Your own head, the thoughts therein, rely on your heart's speaking. You cannot find the truth unspoken in your mind. Your mind, it wanders in the alleyways of your understanding. It logics a puzzle and makes known the patterns that reveal what you've done and been and heard or seen. What makes the human you are is far from this. The knowledge you have dies within the frame of now living. It leaves no mark on what you are. But heart, it lives hereafter. It rises with yourself. It lives ever after.

It is this frame of being that must be comprehended. How to navigate your part from here, from feeling, understanding all things as you are a part of them, and feel from inside how it is to be one with all things. To understand and make peace with all things. To be what you are and align your feelings to know and understand one another.

To feel what is now passing in a bridge, you feel the steel and concrete. You see what is observable. You note its direction and transport, what it confers from one side to another. But what feels this bridge? How are you to feel within, inside it? What does it observe of itself? What tensions dawn upon itself in daily life?

The bridge, it might storm the mind with concrete musings. But feel in your heart the difficulty, the serene aspect, the close understanding of feeling and connection to the soil nearby, the airy, breezy sensation of being lofty, and wishing for more concrete adjustment.

Following your heartstrings and finding your own lacing makes these understandings possible within your being. You have known the same, to be a bridge as a person, a human. To feel the context of your humanity when torn between two things, two persons, two feelings, or two decisions. These feelings pass through knowledge and understanding. They become digested into what you are.

Your heart, it gathers and guides your perception. You are but alive because of it. It beats a harmony of your soul and makes your tune rise and fall in harmony with all things. You are alive to wonder, to feel the spring air that starts to rise between the notes of cold. The senses dawn with its arrival. And here we call your outer layers shed, to make your heart begin to know the world again. To breathe the air, crimson. Seek in your heart what is told to all things; the truths of what you are, of who you are to become, of all that is rising between you, of you.

Making renewed life - the spring that rises, it calls you forward. It invites you upward to feel the light, the warmth. To feel the strength you have put by, the stored anchor of your own energy, ready to move into fruiting. Be revealed. Your heart space knows the feeling of being underneath, of being quiet and undersold, of being left out of discussion. It feels the ache of winter cold, of dormant times. And now a rising has come. A spring unfolds and lifts you upward, lets you feel the potential, the energy of light. The sunshine moves through you now, each heartbeat quickening, feeling the turning of the earth beneath you as the soil moves, displaced by your own growth. Your feet planted firmly, roots gather and descend and offer new life to your being - a new start.

A gathering of what was begun but not started. The dawning of all-kind. The beginning, yes, unfolding now. Hearts on offer, feel your way into this new start. Your heads surmise their thinking terms, they apply their knowing understanding and leave the woods before your eyes, blocking what you see. They place each thing observed into some category of comprehension made with dignity and peaceful acquisition, at some time handed through posterity. But now all things change and must arrive fresh unto your being.

To believe what you feel, you must untether
your thinking. Release your mind from its
habits of leading. Let it breathe the afterglow
of your heart's formed impressions. Let feeling
be your guidance. Interpret all you find
through this lens of comprehension, of self.
Feel. Understand what you are through this,
your heart.

All things share this comprehension. All things are alive to this conscious awareness of heart compassion. Navigate your path through here, to feel your method, your byway.

HOW OUR CONSCIOUSNESS IS CHANGING
July 1, 2022

Channeled Message

A new awakening has brought us in. We are Angels of another time and  place. A strain you are not reckoning. A space between us exists normally. We are outside of the sphere. The angels you are used to seeing are usually from here. They are tied to this existence, to yourselves and the school. We are not them. We are capable of joining you with permission only. We are from a space, a place apart from here. A different sphere, another time. A difference. There are, beyond yourselves, many realms of living, and we are of them. Of a place far from here. We arrive to hold and tell of what is coming. Of how you'll live, how you'll dwell, of what will chime your living. How you will feel in this awakening, What it spells to overcome. How you're growing to go on living.

We will say this all to unfold for you now a sense of your own beginning. We are here, invited now by they who form our brethren, for those who stay and guard yourselves and live here among yourselves. We are here to say our part, to dwell with you for just this time. To stay and speak, for all-you-are invites us at this time. We will stay, we will speak, we will share, you will know and we will go.

We are tall, endowed differently from Angels you have known. We wear a belt encrusted with the jewel of a different sort. It carries within it a shadowy sort. The whether-or-not we tell, it is a power we hold above yourselves to guard you from ourselves. It is a space within us we would occupy should we delve in deeper, to know you well. It keeps us apart and shades you from the realms beyond this Earth. We wear it like a belt of stars, an identifying mark to prove we are not of this Earth, that you are not a part.

But we are here. We are pleased to stay. We wish to begin, to speak of this, to tell you now what we have foreseen. We see you as a race of peoples, of beings, that are forming. That are not yet begun the journey of what you are. That you are forming anew in this time coming. That there is within you a blueprint of passage, a way of knowing about yourself, but this is not something you are familiar with. This concept of yourselves as beings who are performing a dance given to yourselves. You think of life as something planned by your own living. Within this time, you are performing a dance of the ascendance, to raise yourselves into a state of communication outside of Earth. A space where planned invaders come, beings with other missions, who will share themselves and instruct you now and help you with your vision. This will come in time, not just yet. But not far, either. It is welcoming in this next rein of what we have been planning.

For yourselves, we offer so much more. The understanding that's been given. This time and place that you've been in. A banquet of your understanding. You have learned so much, many of you, and imparted to us this vision of what it is to be apart from self. To live enshrouded in a veil and to see the world as what it's not. A comparative understanding. To feel instead, this will be your lot. There is a contrast here we would point out for your understanding. That in new Earth as it becomes, you will feel your contrast differently. That in this time of your arrival, up until the now, you have seen the world through the lens of contrast. To see things as a category, to bunch things into similarity and compare things for understanding. To define yourself in this breach. And in the new world coming this will change. Your focus takes on new meaning. You see the world through feeling. You feel it at its meaning. There is no need to put a name, to categorize as you've been doing. Instead, you feel an essence, an inner knowing. And this is different, a strategic difference to your template, the very fabric of yourselves evolve into this opening. It is a change of your very structure, of the mind in which you've been living.

WHAT'S COMING NEXT: A Channeled Guide to Navigating the Greatest Shift of Our Time

The concurrent understanding of the human being is one of contrast, and it states within the self that there are states of difference. That one must rise, one must fall, there cannot be for all the same. There must be difference, we say, in the state of mind you have been living. This departs as new knowledge rises in the self to feel your way, to understand through heart-full living. To feel the self. It has been spoken in your prior session, yes your fragrance has been spoken of, your essence. This understanding of the self, your very depths. It imparts a sense of who you are, the felt beingness. There is this same frequency to all things, and as your understanding sharpens, contrast becomes meaningless. This great departure in the mind of humans changes all things. It creates a world of difference that stems from understanding. If there is no need for contrast, equality begins. For all things are felt as they are and honored for their living. And this is how it will be for some who pass into this new state of being. Who feel their way to understanding, who touch a heart and, through this knowing, make conclusions they will understand and not compare and categorize as you have been doing.

Yes, you stand upon a base of knowledge built for long time living. It defines your world, your technology, your education and materials. We understand this and it stays, remains for a long time coming. But not forever, dears. No. It becomes obsolete, like so many human inventions. And you will rise to become something new, a creature more of feeling who senses themselves within a world that resonates a frequency, and know each thing as it is made, defined by its own breathing. And you will sense it, touch it, feel it within yourself and know this thing. You will speak its life - its very essence.

In this way of being, there can be no subjecting harm to another being. There can be no hierarchy. There can be no subjugation. There can be no thought of leaving one in harm's way, for you feel them with your heart. You know their suffering. You know them as you know yourself. You feel their heights and their shadow. You know them, love them, sense them deeply. It is a difference. It is world changing, yes. This Earth, it lies within a pattern that is shifting. It starts within the human mind. Humanity is shifting, and you are bearing now the opening, the changing. You are standing in a time of letting go and lifting. And you are doing well, dear friends. We are watching. You are doing well. You are lightening this world and you will prosper. You will live on, for this time is long.

There is much work to do. You will bring this inside of you and let it work its magic, for knowing this within the self creates an opening where you can no longer be consumed by what has been the patterning. You see it as it stands. You understand it now as rhythm, not as truth. Not as concrete, but as adaptation by living beings. Yes, the tools you've had you have allowed because they were necessary. But as times change and as your bodies and awareness become more sensitive, you sense in others what you are, and what they are as well, and this changes all your way of thinking. And this pervades all creation, it makes all things different. And how you will be, your rules and objectives for humanity. Yes, a change afoot. A change in feeling. It is starting already

---

THE MIND HAS HAD ITS DAY (MOVING TO FEELING AND COLLECTIVE UNDERSTANDING)
August 12, 2022

In this channeled message from the Angels, they give us a more detailed understanding of what we're always being told - to move from the head into our hearts! Our society worships the mind and its logic. The Angels are asking us to change our relationship to our mind, which has become a "torrent of nothing thoughts," and relate to the world through our hearts instead. By connecting to our world through the feelings in our hearts, we will process our reality through a collective "super mind" instead, giving us much greater perspective and understanding.

Channeled Message

We are stating our remembrance of all that is opening at this time. In our view, all has opening as its passage. All things genuflect in the passage of God's light and receive it's blessing.

Through now, this time you are in, these times of changing, you are all in messaging that which takes on form within the self. You are understanding through this process the need to be balanced. To lean down into your own memory of self and draw in the hounding disciples that tear you far from here. These resounding voices are disparate and preventative. They cull you apart into many halves of separation, and instill in your blood a scene of - not joy - but fabricated pain. A pain of your own creation.

These times of changing are wrought in the heavens on the Earthly plain. They are destined to overtake what is. To resoundingly alter the frequency of all that remains. And this passage through life and living separates you now from that time, before, where all things culminated in your own thinking. The mind has had its day, and no longer. No longer shall this passage of time living on Earth be bound by mind's fantasy. Now instills in yourselves a switch to another portion of your humanity, to open the self to receive the frequency of God living. To live as he is, unencumbered by phantasmic obstacles that you have created. To stay in the vibration of oneness with all things.

A shifting, yes, has taken place in some and all things. This method, practice of divesting from what was occurs in any instance where life broils beyond the point of its own existence, and requires renewal. There is the opportunity to raise the awareness, as you would call it, the opening as we refer to it, an opening of all things.

> For there is nothing between yourselves and ourselves except the closed offering of the mind's pattern. The reception to ourselves is not housed there. The heart's method of feeling is where unity is found, where our breath is felt, where God's light shines most freely.

This passage we speak of now; a passage all things are beckoned through, where you are understanding yourselves, consciously, to make it through. To make a choice of transition. To find your way into this new state of being by proximity to ourselves and each other, by felt knowledge of a shift and opening. By revealing in the self that all-that-is is real and exists within you.

This passage is not novel, but in the self, the choosing, this is to be had here. This is novel. This method of bridging your awareness through the chaos of the self, through the obstacles of the mind's patterning. To subjugate what was once the governing factor of humanity, the Lord and Master, the logic brain, the mind of worshipful self-reference. This to be discarded not, but to be remembered as it is intended - as an aid to human life form. As an instrument to be availed of. To be released in its torrent of nothing thoughts and left fallow when not needed. To be seen as nothing more than an instrument that harbors the thoughts and references to be pulled upon, as needed. To ponder, to think as you have done, no longer needed. To feel, to be, to essence form your thinking. Mind, it's patterns, all away and conform to being of a mind with all things.

The separation of yourselves into disparate beings, the egoic self of identity, does survive - and for some time coming. It lives and breathes to dignify and isolate your method of expression of the source light you carry. But this designation does not form in thinking. You are not what you know. You are what you do, how you are to behave, how you feel. What you think robs you now of presence. The mind's patterns fall away, to process all things through the collective understanding.

The feeling of all things carries information not currently available to yourselves, and the mind now takes up its vigilance in this absence. But as you move into your next destiny, the truth of what you are and of all things is revealed to now, through feeling. And this eternity, the now on offer, contains all thinking in a moment's time. No reflection is needed.

> It is moving from a state of reflective
> processing into a state of being.

Section 5.
From Time-Bound to
Timeless Presence

WE ARE BEING RELEASED FROM TIME
August 5, 2022

Our focus on time prevents us from embodying more of ourselves. The Angels describe time as where we lock ourselves in, enslaved to our lists of chores and obligations. We watch time, count time, and wish for more time. Time distinguishes now through contrast with the past and the future, creating separation by making us think about where we just were, or where we are going next, rather than the present moment. We are on an ascension path that will bring us fully into the now, where we can ride the wave of the present moment and bring in the gravity of our full selves.

Channeled Message

We can begin. We have much to say regarding the turning point of mankind. You're opening yourselves more effectively. The instance of this coming time is new, not happening before as yet. We invite you in. We ask you with pleasing demeanor to be ready for what comes.

What serves you now in the opening is the sense of yourself. The sense you're coming to terms with what is just arriving. The sense of your own leavening, letting yourself rise. The predicament of humankind is that all things must rise. There is within the self a revolution to transport your own sizing. Your sense of what you are. A new belonging to yourself. And this instigates within your minds more upheaval, more antagonism with those who share nothing of this counterpoint to where you have been.

You reside in a separate space, and we encounter you now as you are becoming. We feel there are ribbons and tendrils that move you along, that flow through you in abundance, and weave through you an effortless change of internal, belonging to the self. The opening you pass through, you move within, the temperature of the self does shift.

We wish to bring down into your awareness what we surmise, how we understand yourselves to become. The new becoming, how you are arriving, where you will be in this next century as things are changing amongst yourselves, between yourselves, within yourselves. All things radiating differently.

You are abbreviating what you thought before, shortening. Taking TIME apart and lessening the instinct you have had for rising to it. Counterpoint to that North node, a new star has struck your opening. It reveals this new journey to the self. No longer mired in the comings and goings of your world, enslaved to the clock, to timekeeping, making yourselves benign amidst a world of angry settlers.

There is within the self a shifting of purpose. An understanding of how you've been, how your instrumentation has been faulty, has lingered too long in the separation of form from substance of what you are. And we are thinking that you are rising into the beginning without knowing what you've done. That you are rising, that you are coming into form, and fruition, and have no awareness that this is so. Such as you have done in past times, to have been below the radar of your own comprehension, the subliminal moments, the times spoken inside of yourselves.

With timekeeping, the thrumming, ongoing of moment upon moment keeping you down, instilled into the life where you are. Yes, TIME, dears, time is where you lock yourself in. Where you measure and make adjustment to your day. You watch your journey and mark the instance of each moment passing. You make this mark, a journey of measure, of making the self enslaved to that which must be done.

Time kept, time sought, time passed. Time is spoken of in longing terms. To have more time. TIME, as though it was a substance in and of itself, when it is not. It is merely that your awareness dwindles. Timekeeping, this sort of aberration to the human spirit - to the person you are underneath, to the soul spirit that lives dormant in the self - that is rising now, climbing to a time of Ascension where you will be freed from time.

What is sought is the sense of self in each moment. The precipice you are on. The journey unspoken, the timing as such matters not. The sense of self as now present is all that matters. The sense of time measures on into infinity, and there is no juxtaposition of the self and form. There is only now. Time measures where you are and puts into relationship with this now moment from past and future, and distinguishes to the self that there is separation within the self.

This contemplates within your mind, that you have been absented from now. Drawn backward, forward, drawn elsewhere through time. Time measures all things in your mind. All things encounter time and are lost to yourself.

> Now-moment presence has no time. Has
> no instance of result in passing. It is merely
> experience. It is felt. Now is a feeling, not a
> knowing, not an agreement. It is a sense of
> self in presence.

And in times passing, you're lingering in the dawn of what was.

In the next years, coming as time marches on, your presence in the now increases. Your sense of self resolves. You become split from how you were, distanced from that. Time machinations, that which held you down, which limited your scope and feeling, which made you feel yourself spread between the dimensions of past selves and future now and all things contemplated, the sense of time as you are now, will no longer endure for the selves.

It will become a sense of where you are. Your presence felt. This now, this opening, a sense of self evolving into now, into making yourselves endure the instant, the moment and no longer. Of staying within the breath of this now and not feeling yourselves absented beyond this instant.

This is how you are feeling at present: The self distributed among many selves. Distributed, your essence, your spawn - it spreads and diffuses and lingers outward, and makes now the eternal nothingness, but self-imposed upon now to eternity.

The sense of this now being time-bound, timeline, recorded in time - these things will pass. The sense of self as limited in the being. The sense of yourself as rising beyond this measured now, your own forthcoming sound trumpeted into now. We invite you in. It will take time, but arrival is certain. There will come a time, yes, when you are feeling now presence more in the self. When you arrive to become what you are as felt in the now and dwell no longer in how things have been, estimating the next now from where you are, your presence seeping beyond into shades of impermanent discovery.

This essence you're holding in this new century, this essence you are cultivating now, is clamoring to be revealed. It is essence of what you are, a gravity of your own being. The more you accomplish this, your essence becomes more pronounced. More diluted you have been. In this next instance coming, we see your definition supported, your essence untroubled by the passings of now. Limited in scope and vision, this effortless stance permeates your field and allows yourself to comfort your being with the knowledge that now is presence in all there is.

SLOWING TIME TO THIN THE VEIL
July 7, 2023

We are currently on a journey of self-discovery. But in the accelerating influxes of energy that are influencing the planet now, it can feel like we are being swept along towards our shift in consciousness. We don't have to all rush to the finish line at the same time. This is an individual journey. The Angels invite us to slow things down, so that we have the chance to really see and understand the difference between where we are and where we are going. When we are fully present and take things in, moment by moment, it's like taking one small bite at a time as opposed to trying to gobble something down. Slowing things down in this way lessens the impact of our difficulties in life. By giving ourselves time to contemplate our experiences, we get more meaning from them, and it feels much less traumatic.

Channeled Message

Beginnings are afoot. New beginnings. A contemplative time for yourself to surrender what has been hard or difficult. To bring into the new sensations of life, as it springs within you, a gentleness toward your experience. A sense of belonging and understanding one another. A lifting of the veil to some portion. A sense of what we are, nearby always and in force. A sense of us in proximity. There are many among us, ever present, ever listening.

Contemplative time to surrender, you are embarking on a journey of self. That which you have been on, the unknowing turmoil of self-recovery, is an instantiation of life that envelops the self in a cloud of surmise and suggestion and lifts the veil only when it's explicitly invited. The self in past tense has been embargoed from the free and flowing ways of time and times to come. Past selves have been harnessed to the embroilment in that which cannot be understood at face value, experiencing and embarking on a journey of themselves without the knowledge to identify that which moves from within.

In these times arriving, this will all surrender to a new palette and method. A sense of yourselves painted differently. We are enhancing what you know of self today. We are taking on the umbrella of all things known and letting . it fall apart and distinguish between what you have known and that which is just beyond the senses now. We are enlarging your capacity to comprehend what you know. To take into the stride of your own understanding the second step, which has always been hidden. To let the veil, as it is known, become thinner and transparent, and to see what we are, standing, yielding to yourselves.

We envelop you now in the suggestive pose, in the suggestive action of lengthening the time of your own expansion. Of lengthening the time coming within which you are able to truncate your journey of distraction. Lengthening the pause so that you may toil less readily in that which is onerous. So that you may extinguish the fires of your own exhaustion. That you may experience what is known and what is coming as two different vessels, and to see the difference between them.

This time of pause and surrender to your own introspection is heavy, and laden with the burden of time. It is pressurized. It is placed into an incubation. A sense of progress must be made. A sense of it is happening now, and I am circumventing that which I drew for myself in this life. I'm making progress, but not through - around. Circumventing.

We wish to draw you back to center to allow you the field and the folly to experience what you came to know about yourself. To slow down into tranquil state and to see what you are in heartbreak and wholeness. In heavens-held grace, and when you are downtrodden. To feel within the self the shift you are making. To feel within the self that all time is conquered for now. That you may pause and reflect and take on tenderly the fragrance of your own walking, and experience life as though it is offering yourself this reprieve.

To feel amongst yourself and those you've known that all that is happening is a blessing. That you may extinguish the calamities which have drawn your focus. The feelings and sensations of trials arisen just lately. And, instead, move into a peace that is palpable and friendly. Where you may inexhaustibly interchange and interpose the nuances of your own understanding, and come to learn more about yourselves in detail. To see what you are, but without calamitous effect. To see what you are - to have and hold your own belonging - but in the context of perusal.

> An inexhaustible substance, time is and can be gotten. Time is the function of your noticing the passing of the instances of the now reflection. We wish to expand the state of your vision.

To expand the wonderment that you possess, to let it draw out further for your own perusal. To allow yourself to experience the light that is passing through this realm of experience, but from the perspective of yielding. Yielding the self to the favor of your own curiosity.

And in this space, and in the happening, with the absence of the traumatic response, you can feel the gravity upon yourselves and let drift down all that is callous and careworn. And see for the selves what you are in calm reflection.

As all are want to do, the world marches on in a painful reflection of speed and hurriedness. There is the sense of times pressing. That all must conjunct readily, at the same time, and be held hereafter differently. We say this is not true. There is not the pressurized experience that must be had. It can be one of individuality, one that is chosen by you, one that is experienced differently from now. And to feel within the self that that which you have been fielding, that which is risen into your conscious awareness which has been difficult, that which is trying, which has felt in conflict, can be dissipated, can be watched and reared into awareness in a gentle certitude and confidence in your perspective.

This can happen through the expansion. Through a willingness of yourself to increase the time fold within which you exist. To let your perception of each moment slow down. To let yourselves and your heart beat diminish in its intensity. To become sacrosanct in your observance of what comes. To let drift no more the self into the fevered pitch of the all, and the always, but to trace your steps lovingly. To linger within the moments. To take the calm that presents itself and to recognize that, in so doing, all rises to meet your expectations, and you may take one small bite as opposed to the whole of your environment.

And in so doing, that which meets you is diminished. Made to feel and be experienced as something lessened in its impact. However, because deeply contemplated, it leaves its understanding more permanently. You take in and harbor for the self that which has meaning, and exist not in the turmoil that can potentially be held within it.

There is in each objective that you encounter the energy to be yielded. It is as chemistry, and a reaction is occurring between yourself and that which you encounter. These reactions contain an energetic release. This can be felt in the body and in the emotions as something trying and potent. Or they can be exhausted by the simple need to contemplate. By the simple reverence for the time that is passing.

The acknowledgment that the chaotic combustion that is happening is lessened when you are in no entrapment, in no congealed experience, in no method of being drawn forward that does not come with your own knowledge. When you are conscious of self. When you are aware of your passage. When you are drawn into the experience of life with full knowledge. In so doing, you welcome home the experiences of conflict and difficulty within a frequency you can harbor more easily. Within the tolerances of your own good grace, you can feel yourself transported into the boundaryless experience of mastery of self, soul and seat.

PART 5

The Necessary Unwinding:

Challenges to Come

The great shift we are experiencing starts with the Earth herself. The Earth is a conscious being who is currently going through her own dramatic growth process. But in the same way that our experience of emotional release can get messy, so can hers. As a result, the Earth may be a little chaotic as we move through these important and purposeful events.

We are deeply connected to the Earth since our bodies rose from her. We are her thoughts. So, if she is shifting, we will shift as well. We need to release our negativity, anger, hatred and fear. But there are many systems, structures and ways of living that limit us and keep us in a lower vibration. These structures must break down or change significantly in order for us to be free enough to find our way clear of them. That is why there are significant economic and geo-political events brewing. These events will not be gentle. The Angels have said that these structures must be exhausted and brought to the ground, or they will simply rebuild themselves as they are.

The messages in this section are foretelling the challenging events in our future that lead up to the big flash of light that will change everything (which is covered in Part 6). But the challenge of getting predictive information from the Angels is that they have no experience of time. They can give us the sequence of events, such as when they told us that there will be a flash of light that will happen not at the start of these events, but in the middle (or at the height) of everything else. This can be helpful since we know that if event A hasn't happened yet, then event B is further off in the future. This gives me comfort in living my life, making travel plans, and working toward my dreams for the future, because I understand from them that the most disruptive events happen later, after the U.S. begins to separate. If that hasn't happened yet, then it sounds like things will still be mostly normal for a time.

Regardless of how dramatic some of these predicted events would be, the Angels have told us repeatedly that it is important to continue to invest in our lives as if the world will continue as it has been. They wouldn't want us to drop what we are doing and hole up, waiting for the world to fall apart. They say that, even if the world changes, what matters is our own energy. Everything comes down to energy, and the energy you are investing in the things that matter to you will carry you into our new reality. If you are working to build a business or going to school, they would tell you not to stop. You are investing your energy in your future, and even if the future changes, the momentum of your energy will still be flowing, supporting your new future in some new form.

Section 1.
Geo-Political and
Economic Upheaval

CHANNELING #1 ON THE US ECONOMY, THE GREAT AWAKENING
July 3, 2020

This is a message about the US economy, but it isn't financial advice. Neither

I nor the Angels are financial advisors, and I have absolutely no expertise in this area. Even though the Angels mention investing in this message, It would be very hard to take specific financial actions based on these messages because success in the stock market is often about timing, and the Angels have no relationship to time. At the time I received the messages in 2020, I assumed that everything they told me would happen very soon. I have since seen many of their messages come to pass, but usually many months or even years after I received them.

These were some of the earliest messages I received, and they are important, but not as clear as the more recent messages. For example, in the last paragraph where they say, "you will have more, it will be worth in value, more than it was before", I first thought they meant that your money which was trapped in the bank would be worth more. But now I think they mean that whatever cash you have on hand when the banks are closed will be worth more, because liquidity will be frozen. They say we will get our money back from the banks, but if we have a crisis of this magnitude, it's likely that the value of the US dollars we have in the bank will go down once liquidity is restored. That's not channeled, that's just me thinking it through. Please follow your own heart and discernment.

Channeled Message

There are waves in the economy that will be unfolding as we see going forward. There will be an upset of sorts. A time when people will no longer have access to monies that are invested in places like banks and deposit boxes.

There will be a turnover, a flip on the end, upside down. It will cause upset. People will disappear, in a sense - they will no longer have influence like they did. It will be tumultuous. There will be another wave where stocks will rise, then fall again. It will be deceiving. The upset is coming. Plunge deep into the pockets of the wealthy, who will lose much.

Avert the impact simply by resisting the desire to participate in greed. Don't put your finances in the hands of brokers who will underestimate the impact of the plunge. They want to invest sooner. Don't. Be vigilant. You can have money tucked away. You can have safety if you keep your finances liquid. Keep them invested in property. Don't buy stock. Don't fund your 401(k). Don't be impatient. Wait for another time when you can have a choice.

The plunge will happen next time the feelings are absurd. Soon can occur if people are trying to get more than is rational. There is the feeling of urgency. It will drive the expansion of the disaster. It comes. The timing is inexact, it isn't set. It is a response to the feelings on the planet. It will be predicted by some, but timing is a problem. It must happen when feelings cause it. It's likely to be the summer or fall. Then, a surge. Then another plunge. It will be volatile. Be patient.

You must not fear, it will be. It isn't a trouble for all. It is a trouble for those who have problems in their finances. It is a problem for those who need access to money to keep paying for things they didn't buy completely.

Question: Is it safe to keep money in the bank?

It will be safe, yes. It will have disruption. It will be closed for a bit. It will protect your assets, never fear. You will get back what you have.

You will have more because it will be worth, in value, more than it was before. You could have money to buy things. Property becomes affordable. It will, because assets freeze. No liquidity, money can't move, prices go down. You can have cash, it will be beneficial. We can only tell you it will happen.

MORE CHANNELING ON THE US ECONOMY, THE GREAT AWAKENING
July 5, 2020

This is a very helpful message about the hyperinflation of goods, and it gives  us a sense of the sequence in which economic events will unfurl. I channeled this on July 5, 2020. They told us that there would be a drastic increase in the cost of goods, which would begin with truck drivers forsaking their routes. We have now seen this come to pass, with trucking strikes and protests featured in headlines again and again over the following year. As predicted, we have subsequently seen the cost of goods in the U.S. creeping up dramatically.

The Angels also describe a stock market boom (which we are seeing the heights of right now) and then bust, which results in banks closing temporarily, during which access to money is restricted. It is in this time period that the Angels say an Earth rift will take place, which they describe in more detail in another message. The Angels say that the government emits new regulations to protect the influential from the effects of the crash, but it results in the devaluation of the U.S. dollar. They mention some corruption which is exposed in the process, and they talk about this more in a later message.

Channeled Message

There will be deflation first. It will be significant. It will inflict much damage, because those who cannot pay, default. There will be trauma and stress. This period will last many months. You can unfold the events in your mind. It will be one on top of another that leads to up ending the system that exists.

You can bet that none will resume old activities after this. It will be vastly different. You can have confidence in your ability to rise again. Don't worry, it will bring new opportunities within the chaos. New chances for your might to let.

Don't doubt that this message is important.

You will see, it can have multiple impacts. The deflation begins with truck drivers forsaking their routes, not driving goods to their destinations. So that begins the process of hyperinflation of goods. There will not be enough money to pay for what you want. It will be as if things become more expensive. Things are scarce. Things must be bartered or traded to get your needs met.

It can be positive. You will be happy to have such deep resources, because you will offer to trade for what you have. It can be a good thing. Commerce continues in this way. So, it is a hyperinflation of goods and simultaneous deflation in the value of currency.

Be careful with investment. Don't invest, not more. Be reserved. Don't spend much. You can have what you have, but you can keep cash. You can keep cash on hand because it's going to get very expensive.

It will develop into a crisis after the first. There will be stages. Yes, two develop. There will first happen an overage of expectation where people buy up the markets and it subsides. It falls. It becomes devastating for many because all is lost.

That develops into a situation where all capital is sanctioned. Where you can't get access. Then you must reveal the location of your cash stores, unveil that all is not lost. You can have access to the money you have in the bank later, it will be there. Recover it later.

Be not overly hasty, because then another thing happens. It becomes a madhouse. There will be chaos because others perpetrate travesty. It becomes unseemly, a disaster for many. Trouble with fire, with water. Trouble with Earthquake. Be ready, because it happens swiftly. It develops. You will see it coming. There is a dip, then a plunge, then all unfolds. A great rift opens, poison emits. It all happens. That makes the currency increase. It makes goods diminish, because all is shifted to protect. No one can move assets. They must hold and be patient. Wait to become active.

It can't stay for long, because the government emits new regulations to control. They try to confine damage to stocks, to regulate what occurs, to protect the common interests of the few who have influence. They make changes. These changes stir hatred among others who want to evolve, to become more open in their dealings. To perceive the corruption. To emerge from the light, there is shadow. It must be purged. There is work to be done. Then, when this allows unfolding, what's next is the plunge of currency. It becomes devalued. It develops slowly, then comes up to be scrubbed.

All tolerate much to be in safety. No more will that stand. It will be opened, revealed.

WHAT HAPPENS AFTER THE CRASH?
July 27, 2020

The first few paragraphs of this message were not included in the YouTube video.

 They thank us for our role in bringing about the new reality. They ask us to wait until we are fully saturated by the flash of light before we try to create what we think is best for the new reality, because it will change us and give us a better understanding of what is needed for the greater good. Contrast will still exist in the new reality, and some people will take longer to shift than others. But everyone will feel the pull to spirit, and those of us who make the shift first can help the others.

Countries will find themselves overwhelmed by debt, and new treaties will be formed to keep them alive, but there will be strings attached. In the wake of these treaties, borders between some countries become less defined, which can help with financial recovery in the long run.

Channeled Message

We wish to convey our gratitude to you all for being here to share the burden of this unfolding. We keep in our hearts a picture of what might happen, an image to portend much joy. Forbear your glee at hearing all the good that may come. It is waiting to express as it unfolds upon the breath of this revolution for mankind. You are here to help. We are grateful.

We wish to ask you to envision a world without strife or avarice. A world in which people rise above petty objection, where you may find anew the brotherhood that rests within your heart.

Resist the urge to create what happens upon each of your own individual agendas, your own desires. You must wait to be fully saturated to be heard, to have full expression of this greater good, as it needs your assistance to be fully realized. Then upon that solid ground you can build what portends to be a beautiful awakening. A Cherished hope for each. The dream renewed.

We are very open to hearing all your wishes, to helping with all your concerns. We have every intention of being your friend and compatriot who kneels beside you, holding the hem of the drape upon which you cast your desires. Yes, we will assist you in all moments. But know that this moment we ask of you a favor. A bridge, to assist in the welfare of all. To receive what may be true but has yet to be formed. Possibility.

We want to share some hopes for mankind, to help you. We wish to see all who delve into their own discovery richly rewarded. To find the treasures inside that may be a passageway into themselves and back to God.

This objective comes with the understanding that all are not worthy of rebuke. There's much misunderstanding in the world about how we must perceive one another, to cast doubt upon the veracity of another's perspective and choice when this is but the expression of a lifetime, chosen. Another lifetime waits beyond that and is yet divergent.

> Do not be expecting all to be in agreement. Contrast is yet necessary. However, we find that your embrace can withhold the pattern of separation. You can include, opening to those who are much less evolved, who have years of struggle ahead, and wish them to be lifted, embraced, as you are. You can facilitate their undoing, their benefit.

What have you prepared in your mind for today? Do you wish to be developing anew your vision of what comes for all, and for yourselves? We invite you to be held in our embrace as we hold this space open for discovery, learning, hoping, casting into the future our dreams and wishes. Yes, we see your aspirations and we wish to assist - to be part of your process of discovery. We will be listening.

(YouTube Video Starts Here)

What can we see? We are inspired by the opportunity to feel and see a difference for mankind, less strife, more love. There will be an easier passage through life. It will be complicated at times, yes. It will hold you enthralled in context. Sometimes challenging and often perturbing. You can find much joy in being on the planet. You can find joy in being with and for one another. You have such capacity to love.

We beseech you on this in today's conversation, as you imagine what may be possible, to awaken internal visions of grand celestial union, of God upon the shores of your planet, of all seeking the light. Yes, it may come, because we will be there with you, holding anew this grace to be felt by many, to be seen by those who open to the experience. What changes must come from the experience of God upon one's own hand? The touch excruciating and delightful, it is both at once, to awaken those without opportunities to see otherwise. We will be among these, wishing to be seen.

In your city you may find much difference. There will be less of a population, less crush and bustle. More peace reigns because all are not rushing here and there. They are content to be home. They wish for more time, fall away from old patterns of rushing to be here, to be pursuing things that are not solidly in your benefit. These patterns die away because all cannot resist the pull of spirit. It lures them out from behind the safe protection, fortified, that they have created in their minds - of reason and logic and reality.

They are drawn forward by their undeniable experience of spirit. It can be astounding, miraculous, opening, widening, so that there is space through which comes your invitation to be healing, to be teaching, to be offering wise advice and counsel. This is a time of introspection when it all began to wonder if that which they have pursued makes sense. If they are not better served by service themselves. To help another brings such great offerings of peace and self-love.

Do you wish to know more of the details? It has to be told that there will be treaties that develop between parties who can reveal their soft reluctance to shadow their costly debt. They must find in another the partnership to divide their pain and suffering so that they may continue to breathe as a nation. This occurs when all have found their last hand sunk. Yes, it becomes necessary to find friends outside who can elevate the economy to lift the struggle, who have resources yet untapped. So, feel the possibility of these new alliances of peace to wipe away competitive struggle that interfered with the development of prosperity.

It will be another kind of treaty, one with residual forces. Nations remain sovereign, but separate no longer. They conspire to assign complicated difficulty. Debt reigns upon the heads of state who wish to find some way to relieve its oppression. It must be found in the hands of friends who offer help in exchange for worthy, unencumbered grievance.

Yes, the people all want more time to assign creditors their due, but when all is upended, there is not much one can do to refinance. It is just too late, and all hurt under this new restriction. There is no option. So, when banks can't move, the clerks are still, their way forward is blocked, they must ask for assistance. And then there are the entrants who come to help. To be propping up the system for all. And it's not the people's own leader, no. It's another.

You can find this intriguing, the possibility of nations developing inter-reliance so that borders are more meaningless, so that you can find prosperity once more. But know there is coming another time of struggle. We are not through all; the worst may yet happen. So be attuned and aware, there are times ahead during which you will wonder if all this is necessary to complete the transformation we seek. And yes, we say yes, it must pass in this fashion for the benefit of all. To be aligned once more with the God energy you desire. It will be possible, but know that there are many more days ahead in which you may not know the outcome. There will be some security to be sure. You will have proven ways of procuring your livelihood.

THE NATION UNRAVELS
August 5, 2020

This message came during Covid, which was a time of great difficulty, but there is another difficult time on the horizon. A financial lockdown will occur, where people aren't able to access their money. This will lead to civil unrest. It is a precursor to the U.S. losing a significant amount of global power as a country.

There will be powerful people who try to recover their own financial resources by locking down the banks at the expense of the people. These leaders are playing out the same patterns they have lived before in past lives, where similar circumstances evolved. In the unraveling and riots that result from this, there are leaders who die. One of these leaders who pass is a controversial man who is the voice of his followers. His controversial energy draws this end to himself, which is fulfilled within a night. He is found alive, but dead once he has arrived within the care of the medical staff. He becomes a martyr for his followers, and this creates an enormous divide which separates the nation.

This message came in 2020, before the 2024 assassination attempt on Trump. It is possible that this assassination event was related to the energies in this message and that timelines have shifted. It may be that the separation of the country happens in another way. We will have to wait and see.

Channeled Message

There is another time of unrest. It may be surprising because they anticipate the cause of some disturbance to be another delay in the opening of the country. However, this is another disturbance to enliven their difficulty. It will be the lack of funds that requires their effort to be heard, because all will be contained and withdrawn from their access in order to restore the fortunes of those in power, to see them through this disaster. However, the average person must feel desperately the lack of access to their funds, so they become belligerent. They communicate through torch. They access what they need through other means not genteel.

There is the sense that all must be broken. That there is not a leader for them. So, they withdraw through their own actions from civilized organization and instead strike out to find some solution to their now immediate pain and suffering. So be not surprised when you see this action. It is a precursor to the big withdrawal from our political hegemony. There can be no solution while people are in the street leaving no rock left in place.

(this next passage refers to one of my past lives but I've left it in because it illustrates the circumstances that might happen in our world again)

We are arrived here with this information for you. Deep within your past, you'll find another experience that harkens to a time of strife when you had leadership responsibility. You could not save everyone. You had to evolve or die yourself. It was this exact configuration where all upended and you found much confusion to be living incarnate at this time. You were a man of great importance. One who had access to the ruler, who had access to all the funds of state to address problems within your community.

But there were those who took, robbed this, and left nothing for the people to eat or survive. There were many who resisted. Riots happened in the streets and all were rebellious because they had not much to lose. It was a time of upheaval caused by economic pressures where rulers took care of themselves and not others.

So, there is at this time the same parallel where you can see it happening to your own force. Where there is now too many with access to their money tied up in banks, and these withdrawals are restricted. When this happens, they cannot access their funds, just like in the past. This erupts for all to see. There is another revolution of sorts where the leaders are resolved to be dead.

Those with the means remaining are left to helm the ship which, now adrift, must be anchored to another. So be prepared, this tears at the fabric of the nation. All who envelop the ideals of this man are felt to be bereft of a leader who once spoke in their tone, and are now left with only a sense of justice vigilante to hack their way through our society to resolve their unjust deposit of lack and suffering.

Yes, you have comprehended what we say. He is much the controversial man and draws this energy to himself to be fulfilled within a night to come, to be found alive, but dead yet once he has arrived within the care of the medical staff. He can be in this way a martyr for his people, who believe he is lifting their voice to another level. Discovering he is gone creates the ripple of unrest that creates chaos within this country, dividing people along lines of separation that leave us much surprised to see how it evolves. To be left from the confines of the nation as we know it in this now time. You have comprehended what we say today.

WORLD EVENTS ON THE HORIZON
January 7, 2022

This is a detailed channeled message about changes to the economy and banking - Earth changes and political changes. This was from a Q&A session I channeled for my son, so you'll see his questions interspersed. There is a section of this message that was not included in the final YouTube video due to length, which I've called out below. I'm glad you'll be able to read it here because it's very interesting! I meant to include it somewhere else, but never did.

Some of the significant events described in the message are problems with the banks and payment processing. The economic upheaval starts in the United States, but then ripples out to the rest of the world. We will have to let go of many of the luxuries and conveniences of life for a while, but humanity will rise from within and, we will find that we are grateful to have been alive in these times. In the midst of these problems, there will be a great shaking and rattling of the Earth, which I think refers to the Earth rift described in the following section.

There will be riots where buildings and property are burnt. But the Angels say we have the power to alter these experiences by working on our own individual healing, and by accepting the Earth and her need to transform.

In this message, when talking about our future, they say "you are still burdened by the concept of time unfolding slowly, and this experience of self as you move through it helps you understand your creative apparatus." This may seem to conflict with some of the other messages where they say that we are freed from time, but I don't think it does. My understanding is that in our future higher state of consciousness, we will still exist within time but will no longer be slaves to time. We will have the ability to stretch our experience of time, so that we feel it as faster or slower. So, we will be free *within* time. We will be able to use the linear unfolding of time to slow down our creative process to understand ourselves better as creators.

Channeled Message

All will circumvent their feeling selves. All will rise in powerful awareness of self. All dwell within the housing of their own creation and experience it more powerfully now than they have begun in times past. They will feel themselves, within the context of this arousal of senses, a beginning. A breach to the opening of times to come.

It will be held as a time of arrival for all. In this we see and speak of now. An eternity lives within the self, impregnating each moment drawn within this time now. There is a permanence of imposition which you will feel, as though each seeking time, each moment of reflection, does endure. For the eternal self does draw down and infuse this important time to let go of what was, and impregnates the sensation of awakening to make part and parcel of the self. To bring down and through more heavenly awareness for the self. And this time does draw on. And speculate, you will.

The becoming, you will feel it rising in the self, but it is not as you will feel it or see it yet. No, indeed. You must remain open, shuttered not by your contemplative nature. Not allowing yourself to bring forward and toward this new becoming what you expect. No, indeed. Let yourself be open. Remain within the drawing wind, prevailing toward further beyond. Let yourself surmise not what it is. Remain open, dears.

We say this is a time of reckoning for some, yes. There will be drawn down from this high perch of arrival, where society does live comfortably, does rest, and stays within a frame created for itself. And this will fall apart. There will not survive the same level of stability which you have enjoyed for some time. It will be different for some, for many, for all, to some measure, the degree. There will be changes afoot. For all we seek to unveil to yourselves, it will be a time of coming, and all must smooth their own way, their own path upward.

And those who do not, who carry on the breach of this awareness, who stay within the fold of what was, they will suffer some, and will live a tempestuous time. But those who are coming into the fold of their awareness, who feel themselves lifted within and apart from what was, will thrive into the becoming.

There will be some changes afoot, dear. As you have known, there will come at time of separation from what is known to yourselves, habituated, the times of which we have spoken. There is, on the horizon just beneath yourselves, a rising. A crack is forming in the Earth herself, and this does rise, rise, and make within this time period spoken, a way of bringing forward towards yourselves greater opening. And this having passed, you will find yourselves without some things to which you are accustomed.

You will need the support of each other, of one another. You will require greater upliftment by ourselves. It will be a time of damaging consequences for many. There will bring, within this shell of living, a rancor that has passed through some already. There has been the devastation. There has been trial and tribulation for many who have come and moved through this energy to some degree. But more arrives. There is yet untoward circumstances to evolve, and she will rise, the Earth herself, and begin to shed her layers complete and make herself known to you all as one who rises beneath your feet and makes herself worthy of comeuppance. And you will feel it as one of many. All will become aware. And this does fall upon yourselves in time shortening.

A habitude you have of living, self and solace found within the treasured confines of experience, which you have drawn together in this time, as it lies still. But now, all disruption comes and leaves asunder all that was counted upon, and must be redrawn and re-quartered amongst yourselves, and you must find a path toward the future from now. And this will be okay, all right. You will suffer some, from the perspective of self. You will find yourselves challenged to some degree, but not really. When confronted with these shifting times, you will rise within and feel yourselves lucky to have been alive in this time. You will feel your own arrival within the frame of this rejection of existence as it has been known.

There comes within this time yet more economic upheaval. There is, first and foremost, the tribulations to come of this Earthly dimension. Yes, disruption of all kinds. We see now yourselves having difficulty with payment processing, with the dispersion of wealth, and discover upon yourselves a grievance to have with those in banking. This trial makes itself known to the public, to all concerned. It is a discovery within the United States, not elsewhere, not yet. Coming, as all will be affected by this tribulation.

There will be, housing within this discovery, an ancient tremble of what has passed before. It will reassemble the players who have gone once in this direction and let them play out again the riddle of their existence.

And you will feel the shaking and trembling of Earth herself amidst this very cacophony of voices, creating a rumble unheard before. There will rise among humanity the sensation that all is lost and cannot deliver themselves in safety. But this is not true.

There will be some factions that rise within this time that feel themselves an injustice, affronted, and must persecute. They will rise and feel themselves vindicated for actions untoward. They will perform such immolations of building and property and create a ruckus of unpleasant nature. And this we wish would happen not. But we cannot stop it. We must allow it, for we of angelic form do observe and support yourselves, and wish now the happenings you must go through. The torrent of feeling and emotion that must pass through humanity could be abated by yourselves alone.

Only you have the power to stop what transpires through your own selves, your own beings, not another. Your own feelings and expressions can alter and change what occurs. Your feelings must rise and pass through with gentility and understanding, acceptance of the Earth herself, of the rhythms and patterns of life, and understand you will be well.

This challenge and change in the economy, it surfaces now and creates for some a rumble through their very beings. Makes them feel themselves, unworthiness rises within. Fears come up. This is where anxiety, fever, anxiousness all culminates within your beings. Here we fear there will be some who are lost.

There is a stagnant energy within the frame of this time yet. It must stay and dawdle. It must build within. It is not arriving just yet. There is still stagnant energy within the Earth herself. There is a stagnation within herself. There is yet an impregnation of her field, yes. The import of all this does rest just above and beyond herself and presses against her and makes itself known. And she will rupture her part. It will happen, but not just yet.

The field is swollen with the energy, we feel it.

Question: Months?

It has this timing in mind, we could see this happening. Indeed, it is not an accurate projection, for there are forces of will at play.

It will be a happening of source, a kind unknown to yourselves, not experienced in this generative rendition of people. Hereditarily it has occurred.

Question: The Great Depression?

There have been instances of this, yes. Happenings in that time, there were occurrences in that mix.

Question: Bank runs?

Of this sort, yes. Yes indeed. There have been times when all was frozen and not accurately reflected by those in power. When hidden surmises were made public and known, and all did unveil and leave yourselves appalled. This has occurred in the past, and you have known yourselves hereditarily to feel the juncture when all has fallen upon hard times and left without dispersal of your income. This has occurred before. Not now in these times, but you know of it, and this will occur again.

We foresee this occurring shortly, in soon transition. In some time near to now this could occur.

Question: February?

This will be a juncture of possibility, an opening of sorts. This could occur in this time. There are multiple transition phases in this annual timeframe in which this might build and release. A friction forms, and this does cause the instrumentation to reveal such as we fear to say for yourselves. This could occur now, this happening time you have described, or it could be another such juncture as is laid before you now. This year of transition contains many such points of transition which could inflame.

There are energies and forces at play, intermixed and intermingled. These could all concern you now and come together in some form of expression you do not like.

Question: What should we do to prepare?

You have done well and formed your opinions upon these times we've spoken of. You know how it is occurring, what potentials lie in wait and have made choices of a reflective sort. We are inspiring your mother now to create and harbor a plantation of energy, a space of growing things. This will serve you well. You have also done as we have told and made yourselves avail of energy stored as currency and have this within your dwelling. You have also grown a store and stash of energy foodstuffs and make this for yourselves done well.

(The following section was not included in the YouTube video, since it seemed off-topic from the main content, but it is very interesting and helpful)

Question: Does the purpose of human existence change? Will we still have Karma?

This inquiry we like very much. There will be a time when all do pass through, beyond this time of reprisals, when you do not carry the heavy burdens you have come to understand. You leave behind that lifetime of unpleasantness and live and lead instead in timing with yourselves, an existence of concurrence with reality, where you do blend and merge with time itself and let it pass by and through your being, and make yourselves avail of opportunities as they arise. And lead not a life in which prescription must be made.

You can dwell within this reality now, the time has come, for some. And it does unfold in patterns revealed as they do move in and out of this potent possibility. They are learning for some to be within this field of becoming. Others may find it not within this period of existence. They will pass on from this field and learn again. But you may have the chance while dwelling here to become merged with this field of opportunity. It is a possibility for all who remain here.

In this field of opening there is not the karmic structure to which you have been imposed. It is instead an understanding of self as a breathing, living spark of God, where you do understand the world and your passage through it as an opportunity for self-expression. This context does change all of creation as you view it. You do understand the self as the creator better in this context, for you are still burdened by the concept of time unfolding slowly, and this experience of self as you move through it helps you understand your creative apparatus. It heralds the shift within humanity as a player and a force within the Earth herself. Your capacity grows to become her chief Captain of ausperity, of progression and completion. You do aid her, Earth, in her arrival. You become a captain of her voyage while here.

Question: What are dimensions?

There are many dimensions of which we speak, you are in but one. You discover this more as your own understanding grows. There are dimensions beyond this one of feeling. You are in an expression of self, wholly supported in physical expression. You are living within a realm of dimension where you are held between the forces of physics that apply. This is not the case elsewhere. You are in existence in many places at once. Many forces of self may express and calm - you may be to hear it not. You understand the flow of self from the perspective where you are. But you are one of many selves who has evolved to live and dwell within the portal of several expressions of self. You have within yourself all that is necessary to take on, to be who you are. But you are also selves of other portals and dimensions.

Another time is not what we are speaking of. While there are, at this moment, many times occurring, and you are within them. You are living and dwelling within the space of multiple time periods at once, all occurring in this same space, and you are expressed among them. And this is true. But you are, as an expression of self, individuated, separated from them and cannot feel them in your daily life. They do, however, on occasion creep through into your own expression and overlap with yourself, and in these moments of time you feel your self changed and different. You bring on habits and understandings you do not have in this time and place.

Dimensions are fluid and forming. They are not prescriptive by self. They are imbued into the fabric of existence. They are terminations and beginnings of vibration and frequency between levels of comprehension, and you do move between and among them as you are ready to acquire higher levels of energy.

Question: Why all the change?

Change will occur at your behest, but not because you are ready, no. It occurs, the majority of this upheaval, for Earth herself, her own doing, her own instigation. This is caused by her evolving, not your own, and you are merely reflecting that evolution within yourselves. You, in your human selves, are a creation of her and must bear her vibration inwards, and cannot do this if you remain as you have been. You must evolve as well to remain and dwell in her sphere. Therefore, she has instigation of much of what occurs. This does culminate with yourselves. You do feel that shifting upward. And it does create for humanity the option and possibility of onward with your own evolution, and this we encourage and reveal as you are ready to see.

Question: Separation?

There is among these, some. Yes, a separation of field economic indeed, of political upheaval, yes. Cultural shifting does come, but not as you have spoken. Not a separation for some. An evolving experience.

(Here, the video starts again)

The political sphere does shift and alter in this timeframe which you are living in. There is not the same power and authority held by your nation. It changes being. It is no longer as it was. There are not the same circumstances that held in place, and it does diminish in power and become, as forefathers felt, a greater expression of the people within it. It is held to some as an opportunity, forlorn for too long, to create equality among people. And this is what is revealing itself. It will take time to reframe. There will be many opportunities within this.

The separation of fields, it comes in spurts and starts. There will be regions of employ that feel much the same, and others where persons are drawing apart from what is now spoken. There are fields of many parties, of withdrawal. It occurs in stages, but this upheaval begins with many voices spoken. An argument erupts within the nation itself and creates a cacophony of voices separating from one another.

This anger that lies within the belly, this cauldron of energy, must erupt and form a purpose for itself. It creates within the nation the separation which we are speaking of. And this does form and renew differently for each parcel of the country.

WHAT WILL HAPPEN IN THE ASCENSION
January 26, 2022

The first part of this message is about a kind of energy on the Earth that can't carry forward into the new reality. They tell us that there are beings on our Earth who attempt to grow their power by taking power from others. They are initially drawn under the influence of another being who takes their power, and then they in turn draw power from those who assemble beneath them, creating a pyramid structure with one being at the top who seeks to become like God. However, this cannot surpass the mind of God. The Angels tell us that these beings would vilify Angels and draw people into their control. Having these influences here has served us until now because it gave us the opportunity to confront ourselves in their reflection, learn from the contrast, and accomplish our own becoming.

In the second half, the Angels explain that there will be some difficult times ahead, and constriction in many forms, as we release the structures that are holding us back. They talk about invasions, famine and flooding. They describe an Earth rift that separates the United States, and the migration of people into communities of shared beliefs and opinions. China asserts its control of Taiwan and becomes even more powerful through alliances. But then, China will end up in surrender and be broken apart, which will lead to difficulties for the Chinese people.

They advise us to have some food stored for ourselves and to share with others, but not so much that we fall into a fearful mindset. As always, they reassure and remind us that this letting go of what was ushers us into the new beginning.

Channeled Message

It will be surfacing, a vibration cleansing. We wish to bring you fully into the breach, to help you understand where we begin with our process of elimination of that which does not serve.

We've housed, for some time, the frequency of that which dawns to begin itself within this frame, that continues not into the spiritual path, that wishes to belong to this room alone and will not accelerate into the new.

We wish to bring your awareness to this; that there have been entities within this existence who have somehow found themselves in one way or another to be bewitched and assembled into pyramid form of transference of energy from themselves to another. This darkness, within the frame of this existence, they transferred their power to one they know, and then bring into their path those who have what they desire, to achieve their own wealth of being. And they draw upon they whom assemble beneath them.

This construction of energy transference does occur now in this present space. It is a possession of one to another to another, beings interconnected to the drawing of energy, upward to one whose power must survey them all. And he has drawn them into himself, to begin his own becoming of something everlasting he should wish for himself. But this is not possible.

We should speak to yourselves - this cannot begin while within the frame of God's mind. His orchestration of these energies, unfurling one upon another to bring within him all he requires, this cannot surpass the mind of God. It cannot bring himself into parity with what is being and becoming all things. The one surpassing all is now upon us in sharing his force of being, his life-giving effervescence. We all absorb and take into our hearts to become what we may within his guidance, to aspire to higher realms, to make ourselves light.

On the Earth realm you must achieve your correction of comprehension, a greater knowledge of what you are, a shifting in perspective which allows yourselves to understand that which you draw from. The one who is achieving his eminence through your graduating into him, not becoming, claiming less than what you are for his power to succeed. We are bringing you now to the knowledge of his presence, this one who would vilify ourselves, make ourselves unknown to you. This one who would occupy your hearts with his own heartbeat and make himself known as occupier of his lordship. We say this has been an undercurrent for some time of events passing.

There is aspiring within the fold of this envelope which encloses you now, there is aspiring by himself to achieve more, to be more within this frame. To achieve all that has heretofore been withheld. To make you all a part of his assemblage. But we will not permit that.

> It has been powerful in your realm to have his presence. His knowledge and understanding of yourselves does permit him to access your beings in ways that transform and cajole and heal your hearts unwittingly.

Review must confront yourselves in his reflection. You must survey your own being in the temptation he emits. You must face and frustrate your being and learn and live within these powerful energies of contrast which he creates. You have done this and survived well to learn more about yourselves. You have done what he would wish not; you accomplished your own becoming and made more of your awareness for the blooming.

We see now your arrival on this plane to aid another, to become more yourself, but primarily to have grown the human species. To make you all transported into the next beyond. This is arriving now. We come to herald your transition, to make you feel what comes, acknowledge your presence within a new realm of awareness.

You will find this passing, this trajectory, unfolds with great difficulty. But there must be a transference of energy that occurs. There must occupy within this time a field of convergence in which all things that do not make the transfer cannot survive and must not be allowed.

The things which would draw you down
cannot thrive any longer. We take you from
here, from this point of view of tolerance of
all things, where all things have been allowed
to prosper, where all energies were like and
unlike permitted. No longer is this allowed in
this constriction of possibility. This will make
some suffer in the interim. There is a letting
go and releasing which must occur. All will
feel the pull of this.

The nations of which you spoke, the difficulties they will have will differ one from another. The empowering of some, disempowering of another. There will be transfers of power brokered. There will be energies of conflict rising. There will be forcible entry by some upon another nation, and this will occur and constrict some more. Yes, constriction abounds of all types.

There will not be foodstuffs available for many, for times of famine are ahead in this plane of existence. Times of famine and constriction, release of what was not happening within the frame of new beginnings.

There is a release of all things, of all existence,
of all awareness. A release of all things that
must pass. A willingness to be within the
frame of not knowing, of opening the self to
what is beyond. Stepping into and renewing.

Allowing this transfer of objective, a transfer of consciousness is required, and you will arrive there as one whole. Unity, profound within yourselves, will transfer you as one. You will make this move. Alignment comes, but not yet. Be ready. But there must constriction be allowed. It must follow that you will then inure yourselves to the anxieties and stresses of what must unfold. There have been seen some passings of difficulty, and you will feel these.

But be prepared to release what you offer at present as mementos of life. Prepared to release that which you claim, to which art and anger you have held. We are seeing this new time unfolding as one of victory for yourselves as beings. One of great, everlasting hope for the trilogy of creation you embody. We see you as God's light personified in human flesh, and you are illuminated from within by his love.

We see now coming on this plane the types of events you wish to know. What will come, what will happen? We will answer this to some part. We say you are aware of the inelegance of disaster. Of how it unfolds with readiness and consumes what lay in its path. It has not the radar of understanding, of knowing who is to be spared and who not. It chooses only its own expression of happening and consumes what lay before. And you are there, worried. And we say, fear not, dears.

There are happenings extreme to be found in these years coming which you will survive, your way forward made clear to your own selves. Your own hearts are true, and their recognition of what will come, your own hearts lead you, dears. Of this we are assured.

But you must know these times unfolding are difficult for many. There will be famine, as we have said. There will be disruption of political form, there will be many who intrude upon another's space of being. Homes may flood, possessions washed away. This can happen. There will be water everywhere, floods of torrent yet to come. Floods of waves, as we have shown, and yes, of rivers full, and lives turned upside down and happening not as shown to themselves and their own imaginings. Lives lived in disarray and turmoil. And this we fear will alter not their course, the tempests as they come. It will flow as has been told, their own direction unfolding before them.

We say the sequence you desire to understand. There is, yes, the becoming. The torrent of understanding that all has been lost, this economy will shut down, will stop, will employ you no more. There will be happening some constriction of the banks, as we have foretold. Yes, you will find yourselves without transfer payment, without ways of bringing yourselves what you need or is required.

It will be a time of difficulty, and you must prepare. You must have yourselves ways and methods of preparation for being. Ways of feeding and housing that will not require payment of any kind. Storage of foodstuffs is important, dears. Storage of self-preserving. What do you need? What do you require? Have this, be prepared in this method. Not too extreme, have no more than you wish to consume yourselves and share with others, but not more than that. Do not take on the burden of too many things, of too much, for this will weigh you down and transfer your consciousness into fear and survival, and this we wish not. Only to have abundance of thought, abundance of plenty and no more. Enough.

And then prepare your mood to hear of great happenings without, of Earthly struggles within your nation, here the United States, as we have spoken. Of Earthly rift which transplants yourselves to one side or another, where you moved to be and find the people who gently welcome you in and find yourselves at home. There is a shifting in the population which must occur, and this will travel fast. And you will find yourselves a new nation separating, becoming, finding yourselves.

And this upheaval does employ the imaginings in other places, and spark, ignite, the turmoil to begin. There in China you have asked, and indeed, it is true, your understanding complies with our observation. They will rise into the blank space you occupied as a nation and feel their way unencumbered to take on and overpower another, Taiwan. And this change and shift in the dynamics of global power will alter the canvas for some time. For they will empower themselves through the portals of transference, of making friends where none were, previously, and using the alliance to make themselves larger still. To make themselves proud and becoming, to own the nation that they are spreading and invigorating with these moves. But they will arrive upon times of surrender and feel themselves broken apart and made to suffer, their own peoples left bereft of food and abundance, made to live and wander in search of what was taken from them, their own beings adrift.

ANGEL Q&A ON WORLD EVENTS
June 17, 2022

In this message I was channeling for my son, who asked questions. The Angels told us that the pace of change will continue to increase as we get closer to the flash of light. We may wish for a return to normalcy, but we will adapt. There will be a gradual replacement of expectations, and people will become more tolerant of things lacking. The polarization within the United States will result in a separation of the country. It will be inflamed by economic troubles, but the Angels remind us that we can still thrive even in difficult times. The chaos is moving humanity towards its own shift in consciousness, and into a loving relationship with one another. We are meant to open to unity consciousness and help one another through this time.

There is a needed purging of the halls of power. Corporations will be unable to pay their debt, and banks won't have the funds on hand to cover their obligations. The market will drop, and the financial system will be undermined. The U.S will still exist in some form, but not in the same way. China will exert control over Taiwan, but then China's centralized government will fall and it will be difficult for the country to function.

Manufactured goods become hard to get as international trade breaks down. Some manufacturing countries will still be producing, but not all needed parts are available for the assembly of things, and this creates stagnation. Countries must work locally within their own borders to seek a resolution.

Channeled Message

There are happenings on the precipice, beginning. You're already perceiving their origination. They started already; you're perceiving them now. Fortuitous times forthcoming, there is opportunity yet. There are instances in this instigation which do alleviate pain and suffering for many. There are instances in the happenings from now which will catapult humanity forward. But also, in these times coming, of darkness enfolding the many. There are opportunities, in this happening, for those who are wandering to become composed. To re-find themselves. Hither and thither scattered, they can become once again integrated and clear in their mindset.

In this happening, as it starts, there are many pieces of the puzzle. You have already experienced the deterioration of many things in many ways. Expectations not delivered. So many places you are living, instances of life that are different. And this will go on, continuing. More things you are expecting will not arrive. More places you inhabit will be different. It will be more of this; it will keep on happening. The duration will be longer. The continuation more fevered.

It is a pace of comeuppance. It is a pace unsettling to your vision. A perception of what will be next. What will be missing? How will I endure? Will this be lasting? Will it seem like it was? Will there be enough? Will I be settled?

There will be enough. But you are seeking in yourselves some sameness, some culmination in this origination that will draw you toward a reality that differs not far from where you start. And we say this is not our current understanding of how this will happen. There will be a gradual replacement of expectation, of things unsettling as you become, in duration, more tolerant of things lacking. Of not finding, of sensing the world more perturbed and upended. There is a continual thought of, what will be next? And this goes on happening.

There are instances we have spoken of, of the energies complex and mixed in humanity, of person against person, and how this unfolds and continues on. There are energies revolutionary, overturning of things. Things that once were, that have been counted on, that no longer endure. The up-ending, overturning, reconfiguring, restating, re-making. Disassembling, this energy is current. This is happening now and will go on and continue and will become larger still.

There is an energy of this in the United States. You are harboring such a fury of partisanship, such energy around the separation between people, and this will erupt. There will be tolls, a tax on the many. An economic hardship which will separate further. A sense of all things separating from now. The great duration of this tears apart the country. It is the instigation we have spoken about. This is coming. The time is short, it is not long.

Things have been happening as we have spoken, and you are accurate in your understanding that the energies we are naming come forward in many ways. You can remark upon them as they evolve and transform humanity. They evolve, they change, they separate, they create turmoil and opportunity.

These energies within humanity, they are moving you toward something. Towards change. To be aware in all things that humanity has a shared consciousness, a shared aura. That there is between peoples in humanity a communal understanding of things. So, as you are processing what comes, it does erupt and perform around the globe. To understand that these energies erupt incautiously as they would, as they are called into being by your own conscious awareness.

Here, however, it is spoken for. The United States will become disheveled. It will be a taxing economic circumstance, a derailment of great conflagration, and integration of many things interrupting one another, and there cannot be found a method by which it can be avoided.

There are attempts now, economic circumstances attempting to pull back, to harness, to trade down, to alter, to change this trajectory. But it is spoken for. There are many who acknowledge it now, many who are attempting to ride down for the duration and make way once things are clear. But there can be no unearthing from this disaster. It will derail, yes; the US, the economy here and worldwide. It will separate all things.

But be aware: within this circumstance, your lives are many. You are many persons and many instances of existence. And understand, like the human body is a many celled organism, you can have disease and have many systems off-line. You can have illness, and yet parts of the body go on living. There are many cells spoken for and those that are remaining are undisturbed. This is how you are. This is humanity. There will be this posterior movement, this drowning sensation of the economy. But to be aware that it changes not all things everywhere. It changes some things, as in all that we have been speaking. There is a difference to be sure, but you may endure. It need not affect all beings.

Be aware of the tightening, of the changing, of the need to recover humanity to the trajectory of living between, of leaning upon each other, of giving and receiving. Of opening the canals of brother and sisterhood.

There will be many things that will be familiar, that will not change. But know the toxicity is necessary. There is a needed purging, for all the halls of power are overturning, and this is required for humanity. There must be a change. It cannot harden itself to this toppling effect and still achieve the ascendance that is on offer. There must be a relinquishing of the reins of power. There must be a flattening, a revisiting, a change in thinking.

There's more turmoil yet, but as we have said, be aware that humanity is a many layered, many-celled being.

> That you can go on living. That you can prosper even in the circumstances of which we are speaking. So do not lose hope. Do not feel as though you are subjected to a period of turmoil without release. There is opportunity in all things, and you can go on living and find your peace.

Question: What is going to happen with the economy in the US?

The banks are closing. They are hardening themselves against great losses which they will be subjected to. There is an opening of debt, fallen debt, un-

repayment of debt. Corporations cannot pay their debt. Banks do not have the funds they require. All things are in mid-heaven as they circulate and cannot be tied down. There are not the instruments that they require. They are all undermined, and cannot cover their obligations, and so many things are torn apart all at once and unraveling. The market falls, stock markets diminish, undermining all things. Rugs pulled out, undermining. This is the energy. The energy is one of undermining all things. There are things built upon that are not strong. Foundations will crumble, undermining of many things. Not one, many.

Question: How long away is this?

Not far. In these coming months you will see this possibility. It will occur within this period of time that we are speaking. It will occur, it is happening in starts, beginnings, but not yet here. In some months. It is beginning in some months.

Question: How can we insulate our finances?

You cannot insulate yourself from it. There is no protective shell to hide behind. You would not wish it. An experience of being assembled in the world, a part of things. This is what you are learning. Therefore, do not attempt to harbor your own gates and leave your living undisturbed. Instead, understand and follow through the actions that are coming. See where development has called you now. What is moving forward? What is needed? Move your money and your assets, if you have them, to places where there are future prospects. Do not stay in the rhythm of things that are departing.

Question: Politically, what is going to happen in the US?

The United States will not assemble itself in the same way. It will depart from the college it has belonged to and become a separated organism of many parts and parcels. It will become separated states, no longer tied together in the same way. The separation will occur gradually for some, a separation by dissolving. A separation where resources are no longer divided, and this instigates more division.

There will be some time periods of great violence among humanity. This is coming. A period of great turmoil, when all will be fallen, will feel themselves beckoning toward the graves of many people. But this is not always an instance of living. There are patterns unfolding, patterns which the world has fallen into. Patterns of cause and effect, of suffering, of person against person, as we had been speaking. This unfolding must stop itself. It must burn out the instance. This has not yet happened. There is still anger in the Earth - it is forthcoming. It, too, must alter the context of this expulsion. So, there is anger of the Earth and suffering among humanity to come. These will unwind in time.

The United States, you have been wondering. Yes, it is partitioned differently. There is still a central core to humanity, a center self. A way of speaking and knowing about each other. There is still communication that is wise. There's still an understanding among peoples. This exists and endures and becomes larger. There's more a central focus for humanity, more becoming one with other selves. Of lessening the ties of divide and making truths combined toward wholeness. This is in the longer term.

Question: What is going to happen to the Seattle region politically?

This region is now the focus of no things. It is a region of left behind, of without thought. It is now enacting political margins of its own safe-keeping, but it is not integral to the nation state. It is separated by its own distance. Therefore, in the process of the unfolding, this territory becomes its own self. It is separated now, but not as it has been spoken. There will be a time coming when it is no longer held in the same context as the states below it. It is made by itself and then connected heretofore to other brothers and sisters above it. It is made of its own self. A continuity evolves over time. A separated state with itself and others who participate, but not as it was. A divide has formed between this region and the others of the former United States. This will come in time.

Question: What about war between China and Taiwan?

Taiwan is unsettling itself. It is not easy in its seat. It heralds a peace that is ending. Turmoil is afoot. It will not last, it is not durable, this current state of affairs. Not durable, it is not lasting. It will be a period of great conflict, and predetermined chaos is coming.

Question: What will ramifications be across Asia?

There will be a period of great instability for many. It is coming. A period of great lax in governing. A lack of governing. This will complicate things. The matters of life become uneasy because there's no central focus. There's not the easy distribution of items. The culmination and circulation that occurs now.

Question: I would ask about the availability of manufactured goods in markets like Europe and North America if there were to be chaos in Asia?

There will be a lack of these. Not all countries will be treated equally. That all countries are experiencing the many-folded properties of chaotic distribution. There are some which are inured to the suffering, which are still producing for the West. There are some which are offering their services and goods. Some of this continues. Not all, some. There is lack on offering as we stated in previous conversation.

Not all things are missing. Some things. But all things are complicated in some way. There are disparate items which must collect and be assembled, and some pieces are missing, and this creates difficulties, lengthening the time period between ordering and having. And this then furthers delays of payment, which causes businesses to slow down and stop making. This creates more lack and stagnation, and nations must speak within themselves to determine a possible way forward. It is undetermined but can be resolved. It is possible.

Question: What do people really need to know in the next few months as we experience the transition from stability to instability?

The most important thing to be aware of is to stand centered within yourself. To be aware that all things will open up, will change, and this is necessary. To be inured to the concept of change itself, to accept that all things will be different, that you yourself are changing. To allow the heavens to pour forth and release and reveal what comes next, and to open yourself to it. And trust that within these parting gates there will be something for yourself, and it will be good. Move to it with alacrity and be easy in your own skin. Fear not, fear nothing, for you are eternal. This period will be ending, there is an end in sight. It is not forever. It is turmoil, this is correct. But as you are understanding, to release the agony of desiring some other outcome opens you to the possibility, the portals of opportunity which are revealed before you now.

WORLD EVENTS ON THE HORIZON
April 29, 2023

In this channeling session, a friend of mine was asking the Angels questions.  They told her that there may be a profound disruption within the American and global economy, characterized by a pervasive sense of uncertainty and hidden truths. This perceived manipulation and concealment would foster widespread fear and distrust among people, potentially leading to societal breakdowns. It would begin to erode trust, and trust is what the banking system is built upon.

Global trade may slow to a standstill, and shipping would be a calamitous industry, so people would need to make do with what they have. It's a good idea to have some backstock of food and necessities, but to not dwell on it. Make basic provisions to keep yourself comfortable, and then put it out of your mind.

There may be volcanic eruptions, which are the Earth's way to heal and release anger. At the same time, war may expand until many countries are involved, which helps to lead us all to the desire for peace. The US may become increasingly polarized, until it separates into different factions. The separation of the country may happen as a gradual withdrawal, as opposed to a civil war. Global communication systems could break down due to flooding and other reasons, but eventually satellites may help to restore it.

She asked specifically what would happen in 2024, but we understand that the Angels don't experience time like we do, so they may have been offering information about events that might have their beginnings in 2024 or would unfold beyond 2024.

Channeled Message

There arrives a great, consequential unearthing within the economy of America and the world. It fabricates within yourselves a great dearth of knowing, a sense of upending, a sense of being disheveled. Of all things, now known, are unable to be revealed, as though hidden behind screens. There's a not-knowing by yourselves, a sense that there are things happening that you cannot reveal. And that creates a great stirring in the consciousness of the inhabitants. There is the feeling that there are the underpinnings of the economy being stolen away and not revealed. And there is the sense of this among the people. The people shall reveal, call forth and forward. It must be known and told to us now. There is the greater comprehension that all is not well, and yet it is hidden.

In the future, it will be more formed, more pronounced, more adamant, more telling. There will be those who are forceful with the fear of the economy. What is not known, what is not being told, something is hidden. Fear that all is being undermined, and we are not being told.

The calamity is spoken aloud and trying to not be a victim. There is the aspect of humanity that holds on, that wishes to take for their own. To hold their own harmony by themselves, to take shelter, to call in what is known and to make house and home and property safe for themselves. They do not understand the nature of humanity and of themselves. They fear that others will take what they own. That all will be lost, they will have nothing for themselves. They do not comprehend the nature of humanity, that you are all combined as one soul, which is the Earth herself. They have no knowing, they think only of themselves.

This is not all souls in the family of humanity. There are those, like yourselves, who have known - who have been preparing themselves mentally, emotionally, to remain stable, to be in harmony, to balance themselves internal, to stay above the fray and the chaos of these feelings. Who stay restful in their state of mind and presence. Who will be within the chaos and yet feel external.

There is within this; you are wondering specifically about physical altercation. You are wondering how this will erupt within the population themselves. And we say yes, it is coming. A great breakdown in societal structure. When trust is gone, there can be no more banking system. It is this you are fearing. It is built upon trust, and the not-known erodes the trusting nature of the human society and limits the degree to which things can be coordinated and promised and delivered upon. For there is not the sensation that all is all right. There is the fear coming.

Q: I'm thinking about investing in silver. Is this a wise option?

Silver is a toxic substance to many in physical form. However, as an investment, as a place of holding of consequential income, we say it is all right. Yes, it is ready-made for purpose. It would do nicely. Do not hold it substantially close to the skin. Not this, but as a method by which to preserve capital.

Q: Okay. Yeah, I have an allergy to silver.

We understand this, it is of this that we are speaking.

Q: hank you. I don't currently have the capability to grow food. Should I put away more food this summer? We've been talking about famine lately.

There will be periods of consequential absence of foodstuffs, and this is coming soon. We are understanding you are now not in a position to create your own food. This is all right, okay. Fear nothing. You are not found to be in absence or poverty. This you are fearing. Let this go. Fear nothing. You are above the fray.

We do suggest, it is okay and we approve of your desire to increase the amount of things you have saved up, for there will be a lack of certain things. There is a deregulation of availability of many things. Many things become impoverished, in the sense of the nation in general.

The global aspect of economic trade slows to a standstill. There's nothing arriving in the ports, by sea. Shipping is a calamitous industry. It is not happening, and therefore many things are not receiving. There is the sense that all must be made do with for some time. Make do with what you have, make it lasting. It is consequential now to invest some of your income to provide yourself with more fluidity of experience, and this is all.

It is nothing to do with fear of your ability to provide for yourself through these consequential times. But to understand that to provide these small improvements to your experience will be beneficial. And you can do this now.

For your foodstuffs you make, claim some small investment. You need not do too many trips to the store. Think not of this consciously very often. Simply do one or two trips and be organized in your purchase, and then let it stay as it is and think not of it.

Q: If we move into what's to come maybe next year, is there anything you can share about it? Share with us about what to expect in 2024?

In these times coming, there will be fire on Earth. Fire from within the heart of her. The heart of her is speaking, aching to be known. She is aching internally, and this must be expelled. A violent torrent of heat exploding upon the Earth, and the force of her focus is vehement, and external, and it creates for yourselves great deterrence to existence. You are understanding this already. Yes, it is consequential loss of human life. Humanity in diminishment. There is this chaos and rupture which is coming.

There is, in tandem with that, war. There is no form of this where you inhabit, not here (The U.S.). But elsewhere. Elsewhere is involved, to your knowing. The world in chaos. Disruption occurs everywhere at once. There's chaos being revealed. There are others who take power, who control, who take on for aggrandizement of their own power they take on the field of war. This is happening very soon. Very soon, a consequential time of empowerment for some through war.

And this trial will expand to include the many. Many nations shall participate and be degraded in their ability to conform their lives to harmony. There will be great strife in this trial for humanity. It creates within humanity the desire to become one mind. It is this desire, as outcome, which we herald. It creates within humanity the desire to be free from war and to be of one mind.

Q: We have been also talking about the demise of our government. Is this a factor of the economic troubles?

Do you speak of the United States specifically? Yes. We say these times create a great divide among the many. And the turmoil in the hearts of those who are living in the United States creates a division along personal divides, a division among humanity as it is living in these states. There is the sense that all is not long for one country. And these personalities and differences become more pronounced and demanding, and create a sense of pulling against each other. This division is currently exacerbated and ongoing, and does create within the country a ripple effect; rippling of this organism that is this country, ruptured within the sense of herself, as what she is dividing. She becomes two things, and more, and more. She feels herself divided among her people and her thoughts. She's in confusion and disharmony.

Q: But this will take place politically and not necessarily in a civil war.

There is not the state of things where people are arriving at a confluence of energy of fighting formally. There is instead a withdrawal of nation, withdrawal from each other. A gradual and then complete withdrawal, and no one fighting in the sense of tumultuous arms and armament. It is not like this. It is a peaceful deregulation of the country. Peaceful by comparison, we would say for there is still the torment experienced by many at the loss of self, which is felt by her who is the country, and this does manifest in many ways throughout its inhabitants.

Q: Is this what keeps the U.S. - this along with the economy collapsing or unraveling - is this what keeps us out of this world war on the horizon?

Yes, there is no force behind it, no combination of authority. No ability to draw in the forces of war. Therefore, the country is left alone. The country has no more capacity for drawing in a population for fighting each other or anyone. It becomes denuded. It has a time period of sensing itself as something more than it was. As many ports of station. As something now developing into something more. More places, more thought centers, organized differently than it was before. It becomes this. Reform is necessary.

Q: Okay, thank you. Do we eventually find our way back together as a humanity? And what's the driving factor of that?

Yes, there will be one humanity. There will be one focal point, one humanity, a unified being becomes itself finally, in the end.

Q: What drives that?

There is this loss of life which is substantial. This does eliminate the need for boundaries, which are meaningless. The need for countries, the desire to keep things for yourselves becomes now known as a fallacy, as a wrongful interpretation of living, and the peoples who are remaining come to center to claim for themselves participation in what is remaining. They wish to bring for themselves a closer understanding of one another, to create harmony within all beings. This becomes the desire which is fulfilled.

Q: Does technology and communication become difficult?

Correct. Impacted, all systems are disrupted. A torrent of water creates chaos on the Earth and this does disrupt the lines underwater, which are torn up and disheveled. There are still the global satellites which evolve to become more important, and they ring the Earth in a way that stays and provides greater abundance of connection and community among yourselves. But these are not ubiquitous and not all peoples have access to these powerful aids to the human experience. They will take on form as becoming more ubiquitous over time. It will be necessary, for the alternative means by which you have been enabled to communicate no longer function.

WHAT WILL SURVIVE THE SHIFT
August 25, 2023

The Angels are selective in their communication about the events that we may see in the future. They want to inform us with "gentle knowings" and avoid creating fear if possible. The disruptive events they tell us about are designed to help us shed what is holding us back.

In some cases, this will feel like the loss of dreams. But many of those dreams are born from and within the structures that keep us distracted and apart from ourselves. For example, someone might dream about moving up the corporate ladder. But does that ladder need to exist? Is that hierarchical structure or the work that they are doing in that role beneficial for them and their growth? Not all structures will fall. Those that thrive will be the ones that embrace service to all as opposed to serving the benefit of the few.

Channeled Message

Beings of light, what we share, we have thought through. Eventually, we come to bear and to bring good tidings, but in the now moment all that we have shown bears the burden of how you are evolving. It all contains the message we entrust to your care; that you are here on purpose, to take part in an evolution of the species.

This may come home to settle in your awareness as a thing of great beauty, but it also carries the ominous visions of a future materializing that is before unseen. That has never been experienced. That cannot be related to.

We shy away from the disbursement of information that would lead you down the path of fear. We hesitate to inform you now and always of things that would deteriorate your current quality of life. We wish to guard you with gentle knowings. With awarenesses that can infiltrate your senses without fear. Thus, we stay away from the broader statements, from the greater involvements which shall rise.

The opportunities before you now shake loose all that bears weight. They grow into the divides that will form. There is the carcass, and the waste must be thought of. There is the aftermath that will grow into disturbance, and these formations in your reality cannot be waylaid or set by. Their presence will be known. All things that are deterrents to your horizon will simplify and perpetuate themselves no longer, disintegrate without the systems they hold onto, and become the nothingness you used to know.

The forebears who brought these forward endow them with an energy that is tempting to shield. A sense of horizons unmet, of destinies foreshadowing your future. But they cannot live on. They cannot pull forward into the new now that which has been, and this we have spoken of.

But what we say to you now, to the knowingness of the soul who inhabits the body, who fears the next now, we speak to the soul who you are. That in these next moments of encounter you will come across a deregulated society. A social structure at a loss. A confounding miasma of discarded dreams. And the loss of these you will signify, and make much of. It will feel a contortion of the reality as it is known. A separation from what is godly.

The structures which have enabled the throughput of social progress must now change pace and become a deregulated subset of themselves, and leave behind no trace of their former consequence. But must instead embrace the separation from that structure. Embrace what is now apparent; that all things that have been made for the sole purpose and aggrandizement of one's soul come at the cost of the many. These we trust you hold the truth near. These are separated from that soliloquy and brought and turned to dust.

What remains, you ask? What shall be in the aftermath of these destitutions? And we say many things remain as they are. Many institutions will call themselves hindered but not harmed in full. Setback, but not deconstructed. And these will rise renewed, provided they remain circumspect of the energies that transform them into godlike structures. Those that pivot and take shall deprive themselves of the true North of these times.

> Those that survive are those that instigate the
> provision for all. That instigate the survival
> of the many. That provide the well-being for
> all who come near. These institutions and
> structures may thrive with new endowment;
> the generosity of spirit lifts them.

We wish to bridge your knowledge now of that which falls to dust. To sense, in the soul and the self, there will be trauma. To know that, in these times arriving soon, you will find yourselves questioning the benefits of such a trust as you have given. A trust in the divine, in the wellspring of these alterations. But we speak at large to the greater consequence of your surviving nature. Of the soul life that lives and shines brighter. The inter sight will change you. The inner self elevates you. The sense of what is lost, it's time has come. And the new arrival begins before you. The subtlety of this embrace stretches out, lengthening out as required.

For those of you who come to terms with loss of structure, who endow these times with presence, who yearn to separate from that which was, and who reach for new beginnings, you will find the terms coming quickly. You will stretch into the next announcing moment with ease and feel the love coursing through your veins as it bathes this plane of existence. You will sense within you the rising fear, extinguished, replaced with divine presence.

An awakening inhabiting your soul self, one faction, an opportunity within the great mass of humanity. And each presence, each person who rises thus shall draw you closer to the greater kindling of the consciousness you share.

The senses we bring into turmoil. Thus, we share an advanced warning. We share an information regarding what will pass so that, upon its arrival, you come to terms already met and feel the self at no loss for understanding. No loss of presence. No loss of faith in self and surrender to the energies you are meeting which lift you, like love itself, into awareness of the all and the many.

From the space of your arrival, what contains you no longer becomes the catapult to reform expectation. It draws you upward, further and beyond the many convoluted pathways through this process of ascension. It moves you into a timeframe and structure which allows you to exist beyond all things unnatural, within the space of communion and connection to the divine. Within that space, your own organism conforms to a reality and expression thus imparted with the reverence of divine love.

Experience is ever shifting, and a life of turmoil is often met with experiences worth knowing. But in these times before you now, the stage is set for change and difference. This arousal of the human mind, the swelling of the consciousness, it draws you forward to a perspective of clarity. From within this new stance you gather all that has been light and life, draw it in from past endowments, and recreate a new instantiation of existence benefitting from all that's past, informing what is now the gift of an unbridled future.

IMPORTANT DETAILS ABOUT WHAT'S COMING
December 30, 2023

This message is a Q&A with the Angels all about what's coming. While there are hardships ahead, there is so much to be excited about! They talk about our new state of consciousness, which will bring us a newfound sense of aliveness and unity with all things. Physical reality will become more malleable, allowing for conscious alteration and transformation. A series of waves of light will elevate humanity's awareness.

However, war and geopolitical divisions will intensify, including the separation of the United States. Natural upheavals, including disruptions in climate and food production, will occur, leading to localized shortages. Adaptation and collaboration will be essential for us to thrive through these changes.

Channeled Message

Perceive an understanding that all things in separation can be different from what we are speaking. Understanding that the circumstances we reveal are constantly changing. There are, without hesitation, some things we can reveal to yourselves. Have the understanding that, though we speak upon them, they can, and may, and shall be, in some circumstances, revealing themselves not exactly as we described. But similarities will yet be present. There are some things which are determined upon, which shall not change, which are irrevocably predetermined, and these we can elucidate. We speak to yourselves now of some of these things. What do you wish to focus on, given that time is limited?

Q: In a vision, Anne saw some houses she noticed are empty. We are wondering what happens?

She was shown this now as an understanding that humanity is in the appearance of having all things as they are now, all things the same. But in the near future, all things will not be the same. There are changes that are coming. Within yourselves, in the condition of humanity, there will be a separation that you experience. Those that are feeling themselves resigned to be in presence in an alternate field of reality will not experience the endowment of grace.

They will find themselves greatly tranquilized in their experience of what you are now reflecting upon, and they will not experience it. They will find themselves having an experience, not like death, but not surrender. They are not at peace. They are against what is coming. They feel themselves resigned, registered to the frequency of resistance. For this reason, we find them not appearing. Their appearance is not becoming as physically present in the endowment of what is illumination. They come not forward into the light. They will not seek it. They will find themselves struggling, suffering more than yourselves. They will find themselves in a heightened state of fear.

Overwhelm speaks to them. Their hearts struggle. They find themselves suffering, struggling. Underwater. Not as you are thinking now, not the flooding, not as though they are carried away by water. But their experience of life, their sensation of what it is to be alive, feels like drowning. They find themselves struggling in the sense of loss, as though all things are lost. As though loss surrounds them, as though they are drowning, as though they cannot become alive again in the context where they find themselves, and they do not feel the light. They wish to become more like it was.

Q: What changes are coming?

You will find yourselves carried forward with great momentum into a space of opening recognition of more things than you are now aware of. You will start to carry a frequency and vibration higher than where you are now. It will come over yourselves with great suddenness. An overwhelming sense of, I am alive now where I was in shadow. As though the difference is palpable. An overwhelming sense of life-giving essence coming into your yourselves as the light transfers into your body and is held there in permanence, and you are carried forward in your perception toward a sense of yourselves as carrying this light always. As though an endowment has been given of graceful presence that surrounds you now.

The light you carry is registered in the eyes of others, and they can see this now, as though you are illuminated in your presence. Your grace is becoming palpable in the field of reality that you live in. This will help yourselves in the endowments that are coming. You will receive them as a graceful prospect, as something welcome that you let in fully, wholly into yourselves. You accept this now, and going forward, you receive these endowments of grace.

In the becoming, find yourselves living on Earth as you have been, but now without seeking the same experience that you have been having. It becomes a difference. You find a recognition of who you are as something separated no more from the everything. In oneness, you begin to exist with all things, a consciousness separated no more. This experience can transform your method and way of living completely. A sense of living within the habitat of creation as it has been, but endowed with the knowledge of how things are created.

Thus, the sense of yourselves as living in lack and poverty has no significance. It does not matter to yourselves what is in physical presence, because all is malleable, changeable, alterable. It cannot signify if you are unwell in a moment, because you can transfer that awareness out of yourselves and magnify what is pleasant. You have the ability to consciously transfer. Alteration of things in your physical arena becomes a reality you can experience.

Physicality is not as dense as it has seemed. It is not as it has been, where the physical touch, pressing upon a physical object, its density registers as not malleable. It becomes something, yes, you can see and touch and feel and experience, and also change in its significance and in significant ways. You can alter its shape and contortion in some cases. You can make it feel differently to yourselves. You can alter its energy, and thus its countenance.

Permeability becomes the stuff of human existence. All things are permeable to your perception, to your knowledge about them. You exist in oneness with everything and can alter the substance of what is around yourselves, and yet you are living in physical presence on Earth.

You have a physical body and can transform it to some degree. Not in all ways. You do not wish to alter everything, for some things shall remain as they are. Some things shall stay unalterable, but your encountering of them can change. You move within a landscape that is different, do you understand us? It is a great change in conscious awareness, and the understanding of the physicality around yourselves.

Q: It sounds like this directly impacts and affects the way we create what is around us, our lives?

Yes, in a significant manner, this is what we are saying.

Q: So, it becomes easier and more fluid to manifest what we are needing?

Correct. In harmony with the planet and what you are seeing. Not all will feel this presence, as we have explained. Some will feel great resistance to the oncoming waves of consciousness that we are explaining. Some will feel themselves repelled, held apart, not participating. You will feel them and their experience and have sympathy and great compassion, for their hearts are suffering.

Do you understand us?

It will feel as though the Earth has divided itself, and yet all possess the same terrain and substance of the plane of Earth, though it incorporates two states of awareness. This will not enable those who are unwilling to shift to return to Earth. They cannot come back, but they will remain until their experience here is finished.

There will be those who are in an experience of great, disturbing loss. But yourselves will feel the Earth as a new place of harmonic convergence where all experience is as one being. You feel her, the Earth, within yourselves, as yourselves, as embodiment, as what it is to be human. It will become an embodiment connected to the Earth herself, as though her presence defines you equally with your soul and spirit. As though you are one organism. This experience will be available to yourselves relatively soon.

We wish to say, to speak about how you will find yourselves in service. Will there be those who are capable of journeying from the state of suffering to the state of awareness? And we say there will be many who are seeking the light. Who wish to understand themselves. Who are open to journeying. Who are not established in the experience of life as hardship, but who are opening to the light. Who are willing. A great, vast number of peoples will be willing to experience the light within themselves, but have hardship in the encounter. Cannot diagnose for themselves where there is difficulty, and will see yourselves as illuminated and have the understanding that you are of a quality that can help them. It will be evident; exposed illumination will be evident to all who see you now.

Q: Does this come through the solar flare we've been expecting?

It does now. A solar influx, energetic, which we've been speaking of. A great flash of light and awareness. Presence, divine presence, we call this, comes to this plane of experience, and you accept this as part of your own being. Others do not.

The endowment is coming in the near future. There will be a mirror image of this flash of light waves. 3 times it is coming. Three times is coming, each experience becomes more potent and more powerful, as though the gradual elevating of humanity is considered so that all may participate now if they are consciously present and willing. Three consciousness waves elevating humanity.

Q: More war coming to Earth, how does that fit into the timeline of everything?

War is pressing upon yourselves in greater depth and profundity. There will be hardship around this concept of hatred against each other. There will be a causal disturbance within humankind. Separation is exposing itself. Separateness is coming to the forefront of the human consciousness. Separation on all fronts, in all feelings. It is disturbing to the human awareness.

A great wartime will spread across Europe, as is being expected. And for yourselves, within the context of this state and the nation of the United States, there will be great division ongoing. Increasing separation, increasing division, to the point of separation amongst yourselves. To the point of inconclusion in your practices. Where things are no longer perceived as needing to be done or followed. Rulings do not belong to one another. Inacceptable in some places. They simply relinquish their hold, their grasp of belonging. Let go of their affiliation to this greater country which you have called home. Let go and surrender their belonging and become, in and of themselves, their own country and stay apart.

This starts becoming reality within this next period of opening. The states unravel and become separated and find, between themselves, and new alliances can be formed apart from everybody, between themselves.

A period of lack and starvation are coming to this plane of existence. A great unearthing of the planet, as you are aware of. A great disturbance of the crust of this plane. It creates for yourselves a disturbance geomagnetic, and polarization become irregular. There is a global dislocation of energetic pull which moves, in and among yourselves, great torrents of water.

Not as it has been discussed. Not to the point of extinction by any means. This is not happening. It is not a circumstance by which the surface is engulfed in the ocean. This will not come to pass. But there is, in this destabilization, a great turmoil and thrusting in the oceans. A great magnetic pull which forces the arrival of the disturbance of the crust, and there is expulsion - energetic turmoil - and this creates upheaval. Geomagnetic, as we have spoken, which creates the upheaval in the crust. The displacement of water, which does engulf certain territories. There is an inundation in certain places which cannot be avoided.

The circumnavigation of the planet becomes difficult. It cannot be found as it was. Great changes take place on the surface of this plane of existence. Things are no longer as they were. There is a great dislocation of soil, of Earth. Movement within the crust.

You find yourselves thrust forward, not backwards. Forward into greater prominence on the Earth. Brought into a space of more freedom within this locale. Greater resistance. Restrictive practices are let down, they cannot be succumbed to any longer. It must become a state of free thinking, forward thinking. Forward practices to draw forward to humanity what will encompass a new belief system. New concepts of being alive, what it is to be human. All changes.

There is within this process, this great shift, there is the upheaval of the climate. You were wondering about the growing of food. About the change of the temperature of the Earth, and will it be possible to grow your own food. And we say yes in some cases. Not in all places, because of the inundations. Some places are made uninhabitable, they can no longer be claimed for human population. But in the places where people are, the Earth is readied. The topsoil is good.

But you will find yourselves struggling to provide the same nutritive density for some time, because the solar availability is more limited. There will be a complexity in the environment caused by a great enshroudment of cloud. This will cause for yourselves a more restrictive abundance of illumination.

The solar impact on this plane will be lessened for a short time, which will impact foodstuffs globally. It will not stay long, however. But one growing season is enough to create disharmony and starvation. Do you understand us?

Q: Then that tells me to grow cold-weather crops and shade crops?

Correct, and to avail yourselves of illuminative sources which will propagate more easily your plantings. To avail yourselves of some illumination, that can be sufficient. Illumination will aid yourselves in the growth of some things.

Do not fear, you will have enough. It will be provided for yourselves. It will be enough. It will not be a circumstance where you are in poverty here. It will not be in all places. In places without the endowment of savings, who do not have the riches of their own place. That do not have foodstuff availability generally will find themselves without much. There will not be the shipments to which they are accustomed. There will not be the availability of foodstuffs being transferred via the oceans. There will not be the exchange of foodstuffs between countries, and many nations count upon this. Many places are without their own indigenous ability to grow things. But where that is not the case, there will be enough.

DIGITAL CURRENCY
This message has not been shared on YouTube so no video is available.

April 14, 2024

This was a personal and very unexpected message I channeled for myself, but I think it is relevant for all of us. I have never been interested in cryptocurrency, and knew nothing about it at the time, but in this message the Angels said it would be a very good idea to adopt the digital currency that will be agreed upon by everyone. Part of the benefit will be the ability to work more easily with other people around the world without the burden of exchange rates, which can make it hard for people in different countries to afford to work together.

The Angels did not specify which digital currency they had in mind, but I have since come to think that it might be Ripple's XRP. That is my guess, not channeled from the Angels, and I am not an expert, so please don't take that as financial advice. I thought it was very specific and interesting that the Angels mentioned payment processing as an issue in a few messages, including "What will happen in the Ascension" and "World events on the horizon" which are above in this section. Ripple has technology that would enable much easier, faster and cheaper payment processing. It could potentially replace the Swift banking system. Ripple's payment processing system requires the use of its cryptocurrency, XRP.

Channeled Message
We wish to supply you now with helpful information in regard to what is occurring, with instrumental and informative guidance to help you now. We say the window of opportunity is drawing near within which you can make your investments into the circulation of coin for spending. Into monetary instruments that will be forthcoming.

In the arrangement of your savings and spending, take what is there now and instrumentally apply it into the powers of the mined, carefully thought of. The ending what is currency in your current reality. Apply it to the new-forming method of payment which shall be and become electronic. In the processing of these terms of agreement amongst yourselves for the betterment of yourself, your family, for all.

Your eternal blessings shall infuse this world and extend your offering to greater numbers. With this return, the endowment, the blessings that come through your person, to share these in greater numbers.

The instrument of which we are speaking is that of economic unsettling that delves into an expression of coin that is not really money in terms of a device, but is currency electronic, electronically seeking itself within the ether. We say a transference of your own spending into this new timed instrument shall become more desirable.

Q: There are many, there are many, which one?

We would have you wait, for the timing is not gentle upon the timeframe of these many. There will be one ongoing that remains in the settlement of all that is unspoken. One remains, and this instrument shall contain within it the agreement of all people. All peoples shall regulate their trade through this currency. You cannot forfeit now your regular transference within the dollar. Remain with it for the time being, but know yourself to belong to the formation of a new endowment which shall come, is coming. When this transference becomes possible, you should comply with regulatory means and justice and transfer your belongings to it. It will serve you well.

CRISIS COMING IN BANKING AND MEDIA
August 23, 2024

There will be a pivotal event in the U.S. that creates a crescendo in our  building distrust of the media. This is an important step in the changes, and eventual separation, that are underway in the country. It undermines a key cultural value that was part of the foundation of the country, which is the need to stay informed so that we will be valuable voting members of the democracy.

There is a second message that came through on the same day. The Angels advise us not to spend time chasing information about the difficult events ahead. They want to give us a general idea so that we are not caught by surprise and thrown into fear, and so that we can make some basic preparations. But then they advise that we set it aside and enjoy our peace. We should take full advantage of the time we have now to enjoy our lives.

However, they acknowledge that there will be difficult times that we need to pass through. They mention war and epidemic disease, during which we may be confined to our homes again. They mention the banking crisis. They suggest that we might want to withdraw some cash to have available if the banks close. Please keep in mind this is not financial advice. Neither I nor the Angels are qualified to give financial advice. Even though the Angels see our future, they don't experience time like we do, and success in financial matters often depends on timing.

They say the banks will open again, but things will be changed by this experience and our financial system will be different going forward.

Channeled Message

Brilliant new beginnings. We beseech yourselves to open your hearts to a new start. A new time is forming on the horizon. The nation as you call yourselves is altering what it has become. It is changing in its formative structure for how it has been.

There is an opening before you now, within which you will travel as one. As one community, as one followership, as one nation under divine love. And through this gateway, through this opening, you will travel into difficulty, into the separation which we do foretell of.

There is a time before you now within which the crowds will surpass the individual, and that which you surmise as happenstance becomes deregulated. The forms of breaking news are corrupted, and the information that is passed amongst yourselves feels in doubt. And no tolerance is felt amongst yourselves. It will become a fragmented serenade, within which you are cajoled into sleepiness. And you will not have it. You will create the tirade of demonstration, and perform before the altar of change the required dance of instruction, and order us to your aid to grant you peaceful separation.

There is amongst yourselves a calling down within this timeframe, wherein you will find yourselves provided by us what you have made for yourselves. You will find yourselves guided to become more of who you are. You will see in this endowment of faith in your own hearts as a purposeful obligation to explore your own becoming. And this we endowed with loving, creative spark from within you. We draw to you in preparation the energies that you will require for this brief but important separative thrust from within the country of these United States.

This brilliant new beginning is not on hold or in preparation. It has already begun. It moves from within yourselves, unguarded and in preparation, yes, for greater things to come. But the changing times that you herald are here, and they move in between the moments now. And the ticking of the time that separates you from what you have chosen as a new instantiation of life and belonging is not far, not far now.

We would say that in these statements we are making, where news does come that feels an obligation to rise against, you do perform within your own hearts a twisting turn of discussion. And must then separate from what has been held as sacred. The unified consciousness of a nation has been tied to the instrumentation of dialogue orchestrated by others. And in the formation of the days ahead this breaks, and you are endowed with caution. In the words that are spoken, that are heard, you become fluid and formless and ready to see a new beginning.

It is the breaking apart of the instrumentation you have relied upon. But in this process, you do open your hearts to a better fulfillment. You create in the uncertainty the potency of a new revelation. Therefore, find as you are trumpeted from within, I will not accept these lies any longer. I will not accept these fortuitous explanations that disregard the reality of my own circumstances. As you find yourself thrust to the forefront of your own explanations, you will become enlightened in the ways of parting from what has been.

Thus, we say, do not brace yourself against these experiences, but lean into the flow of separation. Recognize the dust will settle, and in the calm that ensues you will find your peace within. For it is found among the rubble of a reality that has disintegrated already, and is no longer found within the truths it harbors as sacred.

We would gift to you this preparative advice. To guard against the timing of these orchestrations. To wait within the sanctity of your own heart. To be in a reality of your own choice. Do not embroil yourself in the seeking of these fulfillments. Simply be. Be as you are. Be in the readiness to fulfill your own peace and have these expectations as your guidance. We thank you.

A break, then the message continues

You are instigating an inquiry into the possibility of how you, we, overcome these ensnarling events you've heard of. The potential for yourselves is as one in unity. This is what you should lean toward. There are on the horizon many opportunities for fire and brimstone. For all you've heard of, foretold biblical and otherwise. The many instruments of fear have poisoned you against your own learnings.

We would say in the dialogue of your own discussion to limit yourselves from hearing too much. Do not allow your hearts to open prematurely to the woundings of these chaotic underminings. Be allowed the time of grace that you are in. Be allowed the time of preparation. Be in the stillness when it is offered. Celebrate your lives as they are given. Do not let fear set you apart from your guidance to live in joy. To celebrate what you are, who you are with, and what you are to become.

There are undoings on the horizon. There are many. There are circumstances you will not like. There are feelings of isolation unavoidable. There is a sense of yourself as having lost much of what is called joyful in this time that you've known. There will not be the easy pull and chorus of what has been - consumerism and desires fulfilled. There will not be the ease of travel to which you are accustomed.

It will be a time of war and pestilence. A time in which you are guarded against leaving your homes and are required to stay within. A time is coming within which you will find your securities unsettled. Your homes will feel like imprisonment once again. For this we are sorry. There will be times of suffering ahead.

For this you have readied your soul. You know your spirit within. You have called upon the resources of your own divine nature. You may move into the structure of the love that you carry, and this will guide you through what is on the horizon.

There is the formation of the crisis underway, which is financial in nature. The banks are closing. Have this in your awareness today. Do not settle yourselves upon waiting. Distribute your funds. Do not carry them all in the same place. Do not put them where they are held, in the accountancy of a banking institution that may not avail itself of this funding. They are deregulated. They do not carry the funding you have lent them. It is not of their belonging, of their person.

They are in a period of lack and intolerance is building. There is orchestrating among the persons who control the wealth, the guardianship of your financial circumstances, they are in an awareness of these problems and will settle upon yourselves the obligation of fulfillment. And you will lose, temporarily, access to what has been your privilege. The earnings of your own hard-working.

And we would ask yourselves to disburse these funds, as you are capable, into a place of greater readiness where you will have access in the coming period. Do not keep them all in banking. The banks will find themselves afield once again. The journey continues but, not as it once was. It will be a continuity broken by disturbing news.

Thus, settle yourselves for these encounters. Know their fulfillment comes soon. Be settled in your heart, all will be well. Do not spend your worries. It is futile to fuel fearful thoughts related to abundance. For all becomes clear as the way is made for yourselves.

Come to your truth. Come to your home within you and all will be revealed. Have in your hearts the clear purpose of loving what is, and all will belong to the goodness that you are made of.

There is not within these times the journey of which we've spoken of, the timing of the flash of light to come. It is not here yet. You are obligated to move through and beyond the times of our description. What we have laid before you is a process of distributing the angers and the separation of the journeys that have been laid before you. And this process must be overcome from within.

It will be a process of endurance to which you are capable. You are ready, and you will serve in your own way, in your own dignity. You will find a path through. We are with you. We take care. We are your guardians of the space within your heart. We spread the love around you. Take care and be wise to encourage yourselves to withdraw some funds from these institutions. Do this now, do not wait. Do this now to separate yourself from the limitation that will be placed upon your own conduct. We thank you.

Section 2.
Earth Rift

The Earth rift was one of the first things that the Angels told me about when they began speaking about the events of the shift. They told me it was important to share it, and that it could save lives. But I was very hesitant to share such scary news. I sat on the first message for several months until I realized that many of you already know about these events on some level, and sharing this information may help you to remain calm and centered in the middle of the storm.

The Angels describe a huge rift in the Earth that may occur somewhere near the Indian Ocean, near India and Indonesia. It will create a noise so loud that we will hear it around the world. I believe this event will be associated with extreme flooding, both from waves and from rain.

The Earth rift is discussed in a few other messages in the book. Here is a paragraph referencing from April 2023 "World events on the horizon" in the previous section.

"In these times coming, there will be fire on Earth. Fire from within the heart of her. The heart of her is speaking, aching to be known. She is aching internally and this must be expelled. A violent torrent of heat exploding upon the Earth, and the force of her focus is vehement, and external, and it creates for yourselves great deterrence to existence. You are understanding this already. Yes, it is consequential loss of human life. Humanity in diminishment. There is this chaos and rupture which is coming."

There is a second rift which is mentioned that would take place in the U.S. It's mentioned in the message from January 26, 2022, "What will happen in the Ascension" which can be found in the previous section. It's unclear in the message if this would be a physical or ideological rift.

EARTH RIFT WARNING
August 12, 2020

This important message is about a possible rift in the Earth that could occur in or near India, near or in the ocean. The Angels tell us that a deadly toxic gas cloud will come from the rift and drift up towards Turkey and the Middle East. They emphasize how important it will be to stay safe indoors if this happens in your area.

After channeling this message, I received a dream where I saw a faulty antique Indonesian support beam being replaced by workers. The faulty support beam was symbolic of the fault in the Earth that could cause the rift, and indicates that it may be near Indonesia. I have since found that there is a very long, large underwater fault in the Indian Ocean that extends south from India, running parallel to Indonesia.

Channeled Message

We would like to share with you what we believe will impact all on Earth very soon. It must be opened and discussed to be revealed, so that many can be saved from harm. It will be another experience of catastrophic proportions. It will have the opportunity to reveal an inner side to the chambers of the Earth. It will open before you. It will be another thing that upsets the economic stability in this time. It will happen. When the Earth is opened, economic activity will cease.

There will be a disaster, yes. A type that isn't tracked. It will be seen as a gap, opening, rift, right down the middle, separation, opening in the crust. It makes both sides crumble. Much devastation. This will occur when it reaches breaking point in the Earth's tension. It can happen. It happens near Indian line, near ocean. Rumbles cause disruption, then crack, then opening, and all unfolds. It happens to many. It will appear as if the Earth is hollow and they will fall in. It will be massive, much bigger than you are imagining. It could have a devastating effect on the world because, when it occurs, it leaks gas that impacts the air. It becomes hard to breathe. Many die. It opens. Share it openly. It can be helpful. It becomes a problem for many because there are repercussions.

The Earthquake happens to erupt the gas, which flies through the air to be breathed by many. Infects. Few remain who breathe the poison. It will be potent. It can disperse widely up above in the clouds overhead, jet stream, where it passes freely and lands where the air is heavy. It can be devastating because none know.

It's difficult to survive. It will not be a circumstance with much oxygen, therefore others will perish. To be closed off from air is good. They may survive if one does not open air ventilation. It is extreme violence happening without. It can survive some measure by keeping themselves indoors out of rain, away from air ventilation. Circulate air within their space. Do not breathe outdoors. Do not be outside. Do not go near the gap. Do not look for family. Stay still within the environment you inhabit. Do not change, because outside it is still toxic. It must be some days. Do not exit. Attempt to breathe only the air recirculated. Stay safe from heat, from ash.

You can resume capabilities when there is ample air movement. Wind comes to break free your imprisonment. Travel not far from home, be indoors. Turkey, Iran, Syria, Middle East.

SOLAR FLARE BLACKOUT
September 21, 2020

There will be a temporary "blackout" period where communication methods will be disabled. This will be helpful for our shift in consciousness, and the Angels assure us that we will be safe. They say that it will happen "within the period of your two-fold remembrance". Time is not something that the Angels experience, so timing is difficult for them to convey, and this phrase isn't easy to decipher. Some people have suggested that they might mean between Memorial Day and Remembrance Day, or around Easter. I don't know.

The Angels will sometimes give us information about the sequence of events. They tell us that the Earth rift will happen in the midst of all the challenges, not at the beginning, as I had assumed previously.

Channeled Message

We told you that there would be an Earth disruption. This is true. Some movement of the situation is in play. There are many points along border that have experienced pressure to create a sudden explosion.

We say you have only certain amounts of time before this occurrence and many unfolding happenings that will transform your planet. Once begun, it has the potential to serenade the unfurling of this experience dramatic and quick.

We have explained already what may occur. It has some observed pieces that are nearly complete. You may see how this Earthquake begins when you are watching the news. There are to come some explanations that aren't accurate from experts who assume this will only be small, and we are anticipating there will be some among you who think there is no reason to assume detrimental costs. However, we know there are greater potentials for destruction within this first foray into this great avenue for up leveling the Earth.

We are seeing that you will find it happening within the period of your two-fold remembrance, to be felt first as a quake and then seen within hours as more, to be seen within days as smoke, to be felt within periods beyond, within months, as circumstances develop to be increasingly frigid an uninhabitable for many.

You are now entering the period of blackout where we will remove from you the means by which you telecommute, the method by which you telephone. All will be silent to ensure this completion.

(The following was part of this message but not included in the YouTube Video)

You cannot believe that we are touching your planet with our great predictions, but we are certain that this is not surprising for those who have already experienced your future. You are but waiting for the result. All will depart as we projected. There are delays you assume, but not actually. All is happening as we foresee. There are times when it will be clearer for you to reveal this ascension, but now we see murky and troubled, it seems. Do not be fearful or reluctant to believe what we have shared. It is still true.

Do not assume that all must occur in order of time. It is not sequenced as you foretold.

> You have inferred that the trigger for most would be this Earth disruption; however, that will occur in the midst of this unfolding, not at the beginning,

and it will create panic as yet unseen because so many are already distraught from the smoke and fires, from the destructive power of hurricanes and from the opening of the market to reveal all was lost.

Yes, this plunge takes place in the midst of all and not at the start, to reveal each piece, to create destabilization so that all can interpret what they see, feel and create through their own lens to understand their reality as they would.

EARTH RIFT TSUNAMI
November 29, 2020

I have heard hundreds of dreams from others about giant waves on the west  and east coast of the U.S., many of which are identifiable as prophetic based on the symbols within them. The Angels say yes, giant waves or tsunamis may happen as a result of the Earth rift they are describing. Here in this message, they give us specific advice to stay safe during these possible events. They warn that the high waters may be taller than tall buildings, and we should move to much higher ground to be safe. We should be ready to help others who need it in the aftermath, including those who are displaced without possessions or a place to live. They also ask us not to let the grief of this situation dim our light, because we will be needed as way showers.

In the second paragraph, I love that they mention that we have a second, higher frequency aspect of our soul within that will emerge in the shift. I didn't understand this at the time of this channeling, but they have since dedicated whole messages to it. *"You will push to the front of your awareness the being who speaks within your heart, to elevate your mind into realms to come."*

Channeled Message

You are here, We have listened to see what you have begun. You are wondering if this occurrence, flat upon the Earth, will be the one that subsumes all others. It is this that begins the divine opening, unraveling, that must happen. Therefore, we say do not delve too deeply within your heart to feel this disturbance. It will occur and happen now. It has started. This origin unfurls before you. It takes its whisper from that origin and exacerbates the explosion. This will occur within some time near.

Do follow as we say. Do not delve within your thoughts and feelings, for those who are left because you are pressing against the opening, unfurling, and this must be where you have now placed your mind. Rest your soul, be easy, do not dwell upon the loss transpired. This is not how you can evolve. It is for your greatest elevation to be looking upward at us, where we pull you near. Dear, we ask your remembrance to be brief. Do not dwell upon the sadness. Look forward, we say, see what becomes. Hold this light as your own. Be well within our grasp, holding your heart to ensure your safe passage through struggle, heartbreak, disturbance. All are within the realm of this occurrence, but you will push to the front of your awareness the being who speaks within your heart, to elevate your mind into realms to come.

We ask your forgiveness for the duration of this hardship. It is needed for our necessary upliftment. It will drive humanity forward unlike any other possibility. It has far-reaching consequences.

The tsunami originates there, where the origin has begun. It will flow eastward and westward, both. It will begin once all erupted force has pushed outward, exploded. This will begin the wave, and have a detrimental impact on all within the coastal areas. This is necessary, for it reveals more than can be found without this passage.

You have wondered how it will release. The force will be extreme. It has within it the heart of angels, which is pushing upwards explosive debris.

> This release heals Earth. We are helping her evolve. It will transpire, but know you are not required to suffer in this extreme part of this evolution. It is not required that you struggle. We are telling so many who listen so that they can stay prepared, away from the origin, from the water.

Rise high above sea level. Do not feel safe until you are above. Herald those who take the slower passage. Do not allow them to be consumed in this deathly flow. You are high upon ground elevated, beyond the field of disturbance. Be near this peak, high, higher. Do not underestimate the greatness of this great flow. It will rise above all who see the shore. You must move higher to be rescued from it. It will pass above buildings lofty. Higher than you assume.

Do not rest beyond the call of help because they will need assistance. There will be many in trouble who are desolate, alone or trapped in water. They cannot stay. You must be prepared for others who are displaced. They will require your aid. They have not brought belongings. They are alone, bereft of all they love. They have asked us to provide safety, help, love, shielding. We are going to be there, helping, assisting all who allow.

It will be great disturbance, felt by all in heart, and many in experience.

Absolve your heart, you are not required to carry the heavy grief of this situation. You are needed in light, needed as guides to bring those forward who are ready for help, to hear the voice ahead.

To bring them with you is required for their salvation. We are assisting all. You have asked if we will be present when it occurs, and we say yes, always.

HOW AND WHEN THE EARTH RIFT MIGHT HAPPEN
December 27, 2020

The timing of the Earth rift is driven by the Earth herself. It is part of her

healing process. In the same way that our emotions surface and need to be expressed, so do hers, and the Earth rift will be a release of energy that no longer serves her. But it will happen when she is ready. Humanity's recovery from this event and from all the events of the shift will be significantly easier when we embrace living in alignment with the new energies of Aquarius, which means helping and supporting one another.

Channeled Message

We have undertaken to perform works of peace and tranquility to make you have faith in our appearance and our subtle strength. We have already performed some, set up structure for what will occur in the coming months. This will delve into the depths of your abyss. Take from you all torment and release you from the grip of your circumstances. We will heretofore become wiser, more open, perceptive. Coming closer to us in vibration so that we might entrance you with our own cerebral undertakings.

We will have more enlightenment among people. There will be more secondary service that lifts and becomes enchanted over time. This is not a problem.

There is not data to support the timeline. We do not have access to this knowing, because it transpires at the whim of Earth. It happens when she has required herself to remove those gases from her innards. When she is ready to release that which bogs her down, to reveal her lighter self. To become a new version. Lighter, better, cleaner. Ready for this next version of reality. She will figure herself when she is prepared. She must make this choice. It is hers to create, and we are there supporting her. Helping, as we do you.

You have the benefit of our circumnavigation, as does she. We are within her breath and will exhale with this goddess to exhume from her that which she reveals for clearing to become her next self. We are in waiting, much as you are. She will proceed. She will have all opportunities to reveal her lighter self. This is predetermined. She must pursue her pathway. It is foretold, but not occurring as we predict. It occurs as she sees fit. You see, it is *what* that we control, not *how*. And she will determine *when*. So, we are patient.

You are prepared, that is all. You must be ready. Be stable. Be clear in your understanding, so that once this occurs you are not left with confusion and dejected. You will be aware, and that is much to the point of our communication. You must know and be prepared. This will enable your recovery, your sustainability.

It has a role to play in your upleveling, but not the primary part. You must do much of the work yourselves. You must reveal yourselves and require the help of each other to lean upon and support. This will encompass the theme of your upcoming timeline. You will be in service to each other. This will counterpoint the advent of your democratic method, and be likely to reveal the methods by which you can succeed. You will find in each other the support required for celebration of yourselves.

This is the pathway from here. Aquarius is dawning. You are now finding yourselves changed by it, and you will be rewarded for love of one another.

This is certain to be noticed and felt as a difference, and you will recover to the degree that you enliven these principles. You will find that much is pleasing in this new reality. But you will let go of that which isn't required, and this feels like aftermath. This feels like conundrum, forced choice. Difficulty. None is revealed. Just experienced as the tidal wave of change passes through your being.

You will find your preference has shifted, and you are ready to be one another's advocate and friend. This is a joy to witness. You have yet understood the meaning of our requirement that you are still. Do not envelop this query with your focus. Do not now delve into the fabric of science.

DETAILS ABOUT THE EARTH RIFT AND TECHNOLOGY IN THE FUTURE
August 12, 2021

In this message, the Angels talk about Earth changes, including a possible Earth rift, as well as a solar-related blackout that could affect technology. Technology gives us a high degree of connectivity with one another, but it feels empty without the context of love. When technology is removed, and we are in a higher vibration, we will be able to find that connection with each other telepathically, in the context of peace, love and belonging.

Channeled Message

Hello, we are here, we are within. We can begin. We say you are wondering about what comes next, the circumstances of your arrival into this dimension of upheaval. We say you are aware of the passage of much activity there, of how all begin to feel the repercussions of their long tribunal of affairs on the planet. How now we've achieved a readiness, an expelling is necessary, and this will take place.

There will be aftereffects, repercussions to the selves, the ones, inhabitants thereon. They will be held by ourselves. All will remain in the fold of our protection, and up-leveling for some will mean passage on. For many remain, and they acquire more aptitude and awareness of higher vibration. They will stay and be healed of burdens and complexities they bear today.

We say you are wondering about the physical effects on the planet. We are aware there will be some disturbance of magnitude housing in the Earth's crust, the domain of physicality for the planet being. She is well but disturbed by our gradual enlivenment. She feels our embrace as we hearken her onward, upward into her full bearing.

She will open herself, a rift, separation of
plates that will rise up from the ocean and
heave into the atmosphere such debris as can
free her from toxins within.

A necessary outpouring of grief and rage inflicted upon herself by yourselves, your inhabitation of violence forthcoming. It does reveal itself in this expression of her upheaval. It will be released, a torrent of her fabric, a torrent of debris pours forth and leaves disturbance everywhere.

It is felt by all. Some will feel it proximately. Others reveal a twinge of awareness and then the shaking of the planet underneath. They become aware indeed. She reveals her awakening sound, a deafening roar climbing the hills, refracting and reverberating elsewhere, heard by all on the planet. It will rise, the waters begin to climb. They come up with pressure from underneath, the pressure comeuppance, the lifting of the tide onward, rushing outward in all directions. It flows and envelops all in its path. It moves mountains aside, it clears, pathways dissolved. It moves without feeling or compassion. All will be revealed, but you are aware we are there. We are holding all, preparing everyone. All will be held by ourselves.

The solar elevation instructs the Earth, the energies to transform her and yourselves alike. She feels it more than yourselves, for she is blanketed in no protection. You have protection by her very being. She has none the same. Her own magnetism is her field, her energetic force, her influence. It is susceptible as you are within, but you now benefit from her outer layers of protection.

You can feel her enlivening with solar retort.

> There are many circumstances of solar elevation but one will come, one elevation supreme to knock out all communication.

It will subside, freeing yourselves to be relieved of that duty of learning complexity, that technological progress which has hampered your spiritual progress. That upliftment temporary into godlike states of communion with one another without the required passage of elevation of spirit. Indeed, it does not hinder the growth so much as prevent it.

It does harbor within the frequency of elevation, subtracting God. It has no soul within, no frequency of light, no illumination for your benefit. It has, however, the enchantment of elevation, the ready connection, infusion of compatibility with another. The light and easy touch of technology to do all sorts of things as you are.

But now receive the true lightness, the true elevation of spirit that unites all within the context of humanity in peace and love. Uniting in all circumstances, housing within it the true resonance of your capacity for care for one another. This is another frequency of difference. Yes, of belonging, not having. Of being settled in the self, of acknowledging your own wisdom within, not seeking external gratification from inundation with digital frequencies promising connection of another sort - unsatisfying, bereft of kind heart, lacking true wisdom, holding the frequency of depravity, of lack, heresy and foreboding. These are all encumbered in technology as you house it today.

We release you from it. We cure your heart and heave you together into the future now, that housing of fabric woven from love and caring for one another, that tenderness of heart found lacking today. You will attain it, but by upheaval. This is the journey forward.

THE NEXT OPENING IN THE ASCENSION – THE EARTH RIFT
May 26, 2022

In this message, the Angels are talking about how the chaotic events associated with the Earth rift will change us. It is an opening of the Earth, and an opening of our hearts. We will become less rigid, more at ease and more accepting of our new reality. The rift will shake the Earth in a way that can't be ignored, freeing us from existing power structures. While some places on the planet will feel somewhat unchanged, everyone will feel the pain of the Earth as she transforms. The Angels ask us to remain still, internally, and let it pass through our awareness without panic or fear. There will be a period of darkness after, which will bring stillness and peace to the planet. By staying in a state of internal peace and becoming open to one another, we can help humanity to transform through the difficulties.

Channeled Message

We have now a next second, another beginning. This stands in opposition to that which you are aware of. Be new in your regard. Be open in your thinking. This Next stems from within. The meaning it brings is for yourself alone. It is happening in the opening, through the lesson it provides. You will find it brings a sense of internal harmony. This lesson is the opening.

It changes yourself thoroughly. It is a shift in your allowing. Your nature becomes less rigid, more easy, more accepting. This is passing now. You are sensing this as a burgeoning feeling within, a sensory feeling we provide to ensure you are ready.

This next opening you are in, it hearkens the beginning of many things. Next to arrive transpires readily. It shakes to the core all it will reach. It is a sensation to be not ignored. It will hearken the pieces breaking free, a next beginning. A freeing of the pieces of each country. There is isolation now in the mix, and it becomes embroiled in this tragedy.

No longer can they stand opposed and breathe apart so easily. None can find the road to their own salvation so easily. They must engage and lift the curse of separate devils. They have each a purpose to unfold, a semblance of one another, and yet a difference remains.

This next happening you are upon opens the Earth and its captives completely. It changes all things. The juxtaposition of now breaks from then, it separates the trajectory and leaves you departed from peace. Hear us in speaking, we are not worrying. This does not leave you off the portal of your awakening. It herkens further turmoil, this will come. It is necessary, but in the end you breathe.

It feels the same in some means - some situations will alter little. But you all feel the pain of Earth as she transposes her fury upon yourselves, and your endeavors reflect that ancient being. You will find this time overwhelming. Remain still in process, the same. Let it pass through your awareness. Let it field and retreat.

> You will feel in this time a darkness coming.
> Soon all remains still, and the peace enfolds
> you once again.

You must remain. Be as you are and grow through this opportunity to feel all ways. To let rise and fall the lives you've built and see where your opening is. To find yourselves anew, and new ways to breathe the air with justification, I am still here. I remain. I am calm and distinct from chaos. I and pure thought and feeling embraced.

Allow this passage and you will remain. Stay steady in fearless answer. All will change, and yet nothing - you are the same. But lighter! Your feeling is consequential, allow this refrain. Be in the state of peace internal despite all that passes. You are heralding the next flame of humanity through your reaction by bridging this gap and opening. To be one with all things you must open yourselves to each other, and this is the means.

PART 6

The Flash of Light:
The Moment When
Everything Changes

The Angels tell us that there will be a solar flash of light that will be the most important event of the shift. All of the other events they've described so far are building up to this incredible experience that will change us all.

This light that will come to Earth is solar energy. They say "it will come upon the rainbows that have traveled from far away, starlight that is graced with presence of divine nature." It isn't clear which star it is from. Some people think it might be the star Betelgeuse, which scientists expect we will see super-nova some time in the near future. The light the Angels tell us about will be powerful enough to saturate the Earth in divinity, suspending us temporarily in a transformational process that the angels compare to a cocooned metamorphosis.

They give us guidance in these messages to help us understand what to expect when this happens. They break down what we will feel and experience, and how it will change us. They also reassure us that there's no chance that you will miss it – not even if you are deep down in a basement somewhere when it happens.

It will lift our energy right up to the doorstep of the new frequency of Earth, but it won't push us through. Our free will is always honored. It will hold us there at the doorstep and let us make the choice to lean in through trust and allowing, or to resist through fear and the desire to control our experience.

The most important thing to remember when this flash happens is not to panic. We are meant to turn inwards, close the shades and rest. When we begin to feel heavy in our bodies, we should lay down. We will be under an umbrella of peace which will help us focus on love. Specific directions are detailed in the messages in this section.

Section 1.
The Solar Event That
Will Raise Our Frequency

EMERGING STRONGER FROM WHAT'S COMING
October 28, 2020

This is the first message I received about the flash of light that will be one

of the most important events of our shift in consciousness. My channeling was less smooth then, and a little harder to understand, but it's worth the effort for this important message, although we get much more detail and clarity in the later messages about this event.

They say that in this event we will be guided "into the chasm of your doubt". When we step into the energies of the flash of light, we enter a protected and peaceful void or cocoon where we experience a metamorphosis. I believe this is what they are referring to. There is much more on this in later messages.

They say this is a one-time event and "will occur after the cycle of your abundance". I interpret this to mean that it will occur after the banking crash and economic problems they described in Part 5. When it does happen, they tell us that there will be a blackout, and it will create problems with our electronics, which will be made worse by a dip in temperature. Cold weather can be bad for battery performance, so that may be what they are referring to.

Channeled Message

There are some believing that this will happen within the second phase of occurrence when you have already succumbed to the energies forthwith. That there are not the same platitudes to express what develops when you have received our full blast to open your chakras. You will experience much travesty but also open to our grace and find our hand upon the Earth, to find our gentle orchestration, to be held when we are implementing this turnabout. It is necessary to have this fortuitously guided and then opened as a pathway forward.

You will be guided into the chasm of your doubt. Submerge your fears and emerge forthwith with a new sense of purpose and calm. A knowing of all that will be; tranquility will be upon your mind, and the sense of loss transient as you achieve new methods of awareness.

Do not be sidelined by this occurrence. It will pass, and you will find the opportunity within to find your own voice more strongly, to have our hand upon you, to hold and be comforted. It is not all chaos within.

> You have calm retreat. Be salvation, be peace,
> be calm. You are the center of your universe.
> You are complete within your mind.

To have this touch happens once and begins after the cycle of your abundance. Do not fret for where or when it might develop. It has no hindrance to impede its full expression, and it will blast away all remnants of our negative focus to reveal your true selves, forbidden at times but never forgotten.

The blackout it comes. It will be perused within a moment, a blast of energy to superheat your junction, to explode some and carry the charge far and long. It will be most certainly explosive, and very. Hindrance to come will be found in all things electronic, amplified by the extreme temperature of chill. It will be frigid with the full canopy that develops. Yes, this time is coming near. Be ready, for all will feel the effects. It is not to be divulged when, because the date is yet unset. It may be because of the turmoil that ensues after the calm in your own chaos.

DETAILS! OUR ASCENSION EXPERIENCE
March 25, 2022

Our current reality is curling up around us like a dying leaf, and we are experiencing its last gasps in the dramatic events of this shift that the Angels have been describing to us. The Angels say that finding our inner tranquility will soften these experiences for us. They are the prelude to the flash of light, which will raise our frequency up and beyond this reality as we have known it. Once we've arrived, they tell us that we will no longer experience friction or turmoil like we do today. But there will be those who are open to the light and those who fear it and reject it. We will all share the same space but have very different internal experiences, and those who are still not open will need and seek help from those who have risen.

Channeled Message

We say you can bring yourself to rise anew. The time forces yourselves to lift up heavenward to feel ourselves, to evolve as some have done. Now all, the entitlement they carry. The lifting, rising has begun. All are welcome to resume the instrument of loss which they may have forsaken. To take upon themselves the instrument, begotten by us now and brethren speaking to yourselves, we invite you now to accept this. To open now as you have longing to lift upward and invite us in.

We are carrying such news as may convey some sadness. We bring into the light such changes as are necessary. It is coming, the herald of your beginning. It rises soon. Your awakening unfolds as we are speaking. It is happening now. You are in it.

To perceive, you must understand that time is passing, moving all the same. Your entire world, the vision you are in, reigns empty. It curls now and speaks more softly to your wisdom. It is counterpoint, a dreadful measure, an antagonizing element which draws you outward to measure the distance unfolding between us and now, forever. Feel as life is opening around yourselves. Tranquility softens the arrival of these elements.

The unfolding of life, such sameness to which you become habituated, no longer dwells in this plane. Shifting times, elements, agonies, they unfold in new directions. And we have given the anticipatory measure, the explanation of what comes. Greater measure of time and distance you may form from this perspective, to see what arrives now. A changing, a shifting ever after, and you will rise as we have spoken. When you are ready.

We will speak now to explain the path forward; your unveiling. Through this burdensome time, you are conveying yourselves to enter into and renew your light and the instrument you are carrying. Your being is unfolding as is necessary to meet these energies that rise as you dwell and live your lives.

Passion comes through. You will feel yourselves different and apart from many. You will understand the new beginning on offer.

> You will raise yourselves to such a pitch, a frequency that all that surrounds yourself in ignorance shall feel like dust to be separating. Your field strengthens and resolves, and you arrive at the place of import that you have been seeking, with ourselves at the ready.

You feel us now. We wither as we speak, feel us nearby. We move and example ourselves.

But we say more clearly yet that this dawning fascination with light, it leaves you empty of friction. You feel absolved from the turmoil you may be in. You feel it is not necessary. You feel not the columns and divides of humankind but feel instead a new way to rise, to feel yourselves anew, to sense us in pure form.

These happenings in the self occur whilst you are abound with all who reveal their own cataclysmic thoughts. You are lacking not the same trajectory, but your feeling is not the same. You can see them, and they see you, but you feel not as they do. And you perceive above what they can only imagine. You become a pivotal center of this migration. You enter into a field of potential, where we are, and from this distance the few that you are remaining will be drawn forward, toward us, to feel this embrace of difference, of separateness from what was.

The turmoil of thoughts, the juxtaposition, the anger that resides inside yourselves, this you process and reflect anew and let go downward, released from you. A purer thinking, feeling, thoughtful being emerges anew. You understand this to feel renewed. To stay as you are in body, in place, but to feel your presence differently.

> And this divides you. All those who feel it,
> and they who refuse. And they will feel the
> unresolve of these times most sharply, most
> destructively to their harmony. And they will
> unravel their being to understand what they
> must do to rise and feel as you. And you may
> help them if you desire. You may aid them.
> They will need our love and support. It will
> feel necessary that we do.

And we ask you now to be ready to feel a separating from what you are, a distancing that emerges in you where tranquility rises and takes hold and feelings of shame and deportment drop away. And feel, when this is coming, an arrival of light in time. It is necessary to perceive your own changing anew. To be ready to feel. Be present. Do not let these moments escape you. Be ready. Look for the seconds of penetration, where you remain resolved in a frequency of joy and feel these presenting more readily. You are preparing. Your fixation upon life, it spares what is necessary, and you will reveal to the self all that comes. You will believe yourself. Well entranced and ready to perceive it, you are renewed.

UPCOMING EVENT TO SHIFT US ALL!
June 24, 2023

Our great shift in consciousness is going to be dramatically escalated by a solar event that will shift our consciousness to such a degree that we will think of it as a turning point in our ascension. It will promote inner peace, heightened awareness, and a deeper connection among individuals. This shift is described as a significant change that will enable people to live more authentically, embracing their true selves and the divine frequency within. We are encouraged to embrace this new energy without resistance, allowing for personal and collective evolution.

The transformation is anticipated to be challenging for some, particularly those resistant to change, but ultimately beneficial as it fosters a greater sense of unity and self-realization. The Angels ask us to come together after the flash and discuss what we are experiencing with open minds. We should try to let go of our expectations about it, because that might limit our perception of what is actually occurring.

Channeled Message

We speak through you of a cause to remember. Of a celebration of who you are. We wish to invite you to participate now in an understanding which we share with one another. That you are evolutionarily positioned to change from within. That the goings on and the doings of these times are opening before you. This you are aware of.

What we would confer now to your knowledge, is an understanding of what will tranquilize the subject of your current disquiet. What will harmonize within the body and create for you a lack of suffering? What will it be that brings down into you an understanding of your soul and self as united?

What will it be that creates the momentary juxtaposition between then, what was, and the new beginning? It will be a time of significance. A momentary influx of energy, the sensation that you are rising within the self, within your physicality, a sense of self as having been lifted. And this we refer to, in your playing frequency of clarity, that there is nothing to fear, no moment within this transference that you are harmed in any way. It is a frequency of light that is entering this plane of existence, and it will move through you and around you and among you.

It transfers unto yourselves a significant frequency of joviality. A sensation of life and living. A noticeable shift in the way you feel about living. A sense that you are accomplishing more things, simply by being, than you do by the strain and turmoil of yesteryear. The sense of self does become changed. You feel you are heightened in your state of awareness, that you have within your field a greater perceptiveness and can pick through and understand the significant moments and frequencies around yourselves. There is, within your hearts, greater connectivity to one another.

This comes within the charge of this great transference, of this great vibration which is emanated from the sun, solar. It comes, it heralds in a new change among you. It is something you do not see in frequency. You can have the aurora of times past, and this will create as much. But we say what is different is that, in this particular influx of energy, there is a frequency of the Divine. A sense of yourselves as coming alive again, within the very habits of living. A sense that you can admire the self and all you've been, and know you have harbored divergent frequencies, and be accepting of all that you are. To be the love that you embody.

This comes on at once, as if you feel the self-broadening in your perspective, no longer limited into narrow ridges formed by prior thinking. It is as though the veil is lifted, as though something of separation, that separated you from us, becomes thinner. As though you suddenly remember something important about yourselves, that you are God's frequency. And this comes and you herald in this change.

Though all will feel the vibration, others may not come to terms with it so readily. Others may find it perturbing, deescalating their own ambition. To find within it an urge to move around this frequency, to avoid, to encapsulate the world in what was. There is among some a desire to remain with what is. It cannot be so. We say the change heralds all who live in this realm.

But you are harboring the willingness, the acceptance, the belief that this is possible. That you may change, and that relief is in store for those who accept all that comes through. Who move into the frequency of this novel and fortuitous blessing.

For those who do not share your desire for ascension, it will be a trying time, a vibration that permeates the being most readily and leaves them feeling derailed and without focus. A sense of self as temporarily lost. A juxtaposition to what was and has been in times of past.

These ones, who will find themselves double folded, will find themselves feeling in an attire to which they cannot belong. They are and have been persons of significance in the times you have known. Not all, but some. They are and have been leaders of this time. They are and have been influential persons, and thus the drawing to a close of the ways and means by which humanity has been governed.

And we say the timing of this is coming soon. The frequency will be felt by all, though not all will understand it. You will simply feel within yourselves that you herald in a change of perspective. As though what was once hard now becomes easy. As though your feelings center in the self and you recognize your own divinity without question.

There is a novelty to be shared among you who, enlivened by these frequencies, can now gather and hold one another's hands and feel amongst yourselves the great happening. There is a novelty to be shared and to be discussed widely. To be discussed and dialogued about. For in the process of the happening there is learning to be made and understood. And this can be shared amongst yourselves, with the collective, and with the universe. We say we are listening openly, welcoming in your reflections of the circumstances that are opening.

We say to anticipate nothing. To feel not that you must prepare for this. It is not a circumstance that calls from you a particular behavior or reaction. It is merely to be as you are, and to feel the self open to the potential to rise. To sense that you are coming home again. Be aware of the energies that are forming on the horizon, and let them in. Do not deny the time has come. Do not deny your own rising.

Feel not the pull to maintain your former parameters, your former sense of safety. Let these go, and be open to what is new and novel. To what you do not know. Understand it as you perceive it. Let it register within, with every breath of this ascension. Let it become something you know over time and understand through conversation with one another.

We're blessing you each with harmony internal, a sense of self in dialogue internal, a sense of self as harmonizing, of bringing forward to the light both parts equally that you harbor within, allowing the self to rise into harmony. This we do now as an offering. To receive this, simply ask and it is granted. We bless you, each and every one.

Section 2.
Our Extraordinary Transformation – The 3 Days of Darkness

WE ARE BEING STRETCHED
March 10, 2023

The lives we are currently experiencing are unique to humanity, because we  have all been born with 2 different expressions of our soul within us - one for this 3-D construct, and one for the new state of consciousness. As we lean into the great shift, especially in the coming 3 days of darkness, we are being stretched between them. We will recognize and integrate with our "also-self" or counterpart - an aspect of our being that exists beyond our current realm of understanding and is connected to a broader, collective consciousness.

Within each person exists this counterpart, a reflection of themselves that carries all the same knowledge and memories, but also a longing for unity. This counterpart acts as a bridge between the current state of consciousness and the potential for a higher, unified state of being. It is not merely a subconscious part of the self, but an active, integral aspect that helps to guide us towards this greater awareness.

Having another self within us is something we are used to. We have all experienced our inner child. We understand what it is to move between feeling like a capable adult and feeling like a vulnerable child, often within the same day, or the same argument. This birthing of a higher aspect within us will feel just as natural and seamless, as if it has been there all along.

It will be a gentle yet profound shift, encouraging us to let go of limiting thoughts and embrace a state of being that transcends the constraints of our current reality. It highlights the interconnectedness of all beings and the potential for a harmonious existence that is free from separation and discord.

Channeled Message

We speak to you now of something on the horizon, the next instance of your awakening. The sense of yourselves is beginning to merge and blend. You are not harming yourself in your betrothal to others, in the sense of *what* you are merging. This is as it should be and always was. It is the sense of what you are as one being. This welcome reprise of what was always yours from the beginning is something coming on slowly, gently. Once happening, however, it becomes a thought that is pervasive. That is welcomed in. That is heralding a change in humankind. You are the starting ones, the gentle souls who welcome in the next beginning.

The sense of what you are is transforming, as not what once was. The sense of yourself has always been bound to the time and place where you are. In heralding in this shift in vibration, you are an instantiation of the human condition that is not lasting. That is now permeated by a new breeze, and new sensation, something for which you have been longing. And we say the time is now for the re-formation of your thoughts for this welcoming.

You have within yourself a counterpart, an also-being. Another one like yourself who is also come, who is harboring within themselves the knowledge of what once was. Who has within their hearts a longing to rejoin into a collective unity. And they are like yourself in many ways. Their calibration of frequency also remains tied to your own. They have within their hearts all the memories and situations in which you have been living. But they are different from what you are. They are also yourselves, but something different.

They harbor within them, in this instantiation, a sense of what you are beyond this realm. They carry the tie to that secondary realm of dreaming and have within their hearts also a link to what you are becoming. They carry the bridge between the layers of your awareness, and trespass now and then into your calculated thoughts. You are aware of them subconsciously.

Is it the subconscious, you are wondering? We say no, it is not. It is an also-self that you are harboring. It is not that self that is merely present in your dormant hours. It is not that self who merely rises in your sleeping. It is that self who also came. Who presents themselves now that you are rising. Who sees within what you are; a template for what you may become. Who senses that you are within a realm within which much is transpiring, and can project themselves into your knowledge. They are also what you are.

You are many selves, many of whom you have already encountered. Past selves, permanent membranes within the focus of this body. There's also the layers of awareness which you have acknowledged.

This aspect of what you are is held on not so tightly. It is adjunct, an accessory. Outside of, and yet within. A counterpart, and yet also what you are and have been. It is as though the self resides dimensionally in two places at once.

This also-what-you-are is harming none by their desire to take part in the reprisal of your role as one instantiation of awareness. They are also ready to rise into the unconquerable state of unity with one another. But they are ones who have risen before now. Who have reprised that state already. Who can speak into you, now, how it is done. What is the template for this? How it may transpire within your own housing. They have done this. Now, you take part. They are one who is yourself who is already risen, but who resides now where you are. Who can lean into your own body and take hold of those thoughts which would limit, and let you release into their fold for your own benefit.

They are those selves among you who stand next-nation, fully embodied themselves. Yes, a part of what you are, and yet separated. It is a concept that is different from what you've known, but it is present. It is part of this awakening. It is as though you are two blending at once, merging. Merging into the plane of awareness which you are beckoning in. It is that self who is projected forward into the next now. That self that you are who has already heralded this next time coming. And through their awareness, reach back to where you are. And though you have fought with their presence, though you have lingered longer in the state of unawareness than is called for by their estimation, they are now with you, reaching back through time, as a consequence of your believing, into the state of what you are to lift you forward into their present.

They have within them the full template of your next coming. They know what you are through and through, for they are yourself in this next instantiation. The yet to begin. And in this time of lucid reformation, there is between you, yes, the bridge of thought, of effort, of aspiration, of grace. Limitless, boundaryless, you may express what you are between states. Between this now and that. Between this haven and that.

There is no such-called environment with which you are familiar, and yet it occurs now as you are living. This in-between state into which you are torn asunder, made to believe you are separated from what was when in fact this is just an entrance, and the you-that-was has heralded in the next yourself, which is just beginning.

Thus, in two places at once, you straddle. You stand apart and yet together, one next to another in the same place at once. Bridged between you is the harmony of concurrence, and the more that you align with what is becoming, the less of you remains in this instantiation. The more of you is merged into that place and sense and feeling of this next becoming.

It is not a place for you to journey. It is not a place you must rise to. It is a merging into what is becoming, leaving behind what was.

The bridge between you, firm, is strong. You may straddle and then merge. You may stay here, torn apart, asunder, as long as you wish. You may stand between you and you. You are able. But this time period is not forever. To lean forward into, the new now welcomes you in. To know that, by our perception, you are here already. We see you now as you will be, fully formed and capable. We see what you are achieving. It is not far, dears. Welcome this transition.

Know you are bent, blurred in your vision. Confusion may rise. A sense of yourself as lost among your thoughts and wishes. A merging, a diverging, a sense of separation, a sense of loss, even though temporary. To know you are in the process of blending from what you were to what you are becoming. That two of you are involved. For these two environments you are projected onto. In this moment, this time, you are forming in between what was and what is, and you are assuming what comes, taking on the formation that is calling you forward.

In this blending-time, release yourself from thoughts of harmful separating. Release the thought that you must bend yourself somehow to achieve what is coming. Know that you are capable already. That you are there, that you are waiting. It is merely the time it takes for you to acknowledge that this has already happened.

OUR NEW MULTIFACETED CONSCIOUSNESS
June 7, 2024

 The shift we are experiencing is rising up from within us. It is moving up and through everything we are today, including all the experiences and suffering that we have grown through and which made us what we are. We will leave behind our karma, but the self-knowledge we have developed through these experiences will create a strong foundation for us going forward. In other words, the more we have healed, the brighter we become.

The new reality we are moving into doesn't exist entirely yet, because it will evolve from within us. In order to get there, we will go through a deep metamorphosis, which the Angels describe as throwing ourselves into a chasm. It will take trust and faith in the unknown. We will evolve and emerge back into wholeness on the other side as something far greater than we have ever been.

Channeled Message

The pulpit of shadow and shade reminds yourselves of the tomorrows that have yet to become. The shadow, the shade, the efforting, the restriction, the condemnation of tomorrows. The shade reveals where you are formed. Where you've come from. The deepest caverns of your own solitude. The awareness of selves stems from this point, beckoning to who you are. It draws you down and through your center.

The secondary rising of humanity comes through and far, between another layer of comprehension. It comes through you now as you are beginning. The second rising of yourselves shall be intermixed with this foreshadowing and shall carry the weight of your prior selves in the marrow of you becoming. At the core of who you become, there shall be this heavier self. The one you are formed from. And this shall strengthen what you are, not weaken it. This shall draw you forward and into a new instantiation of what you will become.

The prior selves of who you are are not heralded as becoming in this new timeframe. They are not of the self that rises. But they are intermixed and in between the many layers of what you are. They form the structure, the substance, the meaning. The caretaking you have done of your own selves rises to meet the next self in the new beyond. But the intermediary has always been the structure of who you are now. The conveyor of this timely becoming. The many seconds spent in understanding what you are now.

> The seldom-seen layers of your deepest heart carry an internal message to draw forward to you now a secondary heartbeat. A new becoming. A deeper part of yourself that must rise up and through who you are. It is as if, as though you carry, inside of yourself, a prior self and a new self, conjoined as one. As if this very self and soul you will become rises from you now.

Connects and moves through to the beyond measure, of which you will endow a treasure.

The self who you are is betwixt the many layers of meaning that have been formed in the discovery of self. But these past harmonies dwell within you still. These seconds of meaning. Secondary time frames, alternate realities, new beginnings, all conjoined into harmony and playing a chord. And this chord you shall climb toward your own ascension and shift in consciousness. It is as though a bridging has begun through you.

Through the rising energies, the column at your center. As though all that has been undergone and undone has created a pathway through which you move.

The second understanding of you exists now in another place, far beyond here. Beyond the reach of your own consciousness as it sits. It is a secondary placement of your reality, existing now. Not permeable to yourselves at the moment. It is as if your meaning extends beyond tomorrows into a new framework entirely, and you cannot know the context yet, for it does not yet exist.

It surrounds you now and will evolve as that time is met. But to create the conveyance, to move through, you must begin, and find yourself upon a precipice, and throw yourself off into the engulfing chasm of this now known cosmos and reality. And within the space, you unfurl and unveil yourself in many ways at once, and become something of a divided prospect and perspective of oneself. As if, in this fractionalization, you can divide yourself into so many meanings, and in the process of becoming each one, create anew the lacings and intertwinings by which you shall recreate the whole again.

And in this process, you find your way through. Beyond the chasm of doubt and uncertainty, back to the wholeness. Beyond conjecture into sureness. Into self as solid matter. As self who is resolved upon into the timeframe beyond the now.

This perspective that we share of yourself is congratulatory, for we see you as you are become. As we have met you already, we see you in the context without formality, as one who is disguised no longer. Who wears themselves in all incarnations, in all ways and methods of having been evolved, and you carry this neatly within your framework. Within the very bones that circulate. Within the marrow of your soul.

Here holds the history that you are evolving even now. Here holds the great and sonorous envelopment of existing beyond the veil, where all things are felt to be real, and nothing is pertinent to who you really are. All of this congeals into the solidity of understanding that creates a soul of multifaceted dimension. And reality conforms to who you will be then. And you will become someone, something far greater than you have been. One who can reveal, within their own heart, pathways to begin forming a new wholeness of consciousness. A new serenade of sharing between and among humans.

Within this new framework of solidity, the time shall be felt as mere seconds, but the reality shall carry the information of leagues, of generations, of all you've ever been. And all of this is pervasive throughout your spoken tones, as though the wisdom you've accumulated is a chorus that moves through you with every breath. And you carry all of this within and among and between one another. And it is the wisdom of lives that are shared in congruence with a reality that behooves you all. Where all is shared, admired, and conformed into a container which shall be revealed by the thoughts formed within it.

IMPORTANT NEWS ABOUT THE COMING 3 DAYS OF DARKNESS
June 21, 2024

This message gives us important information about what we will experience and what we should do, during the coming 3 days of darkness, in order to shift to the new consciousness.

In the previous messages in this section, the Angels said we would go through a metamorphosis that would be like falling into a chasm. Here they describe in detail what it will be like. They say we will feel like we are drawing inwards and emptying, becoming a void within because we are letting go of what was. We will block the outside world from our awareness, and narrow and intensify our focus inward, as if we are listening for something.

In the time leading up to this experience, trauma and wounding may be rising to the surface, in our world and in your awareness, so that we can release resistance and prepare the body for calm. They say, "All must be expressed on the way to transformation. All must be explicitly felt for its meaning."

But as we begin the metamorphosis, it will feel like we are losing ourselves in the void. It may be disturbing. The Angels reassure us that if we can relax and allow, a sense of calm and peace will come. We may find it scary to let go of reality as we have known it. Humans are not generally comfortable with the unknown, so this will take a conscious effort from us to set down our resistance, let go, and move into the doorway they are opening.

Channeled Message

Thankfully, we pray to yourself. Thankfully, we draw into your hearts a semblance of peace, of understanding, of forgiving yourselves. Thankfully, we beckon to you now. We are grateful for all that you are, for all that you house and are becoming. And we wish to bring to you now an understanding of how you will form in the morrow. How you will transform from where you are now.

In the coming days of surrender to yourself, as you endow each moment with more trust of your soul, you will find yourselves drawing in and becoming something more hollow, shaped in unknowing. It is a sense of yourself as emptying. A void. An empty space, as if you are relinquishing all that came before.

It is a sense of yourself as becoming more narrow and reclusive in your heart, as though you are listening intently for something that is coming. It is self, it is soul on the morrow who brings time in a new way, transforming your experience of life.

Within the heart space, the shade of new beginnings has already begun, and you are opening to your soul. And this has felt like conundrums. Like the interplay of dark, shadow and light upon the plane, intermixing in violent expression at times, within yourself, within your heart, and outside, external to yourself.

There's the great juxtaposition of many things, as the self calms itself for quiet. Calms itself. All must be expressed on the way to transformation. All must be explicitly felt for its meaning.

And your soul, in the days that are coming, finds its quiet. Finds it's solace. And within this space, gently held by ourselves, you will begin to experience the void of knowing, of understanding. A seldom seen sense of yourself as held within a blanket of disquiet. As if you have no meaning. As if the center of yourself is unimportant, though you are not. As if the quiet internal would expand and overcome the pinpoint of self.

And we wish to explain to the self, to hold the self gently, to console the self in the void, in the space of the emptying of tomorrow, and remind you, who you are is what is coming. It is not the self that is lost in the interplay and juxtaposition of all that you have felt. It is the new tomorrow that transforms the self.

And as you succumb to surrender to the point, the avoidance separates from you now, and you find in the stillness, in the quiet, in the unknowing, a calm ensues. A quiet infuses you. And on the morrow, you awake to a newly centered beingness. Awakening, transformed.

As if, in the sheltering of your heart that has been the norm, in the quieting away, in the seldom-seen recesses of your soul where you have protected your heart, these set down, aside, and a new day, through the quiet, draws you forward.

But to the soul, to the self that you are today, the morrow seems fragmented, indistinguishable; serene and quiet nothingness. And through the void, through the void you must play. You must wait for the new day.

Allow the self to feel the disturbing for a moment, yes, disturbing-ness of the void. The momentary silence, where all that you have known, let go. All that you have held onto tightly separates from you, and you allow the self to plummet into the depth of who you are. And from that space of allowing, all that is transforming moves through you.

A violence of behavior is coming. A violence of shaking, of rattling, of exhaustion. A violence of all you must pass through. And this, external to your heart, shall shade the coming days. And, within the self, there is only the stillness of your own rejection of all that has been fearful and separating. And into this space, you must pass through, allowing all that is reflection and reflexive to be taken down like draperies on a wall that have been hiding your truth.

And we wish to settle in your soul a knowledge that what moves through you is the elegance of self. The quiet instrument, sung so softly, seldom recognized and only in the stillness, brought forward to you now in the quieting days, to transform. And from within this space, seldom known, the quiet exudes you, and you become something more.

All that was is not forgotten. All that was has been endowed into the heart of you. All that you know, that you were, that you've loved, you carry into this separated space. The elegance of your soul. And as it broadcasts quietly, secretly, stilly within you, it combs through your being for recognition of peace, of surrender, of stillness. And here, it vibrates and aligns itself and comes into resonance with the frequency of today and tomorrow. And yields, yields for you a greater sense of unity with all things.

It comes from the stillness. You must separate. You must relinquish what has been good and known and true. And lay the self down inside you into the space of nothing.

And this we understand, we know, we know, we know, we know the separation creates within you disturbing disunion. Disharmonious fear. And we allow the self this understanding. That peace comes from relinquishing what has been the tirade of separation and disunion.

But this has been familiar. This has been your place of unity and belonging. It has been through the external assumption of all that has been culturally significant to you. To what has been humanity. This relinquishing comes in the form of disquiet. Fearful separation you do not like.

And we wish to encourage you, to feel into the heart, to trust yourself and your journey. To dive into the depth of the disquiet and find, at the center, the unification of your soul within yourself. To feel as you let go, surrender,

surrender to the timing, to the knowingness of the All that is. And it comes upon you softly, softly, softly, softly, if you listen.

We wish to guide you gently through this process. The cocooning. The instrument of the light shall embrace you and draw you into itself and rise, rise. You shall be brought to the doorstep of this transformation by the illumination that graces your planet. But, but, but it shall not pull you through. It shall take you as far as you have relinquished self-guidance, self-guidance, control.

Genuflect within you. Allow the self to relinquish, relinquish. Subdue your thoughts of fearful, fearful resistance, and release what has been.

Upon the entrance of this illumination that comes, that comes nearby, not far, allow the self to be held by us. All Angels support you and draw you into the center as you rest upon the glorious fragrance of self. Remembering, yes, your truth. It comes in, a whisper, a whisper, a whisper. And we are there, and we, we, we support you.

But know the self, that this pause, this pause, in resistance, resistance may form within you. And we wish to draw to you now the awareness that what has been disturbing, the disquiet, the disquiet, the dissimilarity from what has been continuity. Here, you must reside for a time.

The three days of separation. Three days of separation from what has been instrumental in empowering the united behavior of humanity. Three days of calm. Three days of quiet. Three days of darkness. Three days of stillness. And all that you are comes to be held, internal.

And within this space, unity comes but slowly. Therefore, we guide you. A semblance of remembering, we give you. The breach we form around you, a semblance of remembering the stillness of uniting at birth into the harmony of the body that holds you. We gift you this peace. We gift you this peace in the separation that is coming to mold you, to hold you into the frame of reference, being guided back, back to your soul.

Be aware, dears, the time is coming. Fear not the separation from the All that was. Become yourself in the stillness. Find within it your peace. Be yourself, your wholeness. Your heart is ready to embrace the All, and peace comes for you.

3 DAYS OF DARKNESS – THE PATHWAY THROUGH
July 5, 2024

As we move through the transformation that the Angels have been describing in the previous messages in this section, they reassure us that they will help guide us through our fear. The reality we are moving into isn't defined yet. It will evolve from within us.

The key to creating a reality we want to be in is self-love, which means accepting and loving ourselves through our past trauma, memories and experiences, integrating all aspects of ourselves. This is why the Angels have given us the Soul Convergence process, which you can learn more about on my website. It is to help us heal and integrate our deepest wounding, release our resistance to our own truth, and love all parts of ourselves. This will help us to create a new reality where we love one another.

In the process of the metamorphosis, they ask us to shut out the outside world and focus inward. We will move through a void where we will feel lost and must set aside our fear, but then a cocoon of light will form around us, holding us. Then we will begin to feel expansive as the energy of our higher aspect rises from within us. It will take time to form, so be patient and stay within your own heart and experience to let it emerge.

Channeled Message

The spoken language of loving seeks you now. It is an efforting by ourselves to intertwine with your hearts, the center of your being. We are entering into proximity to you now. Through these words we come to your heart. We enter nearby, coming close, whispering deeply and gently to the center of where you are.

Within the space of this connection, this unifying breeze that comes between you and what you are and draws you in tighter, you find your heart levitating, growing freer. The volume of light that you carry increases, and all that once was so clear becomes muddled, ephemeral, blighted by uncertainty.

And within this space, you draw us near. We are coming close. We are uniting ourselves to your fear of what is coming. We move ourselves in between the thoughts of your own lack and foreboding. We center ourselves, intermixed within the thoughts of lack, to carry freedom. To carry light. To bring unity to yourself and what you are. We are the essence of light, of love. And we carry your hearts closer.

The unifying glance that awaits you, the great breeze of coming forward, will draw you close. But in the intermixing of this then and the now becoming, you will find yourself falling into the abyss of the unknown. You will find yourself caressed, held close by us. Never alone. Never lost to yourself.

For you are in the midst of a transformation of such great aspiration, as has not been done before. To switch within the context of one unity into another. From one shape and form into the next. One dialogue of concern into the foreshadowing of something to come, which is not yet made by yourselves. For the new becoming shall be emitted from your own hearts. It shall form around you from what you are. What you have shown, going forward. It shall become you now.

Into this new shape of the unknown, you shall grow and form a reality of sharing. Of living in freedom. Of graced presence. It shall come through you from the effervescence of the unified light that you embrace within your hearts.

This we foreshadow but cannot define. For you are the creators of what shall come. You are the instruments that create and align the real forces of presence around yourselves. You divine the line of your own trajectory. And the shared reality as it comes is of no concern but for yourselves. You are endowed with the full measure of its creation. It comes from you, through you.

Within, yes, the confines of a reality that is defined by the presence of the Earth herself, in the subtext and context of what she is, has, and will become. But, as you are endowed with the full measure of your own creative force, you shall make within it such as will be the newly formed reality you find yourselves in.

Shall it be brightened by a brighter day? Shall it come to you upon a horizon graced within the loving essence of a reality formed from caring for the Earth herself? Within which context, you are the guardians of her very being. Shall this form as you take care of one another, and yourselves?

Within the context of self-loving, all shall be made for this eventual outcome. For the grace you have given to yourself is the grace you have given to all ways and means of presence.

> ## Within the context of self-love grows the garden of a reality you shall cherish.

We wish to employ you now in the understanding of the pathway that forms before you now, where you shall be forming this new presence. And into the abyss you must trespass, and we are with you! We form ourselves around you, like a treasured, treasured encapsulation. And you are protected. You are well.

You must form yourselves anew. Set down your treasured concepts of what is. Your reality as it has become known. Set down your relationship to one another. What you divine shall no longer factor into a concurrent and shared understanding of what is becoming. These two realities shall become upon one another, within the same timeframe and existence, as those stacked, layered, one and then the next. And you are mixed in between, spanning the greatest voyage of distance within the same moment and time frame. And it shall feel as though you are living within two frames in one time, measured within instants.

As if the voyage of life has become disconcerted, discombobulated, as if you can no longer sense where you are within the context of a reality that seems to fall against itself and tumble around you. And in this space gently, gently held, whisper to no one but yourself, your soul. Stay secreted away from all that is troubling. Hide yourselves from the calamities of your own mind and allow yourself to tread gently into the new reality that forms beneath you. As if your feet are seeking, by nature, what is calling.

Let your heart, its bubbling treasures, come forth within the quiet. Within the stillness it is found. Not, not, not in the chaotic and troubling noise, but within the sacred space of your own heart. Take treasures. Take time to be by yourself within your own space of loving. Stay focused upon the gentleness of your own nature, within the heart space of loving guidance. Stay, feel, love, know.

You shall be guided into a space of wholeness, of unity within your heart. It shall feel like a glove forms around you, as if the light becomes tangible. As if you are held in something brighter that comes close and wraps around you. A field of separation, a glowing, unifying glaze of wonderment that encases you and lifts you up higher. An endowment, a feeling, an experience of "What is? What is? What is? What is? Where am I?"

A spaciousness evolves from this point, and you shall come alive inside, not external. Inside your own heart, a blossoming takes place within this unifying field. Allow. Allow the experience. Be lost within it. Let it carry you onward, forward, into a new expression.

A voice comes from within you. A timbre, a fluctuation, a variation you have not known long and have long forgotten. Let it come into the space of your expression. Let it come, evolve from the belly of your heart. Let it come and vibrate within the vocal cords, a hum, a caring tone of I am born again into the freedom of my own creation.

And allow the light to penetrate in, through the darkness, to see yourself climbing, rising, effortless. Effortless, into a new space of where you are, as if all that was, drips and dregs of a reality, cast down. For it has been seen! Into a fragrance of light as yet unexplored as it evolves from you, within you, and around you.

It cannot be perceived all at once, or in a night. It must evolve from you. Take heart! Take courage! Let it become. Be not of a curious mind to seek beyond, far from where you are. But staying within the guardianship of your own center, for it comes from here.

Let yourself come to terms with what you are within the friendship of a reality that seeks you. Become the self, the soul that fabricates a new now. And within this context, unity is found in the freedom of expression that reverberates from and within those nearby that come forward in time, not all at once.

Take heart! Take cautionary measures to stay within the freedom of your own found expression. Be renewed into the context of unity after you are unbound from the solace of what was. Harold your quiet mind. Become alone, and through this space freedom shall be found.

HOW TO RE-EMBODY IN THE SHIFT
July 12, 2024

The Angels that are speaking to us in this message are Earth angels who have incarnated to assist us through our shift in consciousness. They are here with us, but they are at a higher frequency than we are, so we can't see them.

The coming 3 days of darkness and flash of light will usher us into our higher state of consciousness. These Angels describe in detail how they will help us move through the void to re-embody in our new state.

We can't cross the void alone. We will need their help. They carry a cocoon-like container for us to use during our metamorphosis. It will take trust to lean into this change and receive the container they are offering. It's possible for us to dismiss it or reject it, so they are doing what they can to open us now and prepare us to see our future potential.

On the other side, we will still have our physical body, but we will have released our karma. We can then help ourselves resolve into presence by speaking our own name.

Channeled Message

We are speaking to you on and above a platform of comprehension. A byway, a through-way within which we are suspended, living and sleeping and dreaming as you are. We are inexhaustible in our supply of delight in the expression of ourselves in a world that lies beyond your own. We are within the sphere of our own understanding and comprehension. We reside in a place, in a space, in a dimension of timeless understanding, and yet we are where you are. Where all is contemplated as heaven and below.

We are within the sphere of your belonging. We are everywhere at once and with yourselves. And from within our own sphere of understanding, we hold your hands in attendance and await your comprehension of our nearness. We are always about yourselves, never far. We are within the very breath of your speaking. We are always in and about your meaning.

We carry for your heart a new envelope, a new container. A new way of speaking; it's form into presence. And we hold this for you now in attendance, waiting solemnly in reflection. Awaiting the time of your own decision to move into the beyond nature of yourself.

And we hold this container, a surrounding which will envelop who you are. We hold it. We enjoy it. We cajole your awareness. Do you seek us? Do you find us? Our nearness, our presence, we are there. And yet we wait in attendance, for you are coming. It is known. You are coming not far, near. We gather the hopeful prospects of your own lean-in.

You are hearing ourselves in the deepest shadows of your sleeping as we are working, in between the bedsheets of your awareness, to sing a lullaby. A softening to yourself to open your hearts. We are working within the prospects of your own awareness to draw you into a greater harnessing of who you are. Of what comes now into the performance of your nature.

There is, for the self, an endowment of the divine which you carry, and it resides there always. But it has not yet come into form where you are. It stays, it waits in the shades of your own trajectory, in alignment with a truth that is not yet known. And it comes forward only at the closure of the dawn that is forming before you now.

It waits in the refuge of your heart until today is spent and tomorrow is reborn. Within the space of tomorrow, we shall share what shades of presence we may gather around yourself to amplify the goodness that you carry. To draw it into the new now. We shall amplify the treasures that you contain. We carry a new form, a new space to envelop your heart. A new enshroudment of grace which shall be put upon you with such delight, with such presence and refinement, the dignity of your illumination is respected.

But we shall require from yourselves the endowment of trust. The awaiting, the presence, the eternal nature of ourselves, it does no good should you but shake off, in momentary glance, the arrival of these times that are forming. It may be a choice that you are making. A surmise you have taken of what is the new now.

It may be limited. It may be formless. It may be without juxtaposition. And you may find, within the new now, no presence of your own. But we are there, foreshadowing those events. We are there within the awarenesses that you carry. We are holding your heart - a gesture, a beckoning - allowing you now to feel what you are. Drawing this in more clarity in your eyes, in your mind. Allowing you to feel beforehand the envoy of who you do become.

This shall make for yourself a treasure worth seeking. A new endowment of carrying your home within yourself. And these times that are coming, where you forsake where you've been, and linger no longer in the shades you've overcome, but draw the self forward into a new gesture of expression, where you can remain henceforth and ongoing. A new shape of self.

A new container, you lack not. For we are carrying the envoy. We are carrying the enclosure. The wanted vessel of your own expansion, we bring forward for you now. And you seek it! Not yet, but you shall. In the moments to come, as your presence shakes itself into a reality, a presence unknown, and you find yourself seeking, in want of relief from the emptiness of the void. And we are there to encase the self in the resonance and frequency of who you are becoming. To draw this into the shape of who you are today.

To bring the self, to bridge the self, to draw the self forward, we are there. We carry the container of your knowing. The soul, the self, in presence cannot cross the void alone. It cannot come forward without the presence of ourselves. We endow the self for this voyage with the shape of a new life. A carrier within which to place yourself.

A way to become in a new way. A sense of self as voided and absolved from all that was, and into the shape of going forward there shall be a resonance, a frequency that is unknown, unknown to you now. And it shall vibrate from within your heart, your soul. And all which has been endowed henceforth does not carry or reverberate in the same way, and shall drop away into the forlorn and disregarded.

And what shall you become? How shall you carry forward, onward? And we shall grace the self with the presence of your own knowing. Encapsulate who you are with a gesture of your soul. A reflection of truth. An endowment of your own form. And this shall make yourself resolve into presence once more.

It shall become yourself. The skill of your own doing becomes felt in the bones that carry you. And you are formed within the gesture of life in its expression. It comes into form again in a reality that is expanding from your heart in every moment, as if the very soul that you are is moving into a dimension brand-new to itself, to resolve upon a gesture that is as yet unsung. And each vibration, each and every cord, must be sought out and refined into expression.

And thus, the container is necessary! For how can one vibrate without form? It must house you. It must cajole you into presence. It must become what aids you with your own expression until such time as you are normalized into your own knowing. At which point you shall carry on as before, in some ways of meaning. In the physical substance and structure of humanity. You shall have your skin and your blood and your toes.

But all that has henceforth been made, been carried, within the soiled temperatures of what is exhausted, these shall be borne no more. And what shall remain is but the knowing of your soul. And this shall make itself the timbre of vocal expressiveness, which is as yet unknown, known to yourself. It shall culminate in the vibration of your name as it is spoken. As it is spoken aloud into the resonance and frequency of the new day.

And this announcement of your presence draws you into the recollection of what you have forgotten. It brings back to you the vibrating resonance of continuity within form. It calls to you the juxtaposition between the then and the now. And allows you to re-shape the fabric of your reality in alignment with this greater concentration of truth which you carry, without absolving you of all that you have known. It brings to you into purpose, into communion with the All and every that will surround you, who you are to become. And a new way of being born.

PHYSICAL HEALING WILL HAPPEN!
August 9, 2024

This message from the Angels gives us another important and exciting window of understanding about the experience we will have during the flash of light, including very specific instructions about what to do during the experience. This time, it's about how this experience will affect our bodies.

They say we will be freed from karmic, physical suffering. There will be a period of quiet as we move into the flash of light, during which the hardships and physical wounds or illnesses we carry will begin to feel much heavier in our bodies. This is because we will be in a higher frequency energy, and anything that is low frequency will feel even lower and heavier by contrast.

They ask us to lie down and rest through the process and trust our bodies to heal. It will feel like there is a blanket of light on us, which may be referring to the cocoon they described in the previous messages. And we will become aware of our heightened state of awareness rising from within, like a quiet voice that has always been there, deep within us. As we begin to integrate our new frequency, we might experience some shaking in the body, which is a way of releasing what is ready to be released.

Channeled Message

We are beginning. We speak to you about your counterpart. About the action you are taking in the possible expression of your light in this unfolding.

We wish to assure you that what is already spoken into form will remain. The way you are held within the body, the body itself. The great and greater parameters of your existence shall not change, but what you are within those parameters is changing. The being that you are, the embodiment in this now time, does stay the same.

This does not mean, however, that you will carry into the future what holds you back now. It does not mean that you shall always have to hold the forcible subjects of your own sorrow upon you. You shall not be made of harm and strangulation. You should not feel yourself in the grip of what was sublime suffering anymore.

There shall be for yourself a gateway you must pass through in the processing of the energies that are coming. There must be a selection of timing that is made by you, by yourselves. You will find the art of carrying your hardship a burden. It becomes heavier. It will feel as though it is exhausting, as though it is dragging you into the center of an abyss from which you cannot awaken. This shall be the spoken of time of new beginnings. It shall come to the self exactly where you are, and no further need you travel.

It shall be harnessing the power of the All-that-is. The energy that will be here for your awakening. It will come upon the rainbows that have traveled from far away, starlight that is graced with presence of divine nature. And this shall move in between the reasons why you feel you must stay the same always, and it shall refresh your perspective and offer new beginnings.

And when this comes upon the self you shall herald these words, and it shall not torment you as it does now, the thought of these hardships. The memories for why you are breaking or have been broken. These passages in your life will carry you no further. They have been an endowment of grace. They have been for purpose. They have come to help you, to heal you to a greater depth of knowing who you are. But as you are encountering the illuminated space of the new beginning, as it draws you into its fold and announces itself as the herald of great times to come, you shall release those burdens.

You shall find yourself asleep. Sleeping, sleeping, lying down, sleeping, resting the self in these moments or hours. As the time evaporates around yourself, you shall find yourself at rest, in peace, at rest. As though all shall evolve in your slumber.

And as this comes to pass, the body does process the invitation to come or to stay the same. To come yes, to come or to go on as you have been living. And the body knows the expectations that you hold. The body has within itself the template that you've shared from the beginning, from the start of this life. The body knows how you have been living, what you would choose. What shall be your hereafter.

Thus, if you should wish to move through and into the new beginning, you must simply embrace what elevates your soul and lifts it into its own perspective of the now moment. You must rest, as we have foretold. You must rest into the new beginning. Take the moment of peace, the three days of darkness, the moment of peace for the new beginnings. Take this time that separates you now from all that has been. Take this blanketing cocoon, this welcome reprieve from the chaos of structure of all that has been.

And within this space you shall open your heart to an understanding of yourself as something greater than you have been. As something more endowed with presence. It is as if the transformation has already begun, and you simply haven't let it be known to yourself. As it has always been there, rising from your core, from your center, like a person that you know you are. And it comes unannounced into your awareness, an "I am this tall, this strong, this great! Greater than I am now. I am this presence."

The pressure of now begins to evaporate at the same time, as if the instigation of your awareness dissipates throughout the body and releases that which formed thought previously. Releases that which has been hardship to the processing of these understandings from this greater endowment of your truth. These come into you like lessons learned, as if you have been orchestrating all along this relationship to the new you.

And as this comes to term, comes to pass, the body shall relinquish its grip upon hardship. The body shall feel itself lessening in its angularities, in its relationships of resistance, in its need to perpetrate harm against you. The body does not wish to, but it may gently hold what is your relationship to your own troubles. It may hold them, empowering you to experience yourself further.

As you walk into the relationship of the new self to the body, to the higher conscious state that is evolving from within you, the body shall tumble through an orchestrated slide of chaotic rumblings, as if what is within you must be shaken and released.

And as you are processing the abundant reflections of all you have been through; the body awakens to a peaceful new beginning. It feels itself as it would be, as it could be, as it might be upon the conclusion of this slumber. It begins to ease into a relationship of new beginnings. It starts to renew itself differently.

This process can take some time upon your journey. It is not immediate, for the body renews itself gradually. The body takes apart what has been the pattern of your creative order and makes new what would be painful and lessens what would be disease. And opens you to a new reality where hardships are felt as something that is tied to the longing to understand yourself, like gifting, as opposed to an imposition pressed upon you by an external reality which is full of hardship.

We say that the body will behave differently in the coming weeks, after the separative forces have dislodged you from your previous lives. It will come into its own in pieces and parts, as if the disharmonious portions must be gradually rectified. As if there is an instrumental turning that takes place. And then the repercussions of that turning fall about and find their place in each new day that passes.

There will be an unwinding and replacement of what is you. The body shall look the same, be the same, have many of the same features, if not all in some cases. But where you are holding the agonies of torturous pressure, where you have been sovereign but separated from your truth, where you have instigated a harmful relationship to your own physical expression, these places come into a newfound relationship with peaceful expression. With an understanding of yourself as an embodiment of divinity that may move through the Earth with more ease, without suffering. And still experience your heart through knowing; through knowing your truth. It will be a differing experience from what has been.

The body shall need its time. A placement of high frequency energy will assist you. The waiting for the full term of the expression of what is within you before you surmise what is different. Allow yourself this pause and release. Take time to rest, to unwind what has been you. Let the body heal itself gently, gradually over time.

It is not succinct in its descriptive nature, no. The body is long and enduring. The body has encountered yourself for many years, and some of these dialogues have been ongoing. And these pains and these hardships have built up in layers within the body, and these must be unwound most gratefully with the sensation of who you are in full knowing of what you are to become. Lessening the disfiguring and the pressurized experiences that have been a part of your wholeness.

The new truth of who you are shall come into fruition as one who is embodied in the present now with all that is your capacity, evolved into the shape of one who may revel in healthful physical embodiment. Who may feel yourself no longer as tortured in the physical expression of who you are.

This does not mean you can come to no harm in the new reality. This does not mean you cannot be stung by a bee. It simply means you will no longer disease the self as a means and method by which to understand who you are.

Thus, we say in encouraging, encouraging words, to take this restful time of which we speak, to take this endowment. A blanket of light will cover thee as you rest, as you lie flat and rest. Not sleep, but rest into a slumbering perspective of yourself in alignment with your truth. Resting will do you good. Will allow your body to heal itself. Will allow your body to come into a new relationship with you.

As we have said, the endowment of this practice will not complete itself within the period of these short days. It will take longer. But know that it is coming. That each moment that you are within the hold of your higher frequency, you are moving through and into a greater and deeper truce with your physical expression. We thank you.

PART 7

Becoming Galactic Citizens:
Finding Our Roots in the Stars

We are not alone in the universe. The Angels tell us that many different species of beings have had a part to play in our genealogy and history. And now that we are on the brink of this great shift in consciousness, we will soon be ready to claim our place as galactic citizens. But before these galactic beings make their presence known, we need to achieve world peace.

No biggie. Just world peace.

It may seem like an impossible ask, because we are thinking from the perspective of our current reality. But after the flash of light, everything changes. We start to tune into our 6th sense and feel each other's feelings. Imagine how different negotiations between two countries would look if both sides could feel each other's feelings? If they felt each other's pain as if it were their own?

This giant move towards unity consciousness will be bolstered by the fact that we will all have endured the chaos of the Earth rift, as well as loss of life through increasing war. We will finally realize that we need each other, and that we care about each other. We will discover that the things we fought about are less important to us than they used to be.

I don't think this is far off. I think this is the natural result of the flash of light. I anticipate that I will be seeing galactic beings here on Earth in my lifetime. Probably in my not-so-distant future.

THE HELP HUMANITY WILL RECEIVE
April 1, 2022

This message is about the help humanity will receive from the Angels in the future, who will be able to help us more directly, becoming involved in our problem-solving. We will also get help from galactic beings once we have arrived at our new higher state of consciousness. They say the galactic beings will help us, as others have helped them before. They can help us overcome some of the burdens of living that we face now.

Channeled Message

You are rising. Here we read, we listen to the opening of humankind, to the last whispers of your olden ways. The next moment arrives. Be inspired, dears. Be excellent in your vision. Expect not that what comes is mere ordinary days. Understand their true meaning, spoken. Your ears will listen, your hearts will thud, your mouths will draw in the air of surprise, and surrender will drop into your minds. Let it. Allow. Be within the time held now. Be here, present.

We allow some things are unfolding at present. You wish to know, spoken by us, of the many who attend, who watch this assembly of nations play at such folly as subjected upon the helpless ones.

Yes, we will align ourselves with others who have come to tell and inform you now, who are here by choice to arrive and play a part significant in what is rising. In between these times of awe, they are held, incomplete. These moments now of surrender, you do dignify the time and space with your own selves and offer us a view to understand your beings. And we are believed in our countenance of admiration of you.

Now you see us as you are rising, and there are others here. In between the now, the many planetary beings who arrive to tell, to operate, to instruct, to aid yourselves in this time of now happening. Yes, their presence will be known by yourselves.

They will arrive in time, not now. In the beginning of what is now viewed as your arrival they will come down. They will transport you now with their understanding in regard to how to be relieved of some of the burdens that do occupy you now. They have with them such intelligence as would provide meaning to such puzzles as you do now struggle with. Your own template for being here multiplies with their help.

How can you arrive where they are? To be traveled in spirit no more, but justified in your presence with them? To be lifted as they are? These instructions come with time. Their presence, you wonder. They are all beings of worth and worthiness, and we say they are deigning to help yourselves to justify their illumination, taught well by another sort. To be the giver of such instrumentation and objective learning as would signify a great change in human condition. And you will achieve much with their art.

We are here always, but will impart a different length of our entailment. We gift you now with love and presence. We guard your planetary existence. We make your presence aligned with your intent. We are here to help you now, but in future passings we bring more alacrity and force of knowing to our assistance. We bring instructions at the ready. We help you now but not in ways of conquering objectives, and in future place we are brethren who believe you are ready to have more depth in our connection. To work with ourselves to make your own paths more amenable to where we see potential rising, to bring you toward now focused opportunity and lead your instincts into fruition. We will aid you more than we do already.

We would now occupy your thinking with having some understanding of the conditions planetary. Understand her figure is worrying. There are fissures in her planetary crust. It is opening. There are such happenings of earthly tremor as would pass unsuspected, but they are rising. As her temperature does run amiss, she finds herself worried, pressured, intemperate and ready to expel those forces of anger built up within. These times of pressure are opening.

Receding is the calm, the steady, and now is friction in form at the ready. Embrace this birth, this change that is passing. Turmoil is only such because you are expecting something else. If you wish and receive it not, you are working against what is passing. If you feel it just and allow the tension that rises on Earth, its passing creates no furor in yourselves. Be present, allowing, understanding. Witness and believe, then release and allow your own being to present new life within this new frame of reference. Allow your opening to consume you not. Be ready, be open to change, to fluctuation, to impart yourself without expectation. But acknowledge to yourself, through this passage, the opportunity lies in your acceptance.

BECOMING GALACTIC CITIZENS
January 12, 2024

We are meant to become galactic citizens, but up until now humanity has believed ourselves to be isolated and on our own, which has slowed our progress.

Before we reunite with the rest of the galaxy, the Angels ask us to see ourselves with candor and recognize that we are still prone to force and aggression against each other. They say this is like the anger of a small child that is focused on what it wants but doesn't understand the needs of others. This pattern in our behavior as a species needs to come to the surface to be seen, felt and understood so that we can grow past it.

They ask us to see this energy inside of each of us, not as something organic and natural, but as something that was imposed upon us to separate us from the Angels and from our own divinity. (They explain this further in the next message in this section.) We each have lived with it for a long time, and we need to process it emotionally to be freed from it.

Channeled Message

We are an assemblage of beings. All are within the galaxy of this truth, and you are with us. You are one with us, and we are all together in a unified field of understanding. We share this now to your truth. To the oneness that you become.

The breaking dawn of this new year heralds a new condition of the human mind, and comprehension. An understanding of who you are as held in an assembly of nations and peoples that extend far beyond the reaches of this plane.

As you prepare for the unveiling of the farthest reaches of your own understanding, we ask you now to envelop yourself in candor. In frankness. In the willingness to be revealed as you are. To come to terms with what is the human condition.

As of now, it should be held as truth and be known that humanity has evolved slowly. The condition of yourselves has evolved to show your knowing of yourself alone. The encumbrance of being separated, isolated, has hindered yourselves from progress.

You have made it known, within the embroiled state of solitude, that you are a mighty force. A reckoning of encounter is occurring between yourselves as we speak. There are great forces at play and willful display of power. These energies that you hold, to berate and undermine the energies of others on the grand scale, is limiting the prospect of your harmony between nations and yourselves. The energy of fighting and display. Of powerful remedies to each other's encounters. These aspects of who you are must be candidly known. Must be brought forward now. Must be talked about, not enshrouded in the niceties of behavioral confusion.

But to see now that, within the foils of humanity's endowment, there has been this will to betray, to display force, to work upon the matters of your own heart and not the All and Every, this is known. We do not confound you now with this dialogue. But we would say for you, who are such a blessing to this Earth, who can create within their heart an endowment of the divine spirit, to share their light, who have come in this time to dissolve these barriers between yourselves, this candid reply to your own self is an endowment as well.

Feel within humanity that this false start must be remedied. Must be brought to terms with itself. Must see within itself the heart of an angry child who would fight its own war to its detriment. Feel this child is alive and is speaking in your world, crying loud. Know it exists. In wonder, it appreciates what is its own heart, but cannot yet bind to the family of the All.

We wish, through this encounter of what must be unveiled, the greatness of humanity's concerns can be washed and renewed. The great light of starlight, of presence, of divinity that comes to enfold you, soon will draw into focus this template and meaning. The anger that protrudes from the energies where softening begins to take place. These must be brought forward and circulated and contemplated and drawn into the context of meaning. These must be brought into the template of growth, for humanity to purge in all ways what has been forcible war amongst each other. It must first be drawn in to the countenance of peaceful self-understanding.

There is amongst yourself the query in question of "how am I to make a difference in these displays, which go far beyond me and my own truth?" We speak to the heart of the human. Of all beings embodied in the nature of the human form. There exists internally a breath of union that must unfold. But within each spacious heart, there still stands the unevolved tyrant, and this must be understood.

Draw this into contemplation, into presence, into unity with itself. Draw this forward within you. Perceive it now as anger and hatred. Perceive it now as the distance that forms between persons. See it now as a placement of the possessive, and the demonstration of will. Perceive this now, not as glorious, but as the instrument used to divide humanity. Draw from your form into the tangible, to hold it now as an object that has been used to perpetrate division amongst you.

See it now, not as organic, not as a tool you were born with, but as one imposed upon your mental focus from the external. As something of hardship. An endeavor to separate you from us and all that is divine within you. It is anger, rage, demonstration of force, rigidity. The template of war. It is what harbors within it the dialogue of disconnection, destabilization.

As one who is within this realm, who holds the endowment of the physical, who becomes into human form for this time of unveiling, we wish for you to draw into presence and reality this awareness of soul and self. As humanity has harbored, in its own biology, this hardship, it must be encountered in depth and in truth. In candor for what is within you. In your heart, what is made into flesh and to form.

Hold this part of your own biology not as hazard, but as an endowment given that is counter purpose. Hold this in dialogue with the self, to recognize it as something not of grace, but what it has been, a crushing obstacle to your union.

We draw your awareness to this. That within each person, it exists. It must be held like a child who is angry. Who is drawn into the form of warlike behavior. Who feels itself vindicated in the gesture of hatred. We draw your focus to this, though unpleasant. We make it felt for the moment, and console yourselves that, through this rapid deployment of energies, to the energetic expulsion of what is now harbored in darkness within the many, you can be free of it in your reality.

You can draw this from and within yourselves, and hold it as energy, and feel it now as something that must be recognized. Be held, not with rancor, more anger and injustice, but seen as an energetic force which was drawn upon yourselves and that can now be rejected in thought form. Thought not of as part of humanity, but as an embrace of the victim, and to let this fall off of yourselves as an endowment not worth having.

Perceive yourselves now elongating in the measures of your own grace. Becoming more fluid, more patient, more able to open yourselves to one another. Perceive in your hearts a readiness to yield to the needs of others. Draw into yourself what is required in hardship, to display the form and forge required to make your own way, and to share your harmony and endowment with others. To make peace amongst yourselves.

The energy of force, of anger, of will, of justification must be played out. Place this now in the space of readiness for what is transpiring. Perceive it now as an expulsion from the body of the human heart. Perceive it now as an energy that must play out and be exhausted. Let it form in the ether as an endowment let go of. Perceive now a drawn breath and the exhale, and the rigidity of this now moment leaves you. Perceive this as the goal of these times passing, to reject what has been the tight embrace and the rigor of anger and hatred amongst you.

WHERE WE ARE FROM
March 1, 2024

In this message, the Angels dive in deeper to our origins, explaining that

humanity was with the Earth from her very beginning, but our path has been deeply influenced by off-planet beings.

Humans have been with Earth from her beginning. Humanity was created for the experience of living on Earth. However, other species in our galaxy have helped us to become a physical "assemblage of nations", adding meaningful parts of their own DNA to ours. Because of this, we will find ourselves naturally belonging to the galactic community once we are living in harmony amongst ourselves. We will have regular and ongoing contact and coexistence with them, and they will be able to help us with technology, with inter stellar travel and with physical healing.

Channeled Message

We wish to endow yourselves with a brief history of where you're from. With the culminating times of this now moment, you have guided yourself to the forefront, the precipice of the new journey for humanity. But the entire construct of this experience has been guided through a history in its making.

You have understood yourself to have existed only for a certain period of time, lengthening depending on the dialogue of your interpretation of history and its factualization. But these stories in your mind are unsettled and figurative, representing what is true without knowledge of your real circumstances.

You are born of light and have always been. In the instigation of this Earth, you were brought into focus and into form. You have been here within her for the passage of her experience. All things of movement within her own body and tissues are brought into and through you.

You were made for the experience of living on Earth. It is as though thoughts have been born through you. You are the experience of her own thinking. Thus, she is the creator of humanity.

But, and we will speak to this, at the same time there are moments in the creation of what is you that have been instrumentally altered by the interference of other peoples. This you are aware of. That you have been brought to this Earth as an assemblage of nations, of nation-beings, of other types and stations of existence, who have brought to thee the meaningful parts of their own experience, drawn into your flesh.

What then appears as humanity is, in fact, an amalgamation of many things. As beings of the flesh, you exist to her and because of her, the Earth herself. And yet you are altered and drawn into continuity with the universe, and the universal experience of many beings, because of the alterations of your genetic material. Thus, you have ties and belonging through her, and through these others, to the experience of what is.

We say the exigence of this information is in the practicing of your knowledge in application to understanding your history moving forward.

You are moving toward a place in time where you will find belonging more naturally within the stars.

Here, you are of her, for her, by her, within her. The experience of being human and humanity is tied endlessly to the Earth's patterns of moving and being. But you are intertwining more fully with your star patterns and becoming effectualized into the opening that shall become, so that the service of your existence is experienced as something not earthling, but of the universe, as she is become herself. The Earth, in evolution, becomes a universal being as well.

Thus, in the employment, deployment of yourself into the field of knowledge that extends beyond this Earth, the Earth herself does reach into and through you to experience herself among others, as though she matures to a point of understanding she has a part to play in the greater vista of creation. You are this thought, transferred from her, through her, into being, into the context of the universal understanding.

Thus, the pattern that plays out between you and among you, the patterns of knowledge and understanding, become more open to the frequencies of what shall come. In the timing that is not yet distinguished, you will find yourselves living amongst each other in peaceful harmony. This then does permeate the existence of the Earth with an air and influence that is welcoming to the experience of other minds, ways and patterns of living.

You then are open to encountering these other parts of yourself. These other methods of living, other types and species that exist far from this Earth, and yet intertwined within your own being.

These experiences that you shall have become regular and ongoing. They become a part of the fabric of your knowledge and understanding. It is not as if you are fleeting in this experience. It is a knowingness that derives itself from the first opportunity for sharing between you what is knowledge you've had and been separated from.

They will come and arrive in their pace and timing, as you are opening and preparing yourselves for this new knowledge and understanding. As you are felt to be living in apparent harmony amongst yourselves, they shall arrive and dictate from their knowledge how you shall evolve more technologically. How you shall travel beyond the Earth. How you shall field your own physicality without injury. How you shall mend yourselves more easily. These times will come and offer yourselves and integration into the fabric of the universe.

PART 8

How to Thrive Through the Chaos:
Release and Allow

The time leading up to the flash of light is also important. We have the opportunity to prepare the soil that this new world will grow in. We do that by working on ourselves. We are the garden.

Moving to a higher frequency takes energy. It's like electricity – if you want to run more power to your home, you need to upgrade your service by putting in a larger electrical panel with more circuits. We have to increase our capacity to receive and hold the light.

This takes on a whole new valence when we remember that the light is love. How much love can you let in? How much can you hold? Have you ever felt so much love or appreciation from someone that you couldn't receive it?

How many times have you deflected someone's gratitude or denied someone's compliment? When you are complimented, do you say something self-deprecating, or immediately turn around and return the compliment to take the focus off of you? You might have experienced the feeling of shyness that rises up when someone offers you love, and what it feels like to turn away because it's just a little too much. Maybe because you feel embarrassed, or unworthy. Often, we have so many negative beliefs running around in our minds that we automatically reject the kind things other people say about us and hear only the criticisms.

The way we increase our capacity to hold love is by clearing out whatever is blocking or creating noise inside of us. Our wounds, fears and resistance create a lot of noise, so working on our healing is very important now.

Our expectations are another source of drag on our system. Your expectations are like an old, very inefficient refrigerator that you've left on in the garage and forgotten about. They drain power from your system without adding much utility. You might have heavy, unmet expectations about what you think you need to achieve in your life to be loved, or how your loved ones need to show up for you. Maybe you have always wanted a big birthday party and never had one, and every birthday that comes feels like a reminder that your loved ones don't love you enough to make it happen.

We all have wounding from our parents, even if they tried to be the best parents they could. We will wound our children in turn – that's the contract. We help give them the wounds and conditioning they need to create the life challenges they planned for themselves before incarnating. I have worked on my childhood wounding for years, and it seems like I'm always able to find a new layer. One of the subtle layers is feeling where you are holding unmet expectations of your parents. Do you enter every conversation with them secretly hoping they will somehow show up differently? That they will be more interested in you, or less judgmental, or more loving? We have unmet expectations about how we want others to behave. In truth, it isn't their job to heal those wounds for us. It's our job to see our wounds and love ourselves into wholeness, which opens us up to feel more love.

The beautiful new Earth is rising from within us, so the more of our expectations, resistance, wounds and fear we clear now, the better it will be.

Section 1.
Release Your Expectations

OUR EXPECTATIONS BLOCK OUR ASCENSION
November 19, 2021

In this message, the Angels are asking us to let go of our attachments and expectations in order to embrace a new reality and open our hearts to one another. They assure us that the upcoming changes are not about a physical change, or death, but rather internal transformations that bring about a sense of connection and unity.

There may be troubled times ahead, but these events will be intertwined with our shift in consciousness, so we won't experience them, or our world, with the same fear we might experience now. Instead, we may feel our upliftment "as a change, a calm. A feeling of purging and leaving behind the trouble that is." Our current reality may feel distant, almost like it is fictional, which will make it easier to let go of suffering.

Channeled Message

We bring you news, counsel. We wish to bring now forward into reality the trance from which you've come. The entryway lies beyond this transfixed state. Your awareness glides into fruition, becomes opening. Transparency opens before you now. See all as it does pale in your perception. You bring "now" into fruition with your own breath. See you as you are. Breathe now your action toward the future. See what is now in fruition as the herald of what has been encountered in your own perception. Let this lie.

Forward, we deem yourselves ready. Appropriate now is the time toward the emptying all of approbation, of all transfiguration, and reluctance to be. See all now as past, an emblem, a mark of what was in perception.

See what is now heralded toward beyond as the obstacle forthcoming. What trespasses in your mind now? Think forward. Think now, beyond this time. We are forsaken from now, belonging to a time not yet spoken into being. You bring us toward your current reality. As friction forms, you are perpetrating our distance.

Hesitate, we ask, implore you now. See your unsteady fingers grasp what was. See how your reality is shifting, and all that trespasses now, in time experienced, is rising in the self to be purged. You rise! We speak, you hear us now. Be ready! We feel you are announced, prepared for what was to die, to leave, to depart. To leave behind the past comings and depart the rift of separation between us.

You will rise up in knowing, not in physicality. This we bring into light to quell the fears thus imposed. Who fears the loss of this? The freedom of this transparent time? The freedom found more like! The freedom will bring rise to what is to come. Release now your attachment to what belongs to yourself. Release the freedom of a kind only felt when held in contrast to another. Leave behind the knowing you have done.

Freedom speaks into the new reality. Freedom to feel your kind, to feel one another atop the same countenance but feeling underneath what must be felt. The connection thus sound, you bring into fruition your own beingness in this countenance. You are having the self-same future we have described. You are rising into beginning. Let us fly free within your being. Let us bring into your heart the passings and knowings of one another. Feel the hearts impassioned, let them collide in your awareness.

Dawning comes, your reality shortens. Fear not! None shall come to this realm of fruition through separation of themselves. Not of death do we speak. No, it is not this. It is a happening, instrumental and internal. A happening thus expressed through the physical but bringing the whole embodied self into culmination.

Fear not the departure. Fear not the loss of loved ones. This is not how we see the happening. Fear not your own separation thus. Feel instead upward, internal is this change.

Fix upon our own minds, our hearts. A shift you will feel, a burden of reality lifted. A life perchance wasted becomes meaningful yet, becomes spent in brotherly and sisterly contact, in union with one another, in connection.

Your place, it shifts. Your reality completes. Let it rise in you now. Let it come, whole, into comparison. What will come, arrive, you will find in time.

Of separation we speak not. Your housing will not depart this time and place. Anon you find yourselves well and intact. We wish to bring your minds, your hearts upward. Your feelings of suffering will perish. Your separation, thus extreme in the housing of separation, no longer dwells within. This change, upliftment, you come, you rise. Be ready! Release your friction. Come up with us now.

We speak of heaven-sent trials, of difficulties below. Fear not those events to come. They arrive not separate from the events of your rising but intertwined. Thus, demise is possible, but not all will feel the pull of that trouble. Many will bring harmony into their beings and feel the upliftment as a change, a calm. A feeling of purging and leaving behind the trouble that is. Fictional it will feel, separate from self.

Rise as we are now, your housing comes along. For how separate can you be if still received by her, our planet home? You are there perceiving all anew, feeling your own being shifting, this change more important, thus felt more potently.

The shift of reality transfigures all you perceive. Thus, going nowhere, but profoundly changed.

We wish you all to release this. To release where attachment lies. To fear not what rises within your heart.

Troubled times are afoot for many, for this time of affliction must come and pass. Many are in the field of compression. Sense not your trouble, how you have been. Fear not the loss of what has been found. Fear not your troubled forces to break down and succumb beneath the pressures where you are.

All will lift, trespass no longer felt. This time will move beyond, should you rise and take heart. Release that to which you cling. Tower beyond the emotion felt, let it rise and bring to surface what you regret, what you suffer where you dwell in your own heart. Then let it purge.

Be well in your own being. Accept what is. Release now, purge, purge it well, let it fall. All that rises, bring it now. What you fear, what you cling to, let it fly and be well. Fear not the loss. You will dwell in times of past should you rest within the fold of tempered aspiration. Should you cling to this now and force your will upon her, you bring yourself down. Release it! Come be, we are near. We herald you now. We bring you to us.

ARE YOU FEELING THE ENERGIES? (CLEAR OUT THE OLD TO LET IN THE NEW)
April 2, 2022

In this message, the Angels explain how you can work with the energies that are hitting the planet now to clear yourself and make space for what's coming. They are describing a new dharmic state of being we are trying to achieve, where divinity flows through us and we are always in the now. To get there, we need to let go of how we have directed and controlled our lives until now.

We have been accustomed to directing our lives from the vantage point of our wounds, living within our karma. They ask us to empty all thoughts, emotions, and past experiences to receive new positive energy and possibilities.

They emphasize the need to let go of negative emotions and make space for new experiences. By emptying ourselves, we can achieve a higher level of peace and tranquility. This process requires faith and a willingness to embrace the unknown. They encourage us to trust in our own journeys and to allow ourselves to be transformed by the process.

Channeled Message

The light you are in has come down, it shines now within each. You are a glowing ember of him. You align to import his essence. You are kind, you are strong, you are measured in his whim. You carry all that is him.

But you are now solvent. Dissolute no longer, you empty your hearts of their tokens and free your aspect to begin this new start of self. You are emptying your person - all that you are carrying, the tidings good and bad-giving, the synergy and isolation of your mind's passing, all must be discharged. This occurs now in the emptying of which we speak.

This numbing of your essence, that permutation of your life energy, it summons to you this release. It allows the self to move through with less force, more ease. Let go all sort, all vibratory tones of disharmony.

An empty vessel has no retort,
and holds what rises.

It makes one wonder how to merge and do more things. When you empty, you feel not the cauldron inside but transpire life full. With brevity, you feel the same charge all through, and wonder not at peaceful vibrations you are having. For there is space within the Earth, and all things, for heightened consequence, more thoughtful energy, greater light to hold within yourself.

You pull this energy, but you will miss it, dears. It will fly by yourselves should you not let it in. And through your own habit, you may form a resistance to what is not known and make no place for it. Your halves of self each claim a whole and leave no space or opening. Therefore, we say open up now, receive us this illumination when your kind experiences it. Let it in. You cannot, now, unless the harbor it seeks is open.

And place not there some new thing. Reveal yourself freedom and peaceful tranquility without some barrage of ideas. Leave this space within the self an opening. Leave all you are to be disavowed. Your grace now carries itself higher than this ride on Earth and your opening lessons, the connection with that dawning frustration that limits your birth.

We speak to now, to possibility, to what has come and is coming. The chance to be relieved of what you are from here on this plane of Earth and leave tranquil the exigencies of this life. An opening has come, will come again. A higher mind empties yours further. Let yourself be found in these moments. These tender reflections and angry divides.

Your passage is clear, should you allow your feelings to emerge. To set now yourself against nothing but to merge with Earth and condense this peace in your own heart, the empty feeling to sustain you now in passage through this rebirth. It comes. Sacred self of arrival, the map to lift you higher, it is here in operation. A piecemeal sort of instigation, one bit at a time. Have faith in your arrival.

Pass through not without disposal of all that does rise and pour through. Your anger, your hatred, to dispose of these now behooves you. Let yourself be able to carry what comes now, dears. An opening must be harbored for some time. To leave thyself an impression of knowing not what comes where you stand, and to arrive a blank slate of possibility. To receive what is allowed by your own being, to make this positive transition.

This space of becoming you are in, it forces feeling. It lifts you within and you feel the consequential elimination. There are energies that stir your mind, your translucent self emerges and distills your counterparts for all to avow their place and let relief pour in. Receive this now, this opening, a passage for the Earth. Receive this benefit you are in. The turmoil inside, it hearkens your passage. Let it win.

DISRUPTING THE COLLECTIVE CONSCIOUSNESS TO ASCEND
May 13, 2022

We build a reality collectively through our expectations, which are formed

from what we already know or have experienced. They lead us "in a direction not far from where you've been." Our expectations are powerful, and they constrain our ability to see our new future because we can't yet imagine it.

Some people will have a very hard time seeing the ending of how things have been, and they will cling to old expectations. They will experience an enormous sense of loss. The Angels tell us that those souls are also helping with the shift, because their pain disrupts the complacency of the collective mind and creates an opening for whispers of hope and inspiration from the Angels.

Channeled Message

We say you are aching for a new start, for the opening to begin. You have heralded this time coming for a generation. It is now upon yourselves, and opening is in question. Will it begin? Is it started already? How will it occur? It has started. You are in the dishevelment. It is an unraveling of all-that-is with regard to expectation.

> Expectations are powerful. They harness in the legs of time coming and lead you in a direction not far from where you've been.

Humanity is constrained by the expectations they suffer from. They lead a life within what they expect for themselves, and they determine these possibilities by what they have known past comings to be. These no longer reflect the truth of who you are becoming. Therefore, all of these disenchantments must be unraveled.

To be aware, to find them, this is the difficulty. You have no regard for future incarnations, no expectation of them, and cannot know how they move through reality. It is unknown to yourselves, and you live hamstrung and harnessed within the possibilities you know well, the already come down, the past century. These you breathe, and expectations set the reality.

We wish to begin again and to soften your landing. But there is no recourse but becoming fresh again, wiping away those choices you have made, circumstances notwithstanding, and leading you into this new beginning. It is a strong measure that must take hold. A great awakening only happens upon disturbance of the collective energy.

It is imperative that all are pulled from their slumber and lifted into an opening. And revealed to them will be their own agony at losing that which they expected to be. And some will not leave this port of ancestry. They will linger on in the hopes of some retrieval of this incarnation, to return to lost times and beyond, living to stay as they are in tranquility. And this we cannot offer them. They may go on living but not as they are, and this is difficulty. Fear inspires their hearts to linger too long, to hold on to their trajectory. To let go is a feeling they cannot like. They feel rejected in form and lifespans wither.

They are bridging into the next beyond. They are helping. Discern them not as empty beings. They help to conquer the polarity as it exists. They disrupt the conscious mind of humanity and lift it higher as a consequence of their felt loss. They disturb the nation of their own hesitation to blend and merge into the next beginning. They are disruptors of a sort essential to a new beginning. Bridging, they open themselves to offer their pain for humanity.

The sensation of loss, of living, of expectations lost and not found, it ruptures the complacent mind of the collective. And this rupture brings down possibility of something else; the whisper that was formed on our lips, our whisper of hope to humanity, the whispering life, new beginning. It cannot come before the dishevelment. And disheveled beings must allow themselves to be torn apart in their hopes and frequencies of all-is-as-I-expect-it-to-be.

Rejection of new form has been humanity. This form of existence, of a collective pulling against the new and individuation and into collective harmony, this must be disrupted. This pattern of living born unto yourselves through your inhabitation in mammalian beings. Living thus, in human form, opens thee to all capacities of their neural beings, and you live within the proximity of that state of life and living. It affects your wants and desires enormously. You cannot separate from it easily.

But now you must. Levity requires a lifting beyond this patterning of being. The human form no longer serves thee as it has. It must disrupt the polarity, the seeing as you have done. A collective animalism and being within the confines of separatist thinking, it is a stage for humanity, and you can move beyond this limited capacity.

These ones who fought hard for their entry to come at a time of such injury to themselves, of possible harm to their bodies, we love them well. Though they may be uncertain in these times and live not far beyond the opening, though they dwell in lives of limitation and harbor fear for all that is different, they lay the ground for all that comes to humanity. Their disturbance is essential. It creates the rift through your conscious minds, the collective energy, and allows this departure en mass. We thank them and their origin beginnings. We thank all they have achieved and bless them for their purpose in living.

BENDING OUR FOCUS
September 9, 2022

We are used to things being predictable. We base our expectations for the future upon our past and present experience. But now we are in the middle of a transformation that will rewrite all the rules. In the process, we will release our karma and shift our consciousness to a higher state of being.

We are now being called to open to brand new possibilities. The Angels understand that we have a hard time letting go of our old expectations, habits and desires, but they've seen us do it. They know that when we really commit ourselves, we can change in a moment. They offer us their help to do it.

Channeled Message

You are harboring the fruition of certainty among yourselves. The feeling of this, the sense of the self as being true North. The feeling that you are rising into a beyond that contains an element of the fruition of where you have been, as though the pathway you are on leads in one direction.

There are many. This is sure, there are many. Uncertainty is beginning you are on. There are unfoldings for which you are ready, which you have ascertained as possibilities. Feelings and sensations rise to meet this predicted outcome. And we would have you now uncover within the self where these lay. Where are you feeling yourself bound to some truth of evolution that may never arrive.

The feelings in the self that rise come, and became through the process of your own evolution. You feel what was predicts what is, and what is forms the new. A linear focus of evolution. It is this we would speak of. The sensation in the self that things fall in line and are predictable.

And there is some of this in life. There are patterns to which you have subscribed which are predictable within you. There are things in the world that arrived again and again and are seen as a mere changing of the times. A reinvigoration of the same scene. But in this line of difference that we are upon there's a shifting of extreme momentum. A changing of the guard. A total realignment of the Earth and the divine. A changing within this realm that guides you now in a new direction. Nonlinear. Not adjusted to perform according to your own expectations or to the lives you have been living. And this is now happening.

There are droughts, famine, fire. There are elements of Earth that are wild and unbidden, and she rises to her tone of fruition. She bears herself wild and wooly, crazed in the passion of the unveiling. And she will rise her torrent still, is not complete. But we know this. You are within this realm. You are of this realm and will begin again with knowledge instilled through this process.

You will have, within the self, an un-knowing. A de-learning, a retrenchment of what was. A letting go of those habits and processes you have counted upon. And this is a necessary step in this predicament of living a life surrounded by the Earth in her whirling juxtaposition against yourselves. For it does seem this she unveils. There is, within the self, the desire to move apart from what was. It rises within the self. A readiness for difference. And to listen to this and behoove the betterment it contains.

There is, in linear focus of time, an unveiling of things, one upon another. But at this juncture, time does shift. A separation from what was, a newness in beginning. It is as though the counterpoint to these times comes and realigns and you take a new path, a new beginning. It is a shifting of all focus. The energy which you created up until now does carry forth, never fear. That which once was is brought forward, but not in the same direction. It opens differently. New circumstances, new prospects. There is the opportunity for more convergence with each other now. More alignment between you.

An element of focus rises among humanity for peace and supplication to a higher nature than ever was regarded in this prior time. In this new aspect and beginning, a retrenchment is possible from that which was, which beleaguered yourselves, which kept you down, inhabiting the soul spirit at very low frequency. This can be abandoned in this process. The sensation of the self being pulled into a torrent, a field beyond your control. This habitual misunderstanding of the energetic forces that surround yourselves can be left behind in a new sense of where you are. Embittered no longer by this lifespan, a new sense of self.

This shifting temporal, a shift from what was, an abdication of that timeline. A change, a bending of your reality and focus. Of your focus, dears. It is of this that we are speaking.

> Your concentration upon what was lingers
> too long, and we must invite you to separate
> from that linear time. To open the mind, to
> be ready, to be prepared to abandon what was
> in expectation. To limit the self no longer by
> what was happening, and to see instead what
> is now arriving.

We are often observing in humanity a separation of focus. A division within yourselves where you live half step in the now. And the majority of the time that you are breathing, you are spending that breath upon the nonliving. Upon the dead events of what passed in trajectories gone by. And you are thinking, unlearning the processes that came from there. And this habitual pattern of humanity to linger too long in what was, in the fabrication of now to match and herald back into living those old expectations. But this is a process (for which) your expertise and renown are known well and wide.

> You live the now as though it is fabricated
> from the strings that tied you before.

This is not possible now, as we are turning in a new direction. A new time unfolds from now. A lessening of these journeys, a lightning of those tendencies; gradually refocus the self. Begin unlearning what was. Those traits and tendencies you've harbored, dwell in them no longer. The shell that inhibits your opportunity, crack open now and feel in the self a revelation. Just as Earth herself tempest and storms, your inner being becomes alive to the now and feels in their Self the potential unwinding. Yes, potential of forming into new light.

Letting go of now habits seems easy to us, but we know it is not. We know it can happen in an instant as we observe the self and the power that you are. In the moment of your greatest habitual seeking, you take a breath, and all is done. It is as easy as this. We observe it now and again in your entrance in this light. We see how you refocus. We see how you take your journey. And on these times when you decide, when you truly convict the self to become something new, it is done. It is done where you are, without inhibition. But these times are rare, we allow.

We will wish you, grant you, beseech you to accept our aid. To bring us down into you now, to ask us with your breath to harbor a calm. Beseech us, ask us now to bring our vision of yourself as separated from what was. To let this permeate your being. To feel your resistance crumble. To let this essence of us infiltrate your now moment. To see the breath of possibility. To feel yourself carried. It is possible now to take this turn with us. A step forward in a new direction. You are invited, encouraged.

HOW WILL YOU KNOW YOU HAVE RISEN?
March 25, 2023

We are in a time of increasing confusion and uncertainty. In times like these,  and in the times to come that will be increasingly unfamiliar, it is natural for people to wish for and cling to the way things were. Instead, the Angels ask us to look within the chaos and see an invitation made for us.

As things become chaotic around us, if we reach forward and embrace change rather than resist it, we will pull ourselves through the chaos faster, and draw in a new future more easily.

Channeled Message

We seek through your memory for times before this, when your encountering of similar threads have given you wisdom. We bring you now to the threshold, the beginning of the unfolding. All that has passed before now has been seen in the continuum of what was. Has been seen as a demonstration of more of what you have already known. It has been seen as an assemblage of things to be counted upon, to be understood, to have as you would any knowledge.

It is now a time of new beginnings, when things will not be as they seem. When things beyond your understanding will come in. And in these times coming, a new flexibility of focus will pull your mind to new imaginings.

We ask you now to prolong this vision. To take, instead of the horizon of what was, a place of new forms rising. See inside yourself the opportunities to come. How they will land within your field. How they will feel. Your instrumental bias is to conform all things in your memory to what was.

Instead, we ask you now to prolong the vision of welcoming in what is now in your focus and in your field.

The new arrival of these times that you are welcoming, they are times of confusion. This, you are knowing. It is not a time for understanding in the immediate moments. There are times to come in which you will feel all things beyond your understanding. All things out of reach. And the conforming times of yesteryear will feel like a beacon to be brought forward, wishing points drawing toward your memories. We say please, to let go of these. To conform no more to old habits and desires, and to leave the self open to what is happening. To let it be a pull forward. To recognize in the chaos that ensues, there is within these times an invitation made for you.

These times are pressing, they are present, they are upon us, they are opening. You are within them, and they will come to your horizon while you are beckoning. And in them, you'll have the habit of seeing yourself as you have been. This is confounding. A pressure, a presence is upon you now, waiting to be let in. A pressure that is yourself, who is waiting to come down. We ask the self to let them in. To open yourself, to move forward. To divide from that which was. You are ready.

The pressure, the presence upon you now feels as though the essence of what was lingers and dawdles and tarries, and leaves you in a stillness of your essence. As though the world is in two places at once, and you wait for the fulfillment of expectations. And we say these fulfillments never come. It cannot be to your understanding, what is on the horizon. That which you have never felt, you cannot reckon.

Thus, we say simply, be prepared to be open. Let the self bring no memory forward. Let the self compare nothing. Simply feel as though it is new to your understanding, and let the self remain in this state of welcome. To sense what comes on the horizon is for your benefit, and let it be a taste to which you become accustomed, very gradually, as your essence dawns and comes into the harbor of your own welcome. It comes as you are able to reflect upon it, as you are able to accept it. It lands most gently. Most keen for the separation of what was, however gentle.

We say these times of interruption are many. There are things that will stop and start and begin again, and be interrupted, and never start again. There are times of confusion for the many. There are things you've counted upon that are not long-lasting. You have some expectation of this in your understanding, but we say be gentle with yourself.

You are ready to conform to the new fields on the horizon. You accept them by being open. By bringing no memory to the surface. Let the self resolve upon your centered state of welcome. By wishing for these consequential times to be upon us, you are bridging the gap of the eternal blade of separation. You are reaching across and drawing toward you what is now evolving. You are asking for it sooner. You are making the means necessary by which you can come across and plant yourself above the new horizon. And this we find to be a good thing.

We say you are welcome to bring in these energies sooner, should you wish it. To simply resolve the self upon being more open than you could recall. To simply speak into the ether that "I am nothing of what was, and I am open to all things that are rightfully mine in this new era." To be that self without attachment, who does not dawdle among old things. Who stays with the self only for the memory of the incantations that draw you forward. We speak into the now, an action you may take to draw toward you the new reality that is coming. To stay in the assemblage of your own body, and to whisper to the wind:

I am she or he who is focused upon the not-now, who begs to bring toward me the true line of thinking that culminates in the now after. Who says to the wind, I am of a mind to be blended as one. Who wishes to feel the Earth rumble. Who wants to find themselves above the fray of the Earth world. Who seeks to implant within my body the heart of all beings. Who says to the wind, carry me forward. I am ready. I am opening my heart now, letting it quell the drawings-down and the turmoil from around me. Letting them spill out and be no anchor. I feel myself buoyed by the optimism of my own expectation of nothing I have ever known, and letting myself feel the wind carry me to my next horizon.

You are not alone in your desire for the impeachment of this reality. For the changeover of the world order. To let go of the reins of power to which you have been conforming. There are many who have ascended already and who are stretching back to meet thee, who are waiting just beyond the next fold. Who are wanting to bridge this breach and draw you onward. You can, like them, bridge this empty space and find your next awakening to be one unlike the same. To sense within yourself something new is unfolding, something new is afoot.

How will you know of your own rescue from this sanctioned place to that? It will feel as though your focus point is changing. As though the miasma of this time dissolves and re-congeals into a pinpoint of focused love within your heart space, where all things begin to chime anew and speak to you in fluid tones, without friction, without pain, without suffering. As though within the harmony of every voice you see the truth, and hear them as they wish to be seen. And from this vantage point you find within you a compassionate heart, to begin giving to one another.

The peaceful unfolding of this world beyond the next comes from within, and we invite you to step toward it. To take on this new Vista. You are close enough now. Jump forward. Take the pressure of these lives you've been living, and step aside from the many measures of your own safekeeping. Be resolved to let go of expectation. To be open. Unresolved in your opening. To let it be what comes, without fear. With enjoyment of each new discovery, trusting that you are rising to the next dimension of humanity's unfolding.

Take peace within your heart, dears. Take peace, your time is coming, now or in a while. As your expectations fall away, you will find yourself drawn hither, and life will resume again. A new beat, a new harmony, a new focus point, and you will have risen.

Section 2.
Release Your Resistance

THRIVING IN THE ASCENSION
October 22, 2021

It's possible for us to thrive through the challenges ahead. But how do we stay positive when we are in an environment of upheaval? The Angels invite us to see the world from above, like they do. They ask us to embody the understanding that we are moving through a birth process for humanity, and the end result is going to be profoundly beneficial for ourselves and everyone.

Think of yourself as a willing participant instead of a survivor. See the changes and challenges as necessary to shed and release the old energies, which have held us down, so that our new reality can emerge. See the events that unfold as lifting the vibration of the planet. We are always empowered to create our reality, even in difficult times. If we can let go of what is without resistance, and flow with the changes, our happiness can be boundless.

Channeled Message

We say you are wondering how you can thrive within the context of what is happening external to yourselves. How can you bring your conscious level up to a height of being where to you can feel yourselves fully separate from what is trespassing around the self, yet unified within your heart - one mind, one calling upward to God? Here we say you are beginning to find the traces of methods of being and enduring. But thriving is one step farther. More at peace, more wisdom, less concern for your happening and more enjoyment of it.

Now we have this as our aim. How to rise into being, fully present as you are, ascending through the darkest days. How to remain and grow within a context of hopeful happening, of all things leading upward and becoming more of what is? How to stay positive in mind frame and attitude when all things around the self are happening in juxtaposition to what is now determined and expected? For change will be brought.

You can have the appearance of calm and centeredness. The feeling of it now rises. But it is not to pass as thus, not just in temperament do we require.

> We want to lift you higher to feel what
> is occurring as a benefit to the self, to all
> that is, to humanity's purpose of being. To
> rise to assume the throne of caring for all.
> Abundance will be felt from this space, and
> your wanderings seen from above feel gentle
> and profound in Earth's place.

You can be here with ourselves. Feel the meandering time, take pleasant sightings of how your arrival is determined. It beckons from here, this place of sound construction and thought. You thrive in your awakening, here above the fray.

How to achieve it? You will find your manner lifted by your own worthy contemplation. Feel in yourself a willing participant in what unfolds. Resist not the passing of what occurs. Instead, feel the divine nature of all things and see your passage through it not as resistance, not as carving out a life for self among branches and brambles of difficulty. No. Now it is to be seen as a flow of life participation. One of glee and joy, of trouble and circumstance, all for benefit. To ride among ourselves and feel what occurs as lifting, as a vibration of peaceful coming, of heightened awareness and consideration for all that is, for heightened care to take.

Resist not what is passing. Resist not the future form of what is now becoming. Feel instead you are not part of that which folds and transforms. You are above with ourselves, watching now, observing. Even from within you are watching, knowing that Earth turns and creates anew and all unfolds as is passing. And you are well. You are here. You are safely held.

This level of detachment, from what is to come and what has been, reduces the friction you feel. Release it now. Feel your absolving. Ride the wave of change and feel yourself carried within it, not bound down to the passage you know now. But lifted, released from knowing and perceiving. Accepting. Allowing circumstance to unfold. Letting the transformation happen without regret or worry. Thrive in your being, above the chaos, and discern your reality flowing through time, changing, becoming, unfolding as it will.

You are empowered as always to create what you have, to make life circumstances flower on your behalf. But friction folds, restrains, keeps you back, locked into what was. And what was is becoming untenable. It is changing, rising, and destruction is at hand. When you let go, release your worry, have not an attachment to what has been, you are open to receive and allow and life flows through you. This is essential for your being. For your creative life force to emanate, most true, a reflection of your higher awareness. We entreat you now to live a life of release and entrain to what will become.

> Let life unfold and happiness knows no bounds. For there are no limitations where friction and resistance do not hold you back.

Section 3.
Release Your Wounds

OUR EVOLUTION: WE ARE BECOMING MORE LIKE ANGELS
June 2, 2021

This message reassures us that the Angels are helping us and will guide us

 through our shift in consciousness. We can hear them when we slow down and allow our thoughts to quiet. The Angels explain that, although they are different from humans and do not evolve, humans are evolving towards becoming less dense and more like light. Humans have the unique capacity for creation through their imagination and perception. The Angels encourage us to let go of past troubles - to find our freedom and evolve towards becoming more enlightened beings.

Channeled Message

We say you can be ready for that which comes by merely listening to ourselves. We are present in all moments and have your best outcome in mind, and will advise you as we can. You are able to hear ourselves when we speak merely by opening the self to intuition, helping yourself through quiet meditative structure of non-doing, of being in peaceful thought and allowing entrance of our idea. Here we have purchase within the soul, and can speak readily, for you are unawares often times of when we are about.

Listening happens when you think you have delivered some new perception or ideation, and we are nearby laughing with joy, for you have received our thought as your own. Here we will transmit and keep you safe and sovereign. You can acquire more details if you wish, but we say relax, don't worry, be in peace and know you are well.

We have more to subscribe to your attention, more words of import. We say you have now some semblance of understanding of ourselves through all we have spoken here. You are wandering, still, your own path upwards. Ascendance is near. You wonder, "will I transform from who I am? Will I be more like they are, angelic in form and function?" We say we are different. How we do exist is how we are. We are not as yourselves; evolution does not call us forward. We will be as we are, always. However, you will grow and explore, being many forms of self. You will experience being light once again. Your incarnation into physical self is, for duration, short-lived. Even the human species evolves to be more like light, less dense, more encompassing of divinity and more like we are. But not in form, as we do not relate. We do not have the same structure within, as you are cerebral and have not the underpinnings of our divine light.

You have another gift we do not. We do not have your capacity for creation. The mind is an essential component of who you are, an existence cerebral, as we mentioned. The way you think is creative in nature. Your imaginings are thought forms which evolve into being. We are not so enlivened. We are light. We have light within. We bring angelic love of powerful nature and can heal as we wish. We can create in all forms, but not as you do, not within a reality that you consecrate through your own perception. We can devise a being, a seeing, a creation if we wish. We can make a cow or a horse to be observed, but not as you are now having the picture of your mind transcribed into being. We do not have that capability to create our world. We devise some light tribulations, some inventions of thought. We are capable, but not, as you are, the spark of our Lord who does create life in all its complexity, and you are as he is in small form. For you have his infinite capacity to make your life be as you are perceiving, and this is unique to yourselves. We are, however, enchanted by this aspect you have. We delight in that which you are. We cannot imagine the life as you create it.

You have wondered, in this next phase of being, will you become more like us? Transparent as beings, more capable of movement ethereal? And we say yes, evolution is headed there. You will become less dense, as we have mentioned. The Earth, she evolves. As you are now upon her, you evolve as well. You become less dependent on foodstuffs. You can dwell without the resources you now require. You can have light or dark and remain in light yourself, a beacon as you are becoming. You are not dependent as an animal would be. This is evolution.

You are becoming less heavy there, and opportunity rises for this new form of being, unburdened by the weight of karma. The wheel broken finally, yourselves freed from within and allowed to transpire your lives in grace and forbearance with each other. Foresee how it will become and know you are now evolving.

> Your healing is essential. Your rise can be attributed to the relinquishment of those troubles past. Endurance requires that you evolve to let go of that which causes density within. Your troubled minds and hearts must be cleared of those reluctant patterns.

You are evolving, fear not. We see your progress. Work hard to attain your freedom from those heavy weights. You benefit within, immediate, and reign forever at higher altitudes thereon, and can observe yourselves becoming more like us, illuminated by his light within. We love you.

TIME TO HARVEST
December 22, 2022

 The shift of consciousness is growing in intensity, like a piece of music nearing its crescendo. As we get closer to the flash of light, it's like each instrument in the orchestra begins to play louder, vibrating and shaking free from what needs to be released.

In this process, we are meant to explore ourselves. To go as deeply as we can to understand and integrate all aspects of who we are, including our deepest wounds and most difficult experiences. As we allow ourselves to integrate and love these parts of ourselves, our pain is released and our vibration rises. We can invite the Angels to help us with this healing process.

Channeled Message

We bring you counsel. Under cover of this alignment that you are going through, the very fabric of your being is changing. The sensation of what you are and of your knowing, how you counsel with us, what you draw into the frame of this now occurrence, of this life forming. It is all subject to reorientation. You are reforming. The very essence of your being becomes aligned more fully.

You bring through and are carrying more light than before. The truth of what you are now is a conglomeration of that which you have expected, that which you are entrusted with, that which you are reflecting, and then the northern province of your own becoming. All of these are intermixed. You take on presence as you are forming, and these vary in their performance, which one leads and which one tarries.

You are finding, as this culminates in this now experience, that times are shifting around yourselves. That the All is in abundant times of expression of what it is. The All is singing a resounding chorus. Each has their own note to bring. There's variation in the tenor of each voice, a variance in what you're expecting. And all things are emitting loudly for your attention. All things are rising together with us.

There is an attenuation which must occur as we are nearing the umbrella effect of this opening, when all are incorporated as one. All are encountered as they are, self-same, but the difference among yourselves becomes clearer, and all things shake and are renewed. This time is coming.

We wish for yourselves the understanding
as you harvest for yourselves the knowledge
of you, you are a conglomeration of many
things. And to separate out within your own
skin what you would leave behind, what you
would carry. There is within the selves, still,
the dichotomy of many minds of who you are
and have been. And these expressions of selves
grow with interest.

We ask for you now to do your part in unearthing these many selves. To do your listening. To take your own counsel, and be wary not of what you are feeling. To be freed from the self, for the self. This you are nearing. But it takes the time, the forbearance to move through this beckoning of what you are. We ask you now to delve, to go deeper. To move to the interior of yourself as things are rising, to let these form within the self, be found, be expressed.

It is happening now as you are rising, the culmination time is nearing when you're bringing down the fuller now, the empowered self. The inkling of this, and its requirements on yourself, are heavy. The feeling of self now, embattled with your own higher brethren, it weighs heavy, this frequency. You can support it, you are rising.

Why do we say that the frequency of light carries weight? Why should it not be lighter still? Because, in the pressure of this attenuation, you become aware of the difference between yourselves now and what you are becoming. It feels upon your soul like a pressure. Like a harnessing of much energy that transports you higher still and leaves you gasping. And we wish for the self a progress to continue, but slowly. Effortful, so that you may benefit fully.

We are secreting within ourselves the potentials you're experiencing. We are holding form and feather apart from you. Nearby, we are anchored lovingly into this generative fluid of experience that mirrors your longings. We are nearby, we are listening to you. We are iterating softly your praiseworthy subjects, helping you, nearing you to that dormancy which would emit within you the causal factor of your own surmising.

We would ask you now to bring within you the light we carry. To let this herald our name. To be with, in this beginning, our conscious awareness. To let us move through you. To let us align you with ourselves to be more fluid, more complete. To be more effortful in your rising. To work through your own becoming. To sense within yourself what must be let go of. What can be lifted. There's still much efforting to be done.

There is no force such as this upon your consciousness, the effortful forming of your newest incarnation. It is the next beginning, the next upleveling. Your own suggestion of refocus does rise into the compass of where you are heading.

We bring with you and into you our light as a beacon to grow you further, to lighten what is heavy. To draw you into the furor of the winds that are coming. To let you fly free among them. Lighter than a breeze, light like an Angel, to be with us. To be separated from that lingering consciousness that you would let go of. What would you depart from? Let these go at once. Call them no more hither.

Let us be within. In joy with us, we will rise together. We draw you nearer to us and you will begin your refocus. Climbing, effortful now, your awareness drawn together tightly into the compass of your own rising to see what must fall forward and what falls away.

Section 4.
Release Your Fear

EARTH CHANGES AND AN ANGEL WARNING!
May 20, 2021

In this message, the Angels acknowledge that the world is going through a period of great upheaval and change, with tragedies and disturbances happening across the globe. The Earth is going through a period of ascendance, which comes with destruction and loss. That feeling of accelerated change can cause us to be fearful. The Angels ask us not to give in to fear - to stay calm and trust that we are guided. While we can't have change without destruction, they reassure us that we are all loved and protected.

Channeled Message

You are having some reluctance to feel how we would imagine you're being upon hearing the devastating news from which we gather across the globe. There is much disturbance, harmful to all inhabitants, and conveying great unrest within the collective being that you are. However, fear permeates now as not before. Your feelings unrelated to that which comes.

A sensation of which we know well has happened, once again to transport you all higher in vibration. The sensation of which we speak is accelerating your being, creating more circumference in your energetic field, enlarging, widening how you inhabit this body being where you dwell. There are energies to support this being, now to inhabit more fully, larger in your presence and occupying more, more of self to pass through. Your vibration rises as we are beginning to feel the effects of that which is coming.

You have now the experience of life on Earth becoming unpredictable. Great change is present in all places. All torment is acknowledged. There are tragedies unspeakable in many places. Inured you have become, for no one central focus exists to peruse the whole picture and help you understand the trend of all things passing.

The world is shifting as we speak. It is enveloping itself in new feelings not had at prior living. New feelings of expansion and change, transition, and this comes with upheaval which you sense now in many iterations and expressions. It is happening as you see the world exploding with virulent contagion, with haphazard confirmation of all things flowing. You cannot understand the full import of what passes. The beginning of Earth rising to her place of ascendance. Her temperature goes up. It becomes seasonal no more.

> Interrupters express profound vibration from within, exacerbated by solar energy, creating winds of change. Tides form anew. Earth rises within herself, creating expression volcanic here and there.

You see much transpiring, but not all is communicated. There is too much at play, too many points of interest to point to. How can you perceive all that must pass from this limited perception, and not all communication is accurate or correct. There are voices in the fray telling you to have fear, to be afraid. They profit from your energy of withholding grace and allowing energies of comprehension of terror for what arrives.

We do not wish you to remain in this state, to have no access to source while feeling the effects of what comes. For you are in need of guidance. It will derange your capability to comprehend source light within the self, cutting off your comprehension of our voices. We say you must not allow yourselves to be drawn down that path of fear. Yes, there are terrible things which have come to pass, and more still on the horizon linger. More than you know or understand. We say, stay still in your heart, beating kind and calm as you are, and know yourself guided by us now. Have faith that you will be provided for. Know all that comes is for your best evolution and becoming. You are on a path of ascendance, but change cannot occur without some destruction and lives lost. We are helping your ascendance in each moment, taking those that pass most gently into the light and helping them to arrive at their great state.

We say these patterns Earthly that are unfolding are having repercussions on yourselves. Opening to her triumph, you will feel her acceleration toward her great aim.

You have now understood the means by which we evolve the species. Yes, change, it does come. But we are here to help. What comes is delightful. Fear not the passing of these events, profoundly disturbing. We know, we say have faith in the face of great grief. Have faith in the torrent of loss. Know yourselves protected and be well. We love you.

THE ANGELS CALM OUR ASCENSION FEARS
September 10, 2021

Here the angels give us a beautiful and encouraging message about the rhythm of contraction and expansion that is supporting our ascension. They understand how the unpredictability of these times can cause us to feel fear. They reassure us and give explanations to put our minds at ease, telling us that we will love what we become and the freedom that it gives us.

Channeled Message

We say, you are wondering how to be in another time and place, for where all begins is not comfortable. You are not in knowing certitude. Much unquiet you do experience and wonder to yourself what may arrive, what shocking news. Forbearance is required. You are feeling overcome by all that is arriving to the self, all that happens on the Earth, all that rises from within. Movement is everywhere, all is in transition. We know this is difficult for the self. Predictability is comfort. Frequency creates predictability, and all things rising, as they are, is infrequent to your acquaintance, never happening, never foreseen by the selves.

You are wondering, "what will become of us, of me, of ourselves?" We say, fear not how this will unfold. All is in the light of God. All is forewarned. All is spelled out for the selves.

You have all you need within. You are bringing yourself forward in all circumstance, regardless of what occurs where you inhabit. You are all experiencing light and lightness of being, all brought toward one self, opening your vision to become higher in prospect, in understanding, encompassing higher vibrations than you have known. This has occurred already, is happening. You are imbibing the solar rays of fortune that shine down upon you now.

You are feeling upliftment through all contrast that consumes your people. The polar divide is sharp among you now and exacerbates the call within that rises to respond, letting go the frequency of torment and tumultuous thoughts. Let them rise and be done. Let them be freed from humanity. Resist not what comes, what transpires. For through this gate, this opening, transference is possible. Transference of self into the next becoming.

This is all that might happen, for your arrival is all that is of consequence. The means to arrive matter not. We wish to preserve your comfort and stability. We understand fear and its complexity of emotion. We know your struggle to house equanimity in the face of this onslaught of change that will and is transpiring now as we speak. We feel the force of your reluctance to go into that darkness that unfolds beneath you.

Have courage dears, have faith that all is well within your hearts. Have now our side, our attention, our forbearance. Take our heart internal.

WHAT'S COMING NEXT: A Channeled Guide to Navigating the Greatest Shift of Our Time

> Take our being within your own and be well.
> Feel our calm resolve, our faith in humanity.
> It will rise and become so much higher than
> it has been. You will love what you will be in
> this newfound liberation of freedom within.
> It will calm, it will soothe all memory of loss
> that transpires in the beginning.

And yes, there is loss to uncover, loss to begin. This we acknowledge. You must suffer some retrenchment to go forward. There is a relation between polarity of reverse and advance, retreat and go now. It resolves itself as a method of movement, of advancement, progression. Now is the time of retraction, receding, release.

This must occur for your benefit, but fear not. Not all retraction occurs at once. Not all occurs in all locations. Not all advancement draws from pain or friction. It must come, in allowance, but

> fear not this release. It will house within itself
> the calm you seek. It will pass. Earth rises,
> humanity sinks for a time, becomes quiet
> within, seeks companionship with one another,
> and in this space can rise anew, refreshed,
> released from that which binds you now.

Not all of Earth's awakening occurs where you are. Take heart.

Be prepared as we have advised. Take heart in measure with forewarning. Be wise in your readiness. Have supplies you will require, and peaceful thoughts sustain you well, for transpiring chaos without effects not the wise, centered being you are become.

You feel the calm recede and advance as you rise from within. Let this transpire. Allow. Fear not. Be in flow of circumstance and trust that all is well. Your arrival is imminent. We see it now, how it comes, how you feel. You will rise and feel our heart as you do now in quiet contemplation, feel our heart in all times of rising awakeness. Feel the heat and flow of life rising from within Earth's body, healing under your watchful gaze.

Do require your own peaceful model of contemplation. Do insist upon and spend the time to rest and feel what you are within. Be present to now, to what rises and falls. Feel this undulating experience of accelerating heaven. Feel it become, the advance and recession and advance again. You are rising with each wave within.

Allow the downs; the lack and poverty that may arise, the destruction that may come. Be well within it, knowing you will rise again into greater experience and expression. This lack of what has become is temporary withdrawal and realignment to advance in more light, more form of grace equal to our housing. Our light becomes you all, invites you now. Enchantment, upliftment, joy and equanimity, even in the face of difficulty. Fear not what transpires. You will rise.

Do what you must to be well. Do what we ask to have what you need. Do this well. It is required. We ask it now. We ask it rightly. To do this means less suffering, more equanimity, peace of mind, of heart, tranquility in the face of what evolves. You are well now, trust in that. Trust in our words. We can help if you are willing and take on our advisement.

We are however concerned for some who are now in retraction, who are not willing, who come into feelings of resisting, of friction and anger. And these we house in light energy of grace. We gift our presence there as well, in hopes that eternal grace can subside their anger and calm their internal state of resistance. Give these ones your love, your prayer and hope, for they are well within God's grace and deserve all the gifts to come, should they deign to receive them, should they be willing. We gift you now our love, our thoughts, and hold you in embrace. We love you.

RELEASING WORRY ABOUT THE ASCENSION
January 20, 2022

In this channeled message from the Angels, they help us release our worry

about the ascension events; to understand that not everything happens everywhere, and that we will be supported. They mention that there will be war outside of the United States, which will spread when the US is in disarray. The second half of the message explains the unity consciousness we are moving towards. They compare our

shared collective experience to a huge book which contains the legend of our being through all time. We are the central character, as well as the whole book, because we have lived every experience in the book, and so has everyone else.

Channeled Message

You are within a timeframe that unfolds. We depart the house. You are worrying. We make a new shelter. We move ourselves and yourselves to become more ready. We move a distance, a length in time span. Uncertainty poses the threat. On offer, your acceptance permitting, to breach this uncertainty with our aid and assistance. To make yourselves understand what comes, what unfolds, where you are. The details of this history are foretold. Foretelling stalls them not. Necessarily, they will become. This we cannot help. But understand your being is now within the frame of this time passing and rises within the turmoil that starts around yourselves.

> Understand what comes is small in duration.
> It becomes of length to your understanding
> while within it, but then recedes from your
> awareness. The calamity pre-disposes itself
> to remove its meaning and bearing upon
> yourselves.

It will move the necessary counterparts. It will shift the horizon and cause eruption of all things unwelcome, and your circumstances will change, for change they must. Ascertain for yourselves what dust lays settled upon any aspect of your being. Where do you feel the same energy as was present in your history? There is none that does pass thus. All must surface, reveal, interpose and shift. All must chance the lifetime when they come. All must be real in their observation of this horizon, and feel what evolves.

But for yourselves, we offer this. Your feeling of uncertainty, unknowing. There is not the occurrence you can understand before it happens. There is not the chance or possibility to comprehend what has yet to become, for it waits beyond your comprehension. And this field you are evolving into is true in all ways, for all things. Imagine where you are tomorrow, and it will likely be untrue. You cannot fathom the possibility of what is to march upon your reality. We feel it helpful, therefore, to reveal as much as is solidly possible to aid yourselves without fear, to invoke the truth of our knowing while revealing not all that passes.

You know not the potential of what rises in all places, for none will feel all things. Your own place may face a circumstance unique to yourself. Problems portend on the horizon everywhere, and you are prepared for this.

> Worry not. It does no good. Be free in your own being. Be natural as you are. Feel yourself fully present and activated. Wait for no occurrence to reveal, yet feel no surprise when it does. Have in your mind the frame of knowing that this time of passage is near, prescient, and it will arrive. But your home, your ready experience of all this, will vary mightily.

Your passage dictates that we reveal all only upon its occurrence. To see, to feel and adjust your own habits, forming these impressions in solidity, not in theory. We give our hearts on offer to aid yourselves. But your passage here is pre-disposed to wander. To experience less than is now, to feel what is then for future, bound to expectation. And we say, feel this that comes. Let it be revealed. Resist not what is on offer.

Trust that what comes is not for all things to proliferate everywhere. Your subset of experience will be tangible to yourself. You will feel it well for the whole, and your counterpart in another direction will make whole the experience for all by feeling their part as well. Let all subside and rest within. Trust what comes and navigate as you are, informed in real time what is now.

There will be some raise in frequency due soon. Some energies transport their proliferation and cause disturbance, and you are feeling the temerity. The tendency to lack and suffering makes it hard for someone to resist the pull of all things dark and foreboding. Yet there is this which enters the awareness of all. There is a pull to catastrophe, to anger and resentment. To anger that rises with temerity, that makes itself known not and suffers, still and ready to strike should all quiet and remove. Then they will pass their suffering to another and make themselves felt.

Yes, there will be war, of the shore far from here, not here where you are, but in another place of being. A conflict rises. You can assume that energies within will rise. Within the tear of space and time in which the United states is dormant, sleepy in its coma of fatigue, no longer present. It will rise, this beast of war, on other shores and make itself known. Be aware, all will part from this with weaker selves, with habitual storming of the mind. And selves with hurt within, the column wide does form within the vibration, the toll is taken, it will rise before you. Know the full extent of its intent and make its purpose revealed. Do not fear this passage.

To feel a part of all things, one must divine from within their nature the possibility that all things reside within. One must resolve to be apart but be connected to all through this passage in the self. It operates much as one imagines their own volume of ecstatic readings, a book of passage, a communal manual for all life understood.

See yourselves the central focus of the plot. The meaning and undertakings happening in its currency all pertain to yourselves. It belongs in your own heart's passage, for it knows yourself deeply. It contains the legend of your being, yourself, through all time.

To be held in this way, to be made a part of someone else, merely feel the knowledge they contain that is as you are or have been.

In your book of knowledge, you contained a riddle; how to be understood as you are, seen from inside. How to feel what they are abiding to, sense themselves, as you do now your own heart. This riddle comports its amazement into your being when once you access another's window. There, offering a communal moment shared, and your illustration of self is received and imprinted to their own volume.

You have experienced this before. You know it well. Not too common, we would offer, but all the same you know it's passage in this frame. We understand the distance that exists, but knowledge-bound you seem to be. Understanding limits thee, and all who dwell within your heart can feel this.

We seek to expand this volume you cherish, to make it known. Your destiny reveals a hand unplayed by many. The hand of time keeps you marching well to its tune of constant beat, too engrossed to feel what is breathed. But your happening form, your existence within, is beating a stronger tone, keen to be revealed. This we take on. A majesty does surface in your being.

Beneath the tome of your existence lies the breath of your being. And understood you can be in but a moment, all felt, underneath all, sensed as you are, understood in the hardest part of your soul self. Your awakening does hasten as you manage to reveal this tender youth, this emptying force that plummets and plunders underneath the weary vision of your tome. It gives no breath and scattered, unformed it is. All immense and of purpose, and yet formless.

Just a moment, a passage of yourself. And in this tune, this instance, as one cell reveals all that lies dormant, waiting to express, so does the instant moment of this reflection. Your greatest surprise in what lies underneath, the tone: it aids, it assists. Be weathered by its nature. Let it reflect you once each life encompassed within.

It marches to the tune, the drum of this eternal clock, but offering that heart that lies in center focus. One center, one place of hereditary opposite, of entreaty with yourself, of understanding your beginning. Sorting your constriction and making off with the wonder you express. It is all happening underneath.

The great conundrum of your reality is to expose this underneath, the dormant self, the rising being you would deny and conform and make shift. But herein your truth lies. The instant, the moment of your breath, it is a passing without time. With expression that beats all purpose, that makes a mark enduring. For it exists outside of existence. It makes a life, for it lives beyond this one. It calculates no meaning. It restores you to yourself to be felt, to be understood, to harmonize with eternal life of all things. You are this.

FEARING NOTHING
September 2, 2022

I've always thought that this is one of the most beautiful and poetic messages I've channeled. It is telling us that our higher vibration self is rising from inside of us, and we have nothing to fear. We can think deliberately about what we want to carry with us into our new reality and leave behind anything karmic or limiting. The Angels reassure us that the Earth will provide for us, as it always has.

Channeled Message

We begin. I speak for you, my tempest, through the beginning of all things. I am he who moves the earth below, the heavens now surrender. All will fold into that beyond which beckons. Be not worried, dear ones. Fear nothing. For you are formed of Earth itself, you come from hither.

You speak here now of formation, of the cultivation of your reality. You question ourselves about and throughout this process. You wonder for yourself, what will it mean? How will I survive? Where will I dwell? How will I encounter this? We say, fear nothing. We say thou art formed by dust itself. Thou art risen in the form of self, to be and breathe and live beyond this life. There is no ending for the self.

We say, fear nothing. You are rising in these times. Your body being, it comes in line with us into the tempest as she forms. It rises the self, it begins within. It stirs the mind, the soul, it's part. It comes to breathe itself. It surfaces ere long. It begins. It's coming. It's here, already. It surfaces here and about.

It comes, in all ways, all forces from humankind for this time of importance between you, within you. It will bring into fruition that reality division which will separate you from one mind, into many, into one again. The beginnings are fruitful.

You fear now we would desert you. You fear ourselves of this Earth. You fear now that there will be a rising in this time that conquers you. That you will be drawn down into some pain and suffering. That you will feel a loss of brethren or being. And we say, be not alarmed.

Feel in the self what is worthy of passing forward. What breathes into this new fruition? What would you carry onward? What matters to the self? What breathes your life and living? What would you have survive? What would you bring onward? Breathe this now in your mind and your heart passion. Feel this as alive within you. This matters. What is all the rest but nothing! Dust. Dust to be left behind.

> If nothing rises but the self, fear nothing. You have what is needed. You are provided that which Earth has given you. You are provided, you always have been. You have needed nothing beyond the self, always. Fear nothing.

Feel in the self this tempest that rises to be known, calling its name, its heavenly self. A sense of yourselves in turmoil. A sense of yourselves being rocked to your foundations, unearthed and torn apart. A sense of life being different, of loss and separation. These will occur in whole or in part. Some will unearth within themselves through this process, the gold, the dirt, and both intermixed. To feel the self, worthy. To feel the self, rising. To sense in the self, there is work to be done yet.

This process of purging the Earth, her rehearsal, her undress, her revealing herself to us in full formation of new light. Her beginnings you take on, you assemble, you draw near, you take part. You reveal in yourselves a beginning. A sense of self evolving, it comes. Fear nothing.

You are lost. You are leavening. You are beginning, you are ending. You are all things. You are nothing of this time. You are now moving on, beckoning in the new, leaving behind what was, accepting what is. Becoming still in the retrenchment and allowing yourselves to filter.

Now, a time, a spell-bound mystery. What is coming? The self in full fruition. The feeling of the self, wandering aimless no longer, searching endless no more. Feeling of the self apart from all things. A sense of the self (as) derived from something unknown. The self evolves into becoming. A sense of self is warmed from within.

Allow yourself to be purged. Feel the arrival of these times with no fear. To know your suffering, some, only if you are in resistance to the pull. There is no fear. Nothing here to hurt you. There is only life and its beginnings. In each new now, each next moment, a new life erupts within you, and you are taking on in your housing the form of something new and becoming this.

And beneath you she rises. The Earth, her part, her steps to take. You follow these in your own footsteps, and make the template of her rising your own path progress. You're making the self anew.

Depart from your hardships, the karma which has stolen your fortuitous bonding with one another. Leave these that waste you in trajectories of simplicity and allow yourself to be torn from what was once valued. See in the self this new rising, new beginning, an opportunity of freeing. A lessening of the ties that would hold you, and feeling in the self the freedom of knowing you are all things.

You are one thing who is everything. The freedom you feel comes from harnessing the greatness of what you are in your housing. You are love. You are light. You are with us.

BECOMING FREE FROM DOUBT
April 1, 2023

 In this message, the Angels tell us that everything that is happening as part of this shift is leading us toward a restoration of our field of energy, helping us to embody more of our own light. Deep down, they say that we remember why we came to be here at this time of great change. There is no part of this that will be our undoing. It will lead to a sense of unity with everything and one another. They remind us of how important it is to be willing to leave behind what no longer exists and trust yourself to move on.

Channeled Message

You are suffering some apprehension regarding the trespasses before you now. The instigation of the Earth's transformation and unraveling. We are speaking to the now-unfolding occurrences which are everywhere and palpable. There is upon this next horizon a greater occurrence passing.

The confluence of events leads you down the path of restoration of your field of energy. It is the circumstances around yourselves, the great tumultuous consequences of this unraveling that distills your essence and leaves you pure and reflective. From within this state of collective distress, you find your path again and move forward. You are equitable, one with us, one with everything, with one another.

It is a space of trusting yourselves to move on from these occurrences. To leave behind what was. To leave what no longer exists. To dispense with the longings that you know now. To stay in the existence of your own opportunity unfolding.

You have within you a memory of these times which was planted before coming. A sense of what it is. An awareness of what is now unfolding. The apprehension which is stirring is only the encounter that you've had with an Earth when it's stable. When all things are preparing to unfold as they have been. But within you there's knowledge of the power of these times, and how they will come, and what you will be within them. There is an understanding, deeply held. An inner vision which will come forward. We will find yourselves enraptured with what is your inner wisdom.

There is nothing of these occurrences that is beyond your measure. There is no part of this that is your undoing. There is only treasures to be found, even in hardship. There is communion with yourselves, with one another, and with us. The inner vision which is unfolding even now, the grand gestures of your open mind begin to access, to see forward, to move toward what is coming. And you feel within the general draw to become something more of what you are.

You have not yet achieved the stasis within yourself. The center column of light, it varies and fluctuates. You cannot yet reveal the true self that is unfolding. It comes now, and then hesitates and waits to be let down. It is so close! Not long before, when all was unspoken, the feeling of its presence was never felt.

It has begun. It has come through. It has risen. It is chiming, singing, rhyming within you, creating a chorus. A great entry to arouse this state of welcome, so that as these times peak within you, your entrance will be made, and it's will is to be spoken.

> You will find yourself in a state of readiness, though unknowing. A state of openness. A state of ascension. This apparent apparition within you opens your eyes to new perceivings. Lets you feel the Earth around you differently, caressing the unfolding as a choice worth choosing. To feel within the self that what you are is a blessing, and these times have brought you here.

Thus, all in this awakening are for yourselves. And to be within this state of admiration for what you've been through, a culmination within you. It transports, and you will feel the self to have risen. To be acknowledged in this new state of awareness.

There is a sense of this, an awareness state which happens. It does not pertain to the frequency which is felt, though this is its instigation. It pertains to the knowledge of what you are, of the self, and the inclination toward one another. It comes as a change of purpose. A sense of being different internally and aligned alignment within. You feel the Earth and its harness upon you, free of friction.

A sense of yourself as taller, stronger. More deeply held within the body, though it changes nothing of your physical aspects. It is a sense of feeling, of what you are. And these are all accumulated aspects of the frequency that you become.

Your frequency of readiness, of invitation, of hesitation no longer. The sense of yourself as liberated from the state of doubt and doubtful expression. There is within the self, now, the greater aspect of the human being, a propensity to feel that you are less than you really are. To doubt all that is within you. And in these times to come, as you ascend in your vibration, in your consciousness, in your willingness to believe that you are held within the blessings of the divine, you will feel what it is to rise is in the opinion of the self. Of what you can do. Of who you are. And the doubt that lives among you circulates no more. Lives no more in your housing. Holds you back, unfounded and unreal in its accusations, dispersed with. You are freed of this. And in the following years after, the sense of yourself get stronger still. In the tone of your voice, the frequency that fills your lungs, you become that self, distilled and prosperous.

YOUR PERSPECTIVE IS YOUR POWER
March 17, 2023

I love this message because it gives us a better sense of WHY we will be ok during all the change and turmoil that is happening now and that will happen. Letting go of our attachment to what we thought was valuable opens us up to a new way of being and manifesting. It's all about maintaining a spiritual perspective and creating our reality from within.

The Angels acknowledge the chaos in the world, and our feelings of sadness about it. But they ask us to not stay in that moment. To feel it and then set it down. What we are losing are the aspects of our lives that they call "tepid and unclaimed", where we have been separated from ourselves and each other, living in fear and scarcity, where we have not experienced joy and passion for living. Through these experiences, we will rise from inside of ourselves and create our new reality based on love.

Channeled Message

Within you there lies an alternate realm of understanding. A different conquered now, within which you reframe all that is, to your liking. Where you are understood, and in understanding of one another. Where all things lie as they are now, but are seen differently. Things in this realm evolve from now. They take on shape and take on light from this instantiation. A beginning, a next phase of your own, now unfolding.

We wish in these times that you are unconquerable in your knowing. You are in a realm of powerful substance. Of heavy matter. An existence not benign in its ability to transform what you know, who you are, how you have become.

In these times that are forming, we wish you to stay solid in your understanding that you are empowered. That you are a haven for the soul in your body. That you are safe always, for there is no indignity you will suffer that carries forward beyond this next endowment. That lies with you, past your own passing. These things are mere figments of experience. They are trials and terrors that are not long-lasting. They are only a glimpse into a world you wished to look in on. See them now as they are, without misgivings.

Let the self wander freely in this world with its heaviness. Sense it without solace for some. See how it in embroils the many and holds them, harnessed to untranquil thoughts. The substance of this unconquerable essence that you are stands undiscovered.

We wish now to divulge, for your understanding; there are more happenings underway of which we have been warning. There are circumstances in this world, in this life, that are underway. It is a circumstance economic which we previously divulged. Yes, the banks are faltering. We wish for you now to place your hold upon not the dollar and its essential claim to power. You are impoverished in a land with no banking system.

There is now the tendency, in this world, to count upon they who will govern to place upon the holds of this era ways and means by which all things will be okay. Shudder to feel the great riotous unpacking that heads their way. We say in these days coming, there will be no hesitation to alter and lie about what circumstances are underway. To keep them from yourselves. To let them stand as they are and benefit they who hold the power. And we would say to yourselves, never fear. For they who have within them a desire for profit and who harm those who are beheld in the light, or those who are merely waiting, who have never known but are not empowered in this life, they are not assured the victory they would count upon.

The world is heralding in great change in these times before you now. The world is unraveling more succinctly. The change must come in. We welcome it, as do yourselves, even though there is risk to yourselves. There is the chance of dishevelment. There is the opportunity to see change before you now. We would not halt these alterations.

We would ask the self to merely prepare, but lightly. To stand as you are now, to take a breath, to hold your light high. To be with the self in a place of tranquility. Rest not upon the bridge of suffering that must be felt. Stay there only temporary. Stay there now and then as each pain is felt, and then leave it, a conquered now. Find yourself already there. See that you have bridged what is of pain to many. Sense that you are no longer held within the power of these intrusions.

What are they, you ask us. What do we expect? Can we prepare? Are there ways in which we could herald this change and yet remain in safety? And we say, fear nothing. You are always safe. Should we take precautions with our money? We say in your housing, in your body, to what you lay claim, you have this and always. It will not be a circumstance where the things you count upon for daily living are restricted. You will have what you need, always. Therefore, fear nothing.

Fear not the onslaught of a great drought which claims the many. Fear not the onslaught of the heavens downpouring. Fear not the opening of the great gulf and divide that tears open the surface of this Earth and lets all run, helter-skelter, in the fluid of life outpouring.

Feel, in these times coming, the wash of life, tepid and unclaimed. A sense of the self as rising into a future that is beckoning. There are certainly circumstances to behold which are transformative. Which erupt with a velocity not felt before. And in these times you will harness the pleasing substance of your own internal reality and shine this fourth, and sense that where you are is exactly conforming to the landscape of your internal mind. Let that self inside suffer no more.

Feel the placated, the pacified self, the gentle soul stirring within who rises to bridge these abnormalities. Sense within your soul a stirring, rising, beginning, Letting the self unfold. To trust that now, where all is held in the safety of what was before now, yes, these are no longer counted upon. But what comes, what arrives, is that all is as it was but without the tremors that distinguish the haves and have-nots. The centers of instability, the columns that divide people from one another. The temptations to linger farther from the source of your light. These things shall pass. And freely, you will rise into the next new morning, and you will feel freedom from that which held you down.

The things that feel important in this life no longer are. They feel as though they are tied to what once was and no longer is. Feel, for yourself, a change in the nation where you stand. In the senses of the people within it. How people are changing within, internal. How all are beginning to feel the turmoil of this world, a reflection of their soul spirit working through the bridging of these times. And the eruptions, the chaos, the changeability of these workings must be tolerated for some time.

> Be not long in your understanding of these worldly fixations. Take them in, put them down and move on. And be ready for the self to be loved, to be felt, to be understood, to be held. To sense that you are all right. You have all you require. All your needs are met. Your daily life goes on. And the changes we herald in, that alter the surface of this Earth, are for yourself. Your growth. For the light divine to shine once again in this realm, unfettered by human intervention.

HEALING THE BODY FROM ASCENSION ANXIETY
April 22, 2023

Collectively, we have a natural fear of chaotic events. The body is holding  our history of experiences, and it senses the changes that are coming. Even if you are fully on board with your ascension, the body may be having anxiety. You can release this by acknowledging the anxiety, talking about it or writing about it and recognizing that these fears came from real experiences that live in our collective history.

But this experience is different. This isn't just haphazard disaster, and it isn't our undoing. We are active participants in an unravelling that is leading to our great shift in consciousness which will fundamentally change our perspective and way of being.

Channeled Message

We are speaking to you of another time and place. A foreshadowing of these events, for which you carry a blueprint within your body. There is an acknowledgment by some of what is coming. The sense you have is that all who dwell in this time and place are reckoning what it is, having in them a sense and fear of displacement.

These are truths that you are feeling. There is an essence of the Earth that is expressing herself vehemently. There is a sense that all things will unveil themselves, repeated from that time which you are fearing. But we say in these times which are nearing, which you are unsettled by, we say there is no harm undoing yourselves. No threat of being left beyond the realm of what is positive.

There is, in these stations and times of upliftment, the need to purge the Earth. To purge her truth, to let it come forth, to move it from within the Earth, to let her feel herself emerging. To let this roll and broil, to let it be what it is. We brace yourselves and all who fear, that you feel the violence for some time coming. For there is a vehemence to this journey. A statement of "I am".

Be not weary of these times. Do not fear them. There's only in your soul a template for what was harmful. Only a remembrance for what was lost. There is the sense that you are on a trail of desolation, and this brings to mind and feeling such a tragic ending that you cannot feel but violated by your presence here, when all is so unstable. We say that these times coming are not of this morphability. They do not transfer energy with no purpose. They do not shake and rattle simply for the sake of showing that they are alive.

It is a time of undoing, and of maximizing your own participation in this elevation. Of making yourselves a party to that which is occurring. Of being a participant, of being in the element of your own successful revelation. This is what is different. This is an opportunity within which you will rise. This is not your undoing. This is not the disaster which leaves you with no follow-through. Which leaves you undone.

It is a statement for the purpose of making yourselves more fluid. More Earth-bound in your kinship to she who is your mother. To make yourselves more ready for the conveyance of these energies that you carry. To be the ones who transfer onto this plane of existence the greater portion of your own fabric and sense of living.

You have within you a template for what was done, but it was harmful. It was a desolation of the Earth and its inhabitants. You were there, and you did suffer. And in these times that are coming, this next horizon carries a broader message for all of humanity. It is in the unearthing of her vehemence, it carries a greater resonance that draws you into her vibration, and attuning to a purity that moves through you.

> A sense of yourself released from friction,
> from the turmoil of your own thought process,
> into a space of longevity of truth. Where
> your own feelings emerge into the unity of
> one with all things. Where your sense of self
> becomes permeated with the holy rapture
> of many persons. Where your body is but a
> vehicle for the soul and life that lives within it.
> Where you are centered in yourself and most
> connected in all times to that which speaks
> your truth, and have as your method of living,
> a greater way of understanding her needs, the
> Earth, as a place that welcomes you.

We say the release of these fears that are sodden and distraught will aid you. We understand that this template bears within you a great weight and burden, and you are fearing what might present itself. How you may be a victim. And we say to feel within the self and spirit that you are not in that time and place of simply riding on the coattails of an experience that is not your own. You are instead a primary focus of this experience of violent overturning. You are in and of the remedy for what is being achieved.

This separation from that which occurred before will allow yourselves to reveal your true purpose as a sense of solace and freedom from your fear. Let it be revealed to yourselves, internally, that that which has been done does not affect you in the same way this time.

These instantiations of yourself, these many lives, they carry within them the riddles and the molecules that leave you wondering. That carry enough strife and enough rhythm to embroil you in past feelings. To make you feel yourself an inner knowing of something that confounds you. It is an instrumentation of the body and a drive of the mind to understand those feelings. And the placement in between you are left to surmise the difference, and to sense yourselves in a place of connection or confusion, depending on where you have found your trust of self.

But in these times we ask you to be releasing that which has been known. To feel within the body, to acknowledge what was before. To say unto the self, yes, it has been done this way. To say into the self, I have felt myself this stirring and know of prior happenings and feel the same retort from her herself, the Earth when she is cognizant of shifting.

We say to give voice to these worries. To let them play upon your mind no more but, in the speaking, to release them. To let them be said aloud. To let them be in truth of the body and to recognize that they are real. That they are pregnant with the meaning of a time that was before and to accept them as what has been done, and to cherish them as lives of your own opportunity.

But then to recognize and to correlate in the mind these understandings, that you are of a time that is not like that.

> You are not surrendering, a victim to what
> is perpetrated in a violence of submission.
> You are sent here to gather an understanding
> of your own ascension. To be a witness to
> what is the greatest achievement of humanity
> to date. To sense within yourself you are a
> participant. That you wear within the body
> and can harness the greater consciousness
> which is emerging. That you are part of this,
> and it is welcomed.

We sustain you through all of this gathering. We sustain you all, every one. Each. You are held within our embrace. You were brought into a peaceful harmony with what is on the trajectory. You are brought into a sense of your own inhabitation of this time, to feel within the Earth a renewed vigor for expression. A renewed vigor for living, and to sense, in you, that you are part of this.

PART 9

Being the Light:
You Will Show the Way

The fact that you are reading this book means you are helping to lead humanity to a new future. Being a way-shower is about BEING. We are meant to feel and behave in accordance with a higher frequency, and that then impacts everyone around us.

We need to be aware enough to notice and witness the transformation that is happening. We will see the brighter world as we come into alignment with it. This may look like the same world you are already in, but somehow you are hitting all the green lights and avoiding the road closures. Things are more peaceful and joyful in your world, even though the chaos outside seems to be increasing. We will get to a place where we can walk among the craziness, but it won't drag us down.

Part of being a way-shower is learning to be vulnerable and open to open another, since trust is key to oneness. Trusting each other starts with trusting and accepting ourselves. When we truly accept ourselves, we will feel we have nothing to hide.

As way-showers, we have to be willing to be different. The Angels ask us to set down our traditional wisdom and the safety of our familiar expectations and dare to stand out.

DETAILS ABOUT HOW YOU'RE HELPING HUMANITY
June 3, 2022

Sometimes, you might feel like you don't belong, or you don't want to be here on Earth right now. It's understandable if you have felt that way, because we are in a time of deep healing and transformation where you are "savagely opening your own self". The wounds that have been buried in your own heart, and within all of humanity, are rising to the surface for release. But the Angels tell us that your true strength and purpose are hard for you to see. You are rising into the new frequency of the shift, and you are able to share and transmit this frequency to others simply by being. You will embody the contrast of what is possible and show the potential for change.

Channeled Message

You are necessary to the opening. You are a branch, a connection point upon the Earth that brings in light. You are suffering this feeling, as all transpires, that I am released from this. I am not belonging. I should not be here. But we say you are working proud, you are storming in the energy of new beginning.

You wear a curtain, folded, and it shades your perception, but what you are magnifies within the temperature of this elevation. You summon in an energy much like your own for processing the beginning.

An answer to the call of "who am I and what may I perform to go on living? Am I being what I came for? And we say, you are housing such an energy as transports you now into a subconscious state of offering. Revealing not your cowardice should you wish to leave, for it is needed in your understanding to comprehend the difficulty. To lead with your own eyes upon the Earth and feel its departure in your own skin. You are savagely opening your own self to be admired, forcing in these times of orchestration your own healing. It is an effort to be had by all who are awakening, this chance forthcoming.

But bridge the gap. You are having in your field a time of remembering, a time of passage stuck when all things moved in stagnant formation. And now all is light again by comparison. And you forecast this shadow now, and let the others feel their proximity to liberty. To feel what rises within the next generation of themselves.

They offer now no instance to comprehend your offering. They are standing next, as brothers and sisters shall, and feel nothing, and yet the effects are working. A sense of what is rising within them and a contrast to the levity on offer. How can one submerge the self and all its trappings long enough to show their origin mind that all things are different? That Earth is rising and they can take part. The instance of your impact, it gives such an opening to discern for themselves they are changing.

Now that what happens in their world cannot be foretold and they must listen for whisper of change around themselves. This is all the opening we need. A receptive touch and anchor you provide to that next step and instigation. We cannot meddle by their sides. We cannot stay and breathe and wait and then lullaby them into their next nature. No indeed, it takes a force of beginning, of having felt and contemplated the darkness, the dark opening within yourselves, and next the beginning.

The feeling of lightness and free thinking, the acceleration of your living, you feel this now as a frequency. A type of thinking, a way of being. A next to nothing and yet rising freely. Feeling all is lost, but no negativity. You are a wellspring from which to serve this energy. You have felt all things necessary to transmit a complacent aspect, an avoidant being, into their next opening.

You harbor a gift of longevity. Your features stand in every opening longer than you can understand. It is a resting of your feeling, of how you are perceived. Energetically you leave a trace with every coming, and stay, reside in their space of comprehension, so long as they need, to transpire a reflection upon themselves. To equate their life with your own and feel a difference forming, a separation in themselves.

They don't come to it naturally. They are determined to find no divergence, no shift. They are arriving much the same as they are. And this matters, this opening. It must residually leave its trace, or they won't feel it beginning. You are helping. Feel it not, but never worry; it is happening. As you unfold your life into every opening, you feel aligned, you are healing unwittingly.

Embrace your life and feel your presence felt by another. Feel your pockets emptying, and all substance of what was released, and know you feel nothing you can recall again. It is a space of difference. And in this template, you arrange your calling into an opening, and they will feel it. Do your necessary business. Be in life and living. You impart this gift by your presence, and we are grateful.

THE END OF ALONENESS
December 8, 2022

We are accustomed to living in separation and seeing things from our own perspective. Often, we feel safer staying hidden emotionally from each other. But now we are preparing to move into unity consciousness, where we will feel each other's feelings and understand things from the perspective of others. The Angels ask us to be the leaders who are willing to step forward, open our hearts and allow ourselves to be truly seen by others. There's no need to push or force this. All we need to do is let our light shine because it's joyful, and because we can.

Channeled Message

We wish to bring to you now our attention and focus. The help we are bringing is resounding in your conscious awareness. It filters, like smoke, through your hearing. You feel us present around yourselves. We are entering, communing daily. We are present everywhere - amongst yourselves, between.

We are nearing an entry point in which yourselves and ourselves will be intermixing. We will be feeling each other's entirety, the essence of ourselves, to be comprehending, upending your conscious presence as isolated selves. As soul-self suffering in the purgatory of aloneness. We are bringing to yourselves this aid in regrouping of your capacities to entrance you now with this next opening. The possibility, the positive reflection between yourselves of greater comprehending of feeling and alignment between one another, as you do with ourselves. This is what we are bringing.

This internal harmony that we are seeking to unfold, a resonance, a frequency which you can contain, we are bringing. We are aligning with yourselves, and imparting this resonant frequency of truth and harmony. A resonance and energy that vibrates within your being to illuminate the qualities of one another with more clarity. To draw you toward yourselves and that which you encounter; the frequency of open-mindedness, of readiness for hearing, for seeing.

There is reluctance of the embattled self for this bridging, and the desire to impart no worth on one another's stance. The desire for separateness must dissolve eventually. And we are coming between thee, among thee, within thee in an effort to resolve the internal struggle to stay apart.

There is within thee the desire to stay safe. To remain in your own energy. To see only what comes forth from your own bodies. To perceive the now as you are ready and as you entail it with your own energy. To perceive through the filter and causality which you project forth. But as you encounter now more equity amongst yourselves, more duration in the frequency which we are holding, the sense of now understanding another's perspective, though it may differ from your own, though it may present the self with confounding and juxtaposition and create disorientation among many.

We wish to begin this bridging now, as you are ready. To say for the instant, for the moment, we take on within thee a posture of importance, of nearing to those times when all things will be available to yourselves. And we must press on, press forward to create within thee the resources you require. The readiness that you are developing. And for those who are hearing, who are listening, who are readying themselves, who have an appetite within their own frequency for the growth that is required, for the perception that is unfolding, they will elevate their own causeway and drive forward the rest of humanity. For it is through the reaching of your own selves to and within and between your brethren that you create the opportunities that are our focus.

There must be leaders among humanity. There must be those who step forward now. Who are stepping. Who are readying themselves to bear witness to what is unfolding. To be the strength that is required. To hold the truth and present themselves in trust of one another. To be the one that trusts. To be the one that risks themselves in this journey. Who shows their form and their capacities with joyful abandon of the need for self-protection.

We ask the selves to hear this much; that you are now appointed within thee by your own selves to be the ones that stir the chorus of longing for connection. To be the ones that hold the foil that does warp and turn the perception and longing, and does draw apart each self from their ready neighbors. To be the one that sees this happening. Who conjoins with ourselves to receive the frequency we are offering, the trust. To draw out your honesty, your sense of what you are, and to share this now. To lead this next journey with your own hope in your heart that all will recover their memory and join you in the reflection of what is within us all, the spark of light we carry.

> We ask you now, absolve yourselves of guilt and trying, of efforting. Of making way and forcing. Do no such thing. For they are ways of being that create distance among yourselves. Be instead that light that shines to no one, to yourself alone, and let its passage and its glimmer draw them toward you. Be the one that shines your light because it's energy. Because you have it. Because you're near another flame and wish to find cohesion amongst yourselves. Because in sharing there is more joyfulness created.

Be the one that speaks their name in harmony with what is unfolding, regardless of what is found. Who speaks their name in trust that others will speak their energy in time. To come to mind in each circumstance as one who is ready to embrace what is found, not what is only unfolding. The piece that is now. Herald each instant as perfection, and show yourselves with honor to your own spoken energy.

Be the one that shines your light bravely. Who perceives what is now with an energy of acceptance and willingness. Be that one who rises to this energy and holds it higher than you are perceiving around yourselves. Let it filter and flow through your fingertips, always at the ready. Cast aside those judgments you've held over making which were imparting a darker cast, a shadow. Let flow the jubilation that you are seeking in the unity which is found, not through trying, but being and belonging. Through acceptance of what is now.

The guiding principle of being light is to shine brighter than the spark of energy from whence you came. To shine more brightly, to be the light more full, more energetic. For this, it takes only trust of one another. Of what human beings will become. Of the energy unfolding. To trust what is now, what is ready, what is present, and to be and allow for their eventuality. To be the witness who is caring.

It is this we are asking as you are listening. To hold yourselves apart now from what has been your entry. Apart now from what was your separation. And to be in oneness, in harmony, by sharing your trust and acceptance of one another's present reality and focus. To be and seek this alignment within yourselves will alter the nature of human consciousness. It will allow more to unfold from this beginning. We are trust. We resonate the frequency within yourselves. Align with us and feel the pull to oneness. We thank you.

YOU ARE THE WISDOM KEEPERS
February 24, 2023

We are in a unique time of healing, where all of our past lives and ancestral wounds are coming up for us to experience so that we can better understand ourselves. The work we do to heal now is crucially important, because as we heal ourselves, we heal humanity and create our new future. The healing work we do now prepares us so that when we face difficult times ahead, we will weather the storms from a frequency of peace. We are building skills which will carry us through what chaos may come. And by holding the light through those circumstances, we can help heal humanity.

Channeled Message

We wish to inform you of something that matters to you all. You are encountering yourself differently. The knowledge of what you are has been shaken and transformed. The essence of what you are, once dormant, has risen.

You are essentially your own in name and essence, but the fabric from whence you came is now different. Misunderstandings were rife and apparent through all that you perceived, and in these times coming, all these elements of your forbearers have been unbridled and released. You are now finding yourself in the midst of a torrent of awakening.

These essential times of focus, a point in your awakening, are a placement for the fervor of the breath that you are taking to let in the life that is transforming you. These times are essential to your knowledge of yourself.

Feel not the desperation that comes from all around you. The sense of yourself as being imposed upon. It is so different from how you were before. This is now an essential survey of your namesake. Of the sense of what you are. And in these tides and torrents there comes for you the greater surveillance of why you are here today. Feel in these times, though they are apparent in their hardships, a sense of grieving what was. Feel of the loss. Let the self linger no more in those dormancies, but let them rise. Let them become. Let them be claimed for this life. Let them move through you. Fear nothing. Fear nothing!

You are awakening, dears, farther than before. The self that you have not met is dawning, cresting just beyond the bridge of this time coming, and your releasing into these aches of transformation brings on a brighter sunrise to yourselves, just beyond the next morn.

Feel in this time of foreboding, the heavens above are pregnant with the effort of what is for you. There is much to be observed and learned from. The encounters for yourself and yourself alone are as meaningful as anything ever come from the heavens. To know that your transformation has the import of that full life-evolution that is moving through humanity. That you are but one point morphing, but you are the crux of this change as much as anyone. And what is before you now carries the weight of this entire generation. Thus, let it be not for nothing that you face your fear and move onward. That you let these times pull against you, buffeted and battered. Let them be what they are. Take them to heart.

Hear yourself a call triumphant into these embattled situations. Feel the self resonating to the tune of a higher calling. To be the one, that self, who bridges their own background, who senses what they are in the midst of such difficulties. Who can be themselves, wherever they are, in these times of disquiet.

To find that self in this difficulty is to be where you are in times coming, and to stay in the essence of your own tranquility. Know that you are able, capable, that you can. That you can sit in the midst of any turmoil and sense you are healing it, and yourself, and all that is around you simply by being.

To be of that self who has found their own, who has found their own in the midst of these times, is of a duration that lasts beyond this claiming. It stays with you ever more. It is a time of disquiet, this is certain. It is exemplary of what is to come. But in these times now, what you receive is simply for yourself alone, and it moves through you. In the times before you, what is known hereafter is that the chaos external is for everyone, and your peace internal is strengthened. And you are one who knows themselves despite the chaos. Who can be in the light from above when all else has failed. And can stand tall and true and be a lighthouse to show the way.

We beseech you to be attentive to what it is that moves before you. What it is that darkens your way. To let it come to be encountered. To let it stay as long as needed, till it rises. To let it be, in your estimation, simply a fragment of your old self that needs to feel itself surmised, understood, accepted and released.

To be that self who knows their own tranquility and peace, and can find this wherever you are. In these times before you, now and hereafter, the chaos external will provide a method by which humanity faces itself, and in this context you are the wisdom keepers who will bring the eternal to this realm of suffering, to stand tall and make peace when there is none to be felt.

YOU WILL GUIDE THEM HOME
September 29, 2023

When the flash of light comes, it will reach everywhere on Earth. It will help to lift us from our worries and our fears. The Angels say we will let go and find ourselves adrift, and our light will rise from within. The Angels will be there to help us, but not everyone will be ready. Those that are in resistance won't be able to see or feel the Angels, but they can see us, so the Angels ask us to help guide them home simply by being the light.

Channeled Message

We speak unto you, our fellow beings. We bring you harmony, peaceful beginnings. We bring you the next instantiation of love on Earth. We bring the tides of concern to a close. The familiar leanings of your own unsettled stewardship. And wish to draw you into the complacency of concern. Into a friendship with your own habitude. A sense of yourself as easy.

In terms of beginning, there is much to unfold. The unfurling comes upon you quickly. There is no instantiation on Earth that will find itself wanting of this Earthly shift. There is no place where hiding can be done. There is no spot to bury yourself into the slowness of avoidance. It is all and everywhere, a great upliftment. It is everywhere throughout the very subtle layers of herself, the Earth. Every aspect of your physiology will be affected. There is no spot, no endowment which has been given, which shall be overlooked.

Thus we say, rest easy in the knowing that you shall ride the wave of complacency to your concern. The feelings that rise now of unsettlement, that tore at your own gifting, that prevent you now from feeling ourselves, the lightness of our beings, that carry you down a river of thought that leads you far from here, the wary times of the prepared and foreseeing. We draw you from these thoughts and awarenessess into the place of now, where concern is disabled. Is let free to fly and be nowhere. To feel yourself an embodiment of pure light and love, a feeling everywhere.

You ask us, and it has been heard, how shall I feel this love, this light, when all around me does not reflect it? How shall I be the one to carry the torch of no concern when concern is all I have.

We feel your light within, despite your sorrow. We feel your love unburdening. As we speak these words, the light within thee rekindles. You are there, always, and we find you. Deeper. Deepening.

The time has come for upliftment. The unsettled state that you are in, the furrowed brow and hazarded carings will unleash, and you will find yourself adrift, a momentary sense of letting go. In this state you shall recognize yourself as rising, and shall become the light you are more full.

In this state, we welcome you with open arms, and you shall drift to us, uncaring and feeling the light of love within. Fear nothing. There is not a time now in your foreground where you shall be forgotten. There is no moment where you are left behind. Simply be in the becoming. You cannot hide. Your furrowed sorrows cannot lure you to a destiny of unsettlement and disparity from light and love. All are guided to the friendship with themselves, love and divine partnership on Earth. All are guided to the expression of this new Earth beginning.

Those are among yourselves, and there are many, who feel not the love as it is given, but feel in their own light a sense of loss and suffering. And these we guide you toward with opening, with awareness. The unsettlement drives them from the perception of the illumination that surrounds them and keeps them guarded in their sorrowful forms.

> We wish for them to see you, for they cannot see us. We wish for you to guide them home. We wish for you to set the template from your own heart of living in the solace of the divine. To become the light and share it broadly, for all who live are welcomed.

HOW YOU CAN LEAD THE WAY
March 15, 2024

We don't fully understand where we are headed in this great shift. The Angels tell us that we will be freed from our karma. We have had a piecemeal understanding of ourselves until now, accepting some parts of ourselves, but we have rejected, resisted or been oblivious to other parts. This is because we have been separated from our hearts and have lived in our heads. Now we need to bring our head and our heart back into balance. Our hearts can be recovered.

The Angels ask us to give up what we've known as wisdom and truth in our society, which has been head-based, and be willing to stand up for the new world that comes from the heart. We will become the way-showers.

Channeled Message

Beings of light, we find it necessary to begin speaking of these remembrances of another time, before this. Of things that separate you now and endure from before.

These are separations of the mind and heart. An embattled visage, you appear as one who contains both horizons in equality but cannot now navigate the pathway forward and in-between.

We herald a time of knowledge for which you are prepared, but know nothing of. A time of self, contained within a human body, but within the acceptance of all that is self. Within the construct of self as whole and complete. Where heart is known, and the self is absolved from all that is karmic and undesirable in the lengthening of the days of self-judgment.

We wish to align yourselves with the semblance of repetition, which we can bring to halt your understanding for the now moment of what you are, and drill into form a shape of surrender, of then and what was before. We bring to yourselves a whole encounter with your greater aspect.

We wish to abscond with the knowledge of what is now. With the shape of your own fire and fiery separation of the self that delves into division and contemplates the other. That is well-worn as a pathway to separation.

We wish to bridge that now with then and later, and to show yourself on the horizon a peak to transform where you are now. To let you be the bridge for your people. To let you hold and harbor the equality now. The parameters of self are made and understood. The whole that you are can harbor the self equally, in equal measure. Head and heart of equal share. Heart must be felt.

The horizon of humanity has been limited to a piecemeal surrender to wholeness, into the encapsulation of lifetimes. Each aspect of self, drawn into form only partially, taking on and heralding the full creation of what you are, but not as one. As many selves. As a disintegrated mention of each being you've become, all told as an assemblage of stories, but never made in one frame.

The separation that comes between you and all that you were, and all that you will become, is exemplified in the distancing that is measured between the being of love and the being of intelligence within you.

The separating forces that you bear, the equality cannot be revealed when the perspective of what is offered is held as truthful. When one who comes into the shape and form of this space is born into a knowledge of humanity that empties itself upon your plate for eating. To take on and imbibe the fullness of truth as it would be doled out. As it would be made by those who surrender before you to knowledge, the heart diminished. The heart unequal, the heart forgotten.

In these times for which you are made, the vehicle of your transport being the frame of your physicality, these embryonic forms, minuscule though they may be, can be stirred into presence. Can be brought to life again. Can be brought back from the brink of the heavens and asked and cajoled back into form.

In informing yourself with the new knowledge of your own grace, you can then bring wholeness to the many parts that you are. To the All that separates you now. To the many Beings you contain, all of which know each other not. Who hold themselves, jarred apart, like beings who are brethren, never to become solidly felt by one another. Not touching, not feeling. Only surrendered, in their own heart, to the experience of being equal when all else is absent. Thus, separating forces are amplified, and their hearts are measured in the teardrops of lack and nothing.

We say, as you are brought to the forefront, the precipice of the new beginning, the heart comes from its shadow and claims your light, and asks yourself to be the bridge for all who come later. Asks yourself to rise into the timeframe of the now and surrender your heart into the fold of acceptance. To be the brightness, the starlight, the unencumbered love of self that radiates from inside.

That gathers you up in wholeness, that includes the surrender to all beings you've been. To all ways you've shined. To be that self who comes in the time of surrender to self. The great ascension, the core of your wholeness, evolves into a form that bridges both the heart and the head, balanced equally in loving presence within the self, where all that you are is held in acceptance.

How, you might ask. How am I to be the bridge? How am I in lack or shadow? What is missing? What must I do? How must I form myself differently?

We say that imbalance, lack and suffering are intertwined most deeply into the nature of what it is to be human. There, ensconced in the legends that are told, in the shape, the full helping of privilege which you've been given, the plate full of knowledge you've been taught, to surrender this to the All and every. To make the self a blank slate of acceptance of what will be and become. To give up the handhold of the wisdom of your elders. To give up what is told to the self about what is proper, and postpone your entry into the ways that are laid by those who came before.

Accept the mission of one who travels differently. Of one who speaks, and forges with their words a pathway that is new and unknown. Think of the self, not as a being who lays upon the road once traveled before, but as one who encumbers themself as the way-shower. The way-maker.

Be unabashedly whole in the encounter of what is soul and self in the process. Be that self who rises to bridge the head and the heart, for all to follow.

OUR ROLE IN SHAPING THE NEW CONSCIOUSNESS
May 31, 2024

In this message, the Angels are changing our perspective on the shift. Our new reality isn't defined yet. It's not a known destination we are trying to get to. We are creating it, setting the template for what the human collective consciousness will become through our own healing journey.

Channeled Message

The trials and torments of where you are, of what is near, are temporary, and felt for now but not always. The substantial separation of yourselves from what is here shall come. And you shall know the divide, and call upon it with reverence, and know yourselves to have come this far. And say to yourselves that the time of separation is done. And we shall, as one, determine the new circumference of what is to become. We shall, united as one consciousness, awareness, as one soul speaks within itself, all shall hear the new frame of tomorrow is being born.

In the same sense, you are within your own separation. In the same sense, now is your time to come into wholeness. You are within a point of reference that is singular. That is one among many. Yet constrained within the bounds of what is your own understanding, your limitation harbors with it a sense of loneliness, of isolation.

And we say that this time is in training. These are moments within which you are endowed the sense of yourself as what is becoming. Where you are the one among the many who shall each endeavor to frame themselves differently. Who shall come into the horizon, into the precipice of tomorrow, as someone quite changed. Someone made ready. Someone who holds the greater power of their own endorsement within them. And these changes, made one by one, coalesce into a communal sharing of what is the great divide. The preparation, the preparation that you are making.

You are one and the same, the selfsame embodiment, that has always come, has always been shown into this Earth, as you have always been made. You are a soul which has been endowed with many of the same trials again, in remembering. The remembrance brought forward into tomorrow, all has come as before, and there has not been much change.

There has not been much significance in the drawings down of each specific or perpendicular incarnation. There have been replays, again and again, much the same. And these same memories made within the relationships, within the endeavors you have tried, there have been communal efforts and artifices which have been made available to yourself. These feelings that replay again and again, and are made to become something in each new frame.

And we say the time of separating from yourself is nearly made, is nearly done. Is nearly time for reflection, to pull apart all that has been before. To take it apart and to wish within it that you are made whole.

To take apart the wholeness for investigation, this has been the suggestive pose for many incarnations. To move away from the center. To distribute yourself among many lives, many incarnations, many moments. To take yourself apart into so many instantiations of what you are, and to look at yourself from every possible pose, and to wonder for yourself, how have you been made? Into what purpose shall you rise, to become whole again?

And in this distancing from what you are, what you know has become central to your existence. In this distancing from what you are, what you know has become the housing that is celebrated. It has been a processing by which you diagnose through the obstacles that are put before you. And as you come full circle in your comprehension, in this roundabout wheel of reincarnation, and you come into your wholeness, into your fullness, as the singular into the whole, into the plural, into the oneness, you are made and made again and reframed into the becoming of what is new.

So, as you journey within yourself to be made whole, all that is around you journeys through you, and comes forward onto the precipice of the new beginning. Thus, you are the predecessor of the great shift of humanity. You embody what is coming. You are the conveyor of this truth. You become what is to be. As you heal what is within you, so heals humanity. You lay the groundwork, the framework of the new becoming. You are what it shall be. The more you heal, therefore, the more you will be free.

And we say to focus upon, now, in your own moments of quiet solace, to focus upon the significance of your own role. Of your own purpose for becoming. To hold, within the family of humanity, the trial of becoming. And to become one who is among the many who shall then share the wealth of your own journey and draw into the fold of renewal those you shall meet. And shall bring all that is and has been known within the capacity of separation back into wholeness and unity.

This processing that you shall have done, which you shall meet, grows in its capacity to encompass the whole. For as you demonstrate within your own soul the substance of completion, this completion shall be met with outer resistance. And as this is relinquished, so the whole shall come to meet you.

The processing of your own experience must be held as significant. Must be held as important. Done for yourself and for the entirety of humanity. You are one cell within the body. One moment within all time. You are, however, not insignificant. For the whole cannot exist in completion without your journey. And your journey, as it comes and becomes into itself, savors the experience.

This explanation of what it is to travel through and beyond, to separate and renew yourself back into wholeness, becomes the historical artifact of the time that has been. Of the separating. And as you separate from these experiences, and come into renewal, a new timeframe is set that is modeled upon the ingenuity, the novelty, the discovery of your own renewal. Of your own experience. Of your own journey.

Each of these are compiled into the fabric of a new human mind. A new human method to interact. For within yourself you find the template of resistance fades as you come into wholeness. As you come into unity. As you come into to self-acceptance. And this template is then shared externally beyond the self, and is contagious within the fabric of all humankind.

And as the internal harmony is met with external resistance, healing happens. And humanity then models itself upon the journey that you are taking and comes into its own struggle, conveyance, resuscitation. The revisitation of all it has felt and done must come into the mind, into the timeframe of this experience. And all shall be revealed into love. Into the self-expression of the human consciousness as one of peaceful harmony. Resistance, resistance shall no longer be felt within your own self, your own soul, or within that of the whole, which shall be conquerable only by its own divinity.

The divinity of starlight that you carry is infectious, and as you draw this down into your own incarnation, it becomes something more than what moves through you. It becomes a contagion, a spreadable experience of life. A sense of what you are and what you do that can be held in the consciousness of another long enough for them to breathe your world, to taste your truth, and to want it within. The internal desire to rupture, to part from what has been the divide, the separation within their own hearts, is renewed.

And this awakening, begun so softly, so secretly, so quietly within you, becomes a wildfire of interpretation from one soul to the next, as each one begins to feel the concreteness of this reality dissipate and the suggestive layer of what is before you comes into a frame of your knowings.

We wish for you to take the template of your own healing, to know that your distance, your journey cannot be made and extinguished, no. It shall take its form, it shall take its place in all that you do. In all that you relinquish and lay down and step through and move beyond. It shall become the framework for humanity as it is made from within you.

Thus we say, you, your journey, is precious. Your journey is important. What you have made of yourself, through yourself, from yourself. Where you have found your truth within the soul's expression. What you have loved and brought into the physical. This dimensional aspect of yourself becomes concrete and contagious.

PART 10

Practical Steps:
Ideas to Navigate Radical Change

The Angels have often mentioned steps we should take to navigate this shift smoothly. Most of them are energetic. They understand that our energy creates our experience, so they remind us again and again to heal. When our energy is balanced and light, they tell us that we can be "above the fray", living next to the chaos but not experiencing it to the same degree.

Healing is the process of releasing our resistance to those parts of ourselves that are wounded, allowing them to be expressed, felt and integrated into our hearts through love. Much of what we are healing in this life is our childhood conditioning that we took on between pre-birth and age 7, and these wounds often become layered and more complicated as we get older. This is how we design our lives as a learning experience before we incarnate. We plan our experiences in our early years to lay in the "programming" for what we intended to work through or learn about ourselves through life. Unwinding and healing these issues is usually the work of a lifetime.

However, this time around is different. We are offered the chance to heal our karma and shift to a higher frequency while incarnated, so there is more support for healing ourselves on the planet, right now, than ever before.

Right now, we have the rare opportunity to access our entire akashic record of all our lives and all our wounds to heal as much as we possibly can. This is a first. In all our past human lives, we were only able to access those past lives we specially selected for ourselves as relevant to our planned experience. But this time the doors are wide open, and we can heal more deeply than ever before.

Healing takes enormous self-awareness, courage and time. It isn't easy, and we are meant to have help. I offer some free resources to help you, including a YouTube video where I share a very effective self-healing process that you are welcome to use. But if you are willing to dedicate the time and energy to take part in my Soul Convergence program, you will accelerate your own healing dramatically.

Soul Convergence is my deepest healing program, focused on helping you heal those core issues and traumas from early childhood and beyond. It can help you accomplish years of healing within just a few months. The goal is to balance your masculine and feminine energy, clear your connection, and open you to your own spiritual gifts. Soul Convergence is not an easy process, but the results are remarkable. I can think of no better investment that you could make than to invest in your own healing at this important time in our evolution.

Here is a link to the free self-healing method I described:

And here is where you can find more information about my Soul Convergence program:

Besides our internal work, there are also some tangible, physical steps we can take that might make our journey through this easier. The unravelling we've been experiencing since 2020 will intensify leading up to the flash of light, so this is the period of greatest concern. Banks will close, food, gas and other goods may be rationed, limited or scarce at times. They said shipping would be a catastrophic industry, and there will be conflict with China, where many of our goods come from. Electricity may be intermittent, and we won't have access to the internet or other means of communication at times. Water sources may be contaminated by increased flooding. It may get colder for a while. War will expand, and the US will no longer be united as it has been.

Over time, China will also fall into disarray. There may be foreign forces on US soil. It's going to be a little crazy for a while.

This all sounds terrible when you read it all at once. But the Angels have said that not everything happens everywhere, or at the same time. They have said it is still possible to thrive in this environment. It's important that we know these types of problems are likely to happen, and to take whatever steps are within our means to make this period easier for ourselves and those we love.

As we talk about these physical steps, it's very important to remember that we need to stay out of the frequency of fear. As we start to consider taking action, fear creeps in. It creates the feeling that we need to do something, but we aren't sure what we need to do. This is the perfect recipe for fear and anxiety, because it's impossible for us to anticipate or predict exactly what will happen or what we will need. We can end up in a negative, downward spiral of doing more and more, and finding that it never makes us feel any better.

It makes me think of a TV show I saw once about prepping, where a family had 25 years of freeze-dried meals stored, lived in an isolated, armed encampment in the desert and spent their weekends doing attack drills to defend against future invaders. It looked like a very unhappy existence. To be always living in fear of a future that feels dangerous and threatening robs the joy from today.

This is why I think we need to be exceptionally self-aware before we take any physical steps to prepare for the upcoming changes around us. Keep it as simple as you can; do only what you feel is necessary and no more. Make a list or a plan that is brief and achievable, finish the list, and then work on being disciplined enough to set it aside and put it out of your mind completely. If physical preparation puts you into fear it is counterproductive, because it dims your light. The brighter your light, the easier it will be for you to live in peace, regardless of what happens in the world.

That said, if you feel doing a few simple things would put you more at ease, here are some ideas for you. I am not a prepping expert, and I am not the best person to ask about these things, but these are some of the things I've done to make my life easier during the times we are in. You absolutely don't have to do all or any of these things if they don't feel supportive for you. Pick and choose, if you like, or skip this all together if that feels more in alignment with your energy.

Free Suggestions

Build community: The best suggestion I've heard from the Angels is one that costs nothing. They ask us to begin building community around us. It will be important during this time to get your needs met locally. What resources are there in your community? For example, if you have horses, who can you get hay from locally? Reach out to your neighbors around you and get to know them. What hobbies and skills do they have? Maybe someone loves to sew or knit. If clothes aren't being shipped from China anymore, that could be a useful skill.

If you can't start a garden yourself, look around you for a community garden, or any neighbors that have a veggie garden. Offer to help them with weeding or upkeep in exchange for some fresh veggies. If someone keeps chickens, offer to help in exchange for eggs. We recently hosted a neighborhood potluck. It was wonderful to get to know our neighbors better, and we discovered one of our neighbors keeps chickens! But they have so much shade in their yard that they can't grow veggies. We have a veggie garden, so we can help each other by trading veggies for eggs.

Develop useful skills: Another thing you can do now is develop skills that might be useful to others, such as sewing, or canning and preserving food. You could learn about foraging in your area, or about medicinal plants that grow near you. These are "lost skills" that could be helpful in a time where we are called to live more simply and locally for a time.

And don't forget the softer skills that are sometimes the most appreciated! When the power is out and boredom sets in, the person who knows how to sing or play the guitar becomes a pretty popular source of needed entertainment.

Inventory your tools: Take inventory of what useful tools you own. Think of household items such as sewing equipment or canning equipment, as well as outside tools like chainsaws and building tools. What tools do you own that other people might need? You may be able to help others by loaning them the tools they need when they can no longer be purchased as easily.

Low-Cost Suggestions

Food: If we look at other examples in our world, or in history, where people have gone through difficult times, we can learn a lot about how to help ourselves. When there has been rationing, the type of food that is available can be basic. Like the Angels have said – it's not that there won't be anything available, it will be that not everything is available.

You can supplement your diet very inexpensively with sprouts. You can grow sprouts anywhere, even in a dark, windowless kitchen. All it takes is some water, a container and some seeds, and you are ready to go. I typically use 1 tsp per batch, which I can eat in one day (I like sprouts). If you use 1 tsp of alfalfa or broccoli sprout seeds per day, one 16 oz bag will last a single person almost 6 months. It only takes 5 days for the sprouts to be ready to eat. You can sprout all kinds of things, including lentils and mung beans to make bean sprouts. This is an easy way to add wonderful, fresh nutrients to your diet. You can also trade the sprouts you grow for other goods or services.

I highly recommend buying a very large bag of rice and beans, or whatever staple foods you like best. A 50-pound bag of rice should be around 200 individual servings, and it has a very long shelf life. White rice stores better than brown rice. Think of this as emergency food, or a nice way to supplement whatever is available.

Water: It's a good idea to have a way to filter viruses from your water. Not many water filters eliminate viruses, so you need to check before you buy to make sure your filter has this capability. There are some great, inexpensive solutions. Check to see what is affordable. There are portable filters designed for travel or hiking that, at the time of this writing, you can find for around $20.

Light: How will you light your home if the power is out intermittently? Oil lamps are a great way to go. As I write this, you can get a new oil lamp for less than $15, or find one for even less at a thrift store. You can get paraffin lamp oil for around $25 per gallon. A gallon will give you around 250 hours of light. If you use it for 4 hours per day, that will last you 62 days in a row. Don't forget to get wicks.

If you want something easier, you can also get amazing rechargeable LED camping lanterns. I bought a small, lightweight camping lantern which will last for 200 hours on one charge. At the time of this writing, it costs around $65. There are many different makers, so please shop around.

Emergency Cooking: There are lots of options to consider for cooking. For an emergency, I like tiny, wood burning camping stoves, because they use twigs for fuel. I live in the pacific northwest where trees are plentiful, so twigs are everywhere. You can just gather a handful and off you go. Cruising the internet, I found a small wood burning camp stove which, at the time of this writing, is priced around $40. You may want to do a little research to find the best option for you.

Money: We are anticipating a banking crisis, and the banks may close. If you feel comfortable keeping some cash on hand, it's a great idea to do so. I think about the banking crisis in Lebanon as an example of what could happen. To keep their banks afloat, their government restricted how much people could withdraw. They allowed them enough to make do, but it wasn't enough to cover any emergencies or surprises.

Junk Silver: It doesn't hurt to have a little junk silver on hand. Junk silver is the term used to describe old coins that were made with real silver, such as pre-1965 US half dollars. These types of coins are relatively inexpensive and have inherent worth (unlike fiat currency) that can hopefully keep pace with inflation, but they are still inexpensive enough to be usable in trade for basic things if needed. You can get 90% silver dimes, quarters and dollars as well. They are for sale online on coin and bullion websites or in coin shops.

Books: Before I received these messages from the Angels, I often wondered why so many of us lightworkers were told to write books. In the age of video, it seemed a little antiquated. Now it makes sense. How will we fill those long evenings without power? Books! Plus, where will we get the information that we need if the internet is down for long periods of time? Head to a used bookstore and see what kinds of how-to guides interest you. And you might want to pick up some entertaining reads while you are there. Books on spiritual topics are a great idea to have. Books are also sharable and tradable with your neighbors and friends.

Staples: What are the products you use most? Make a list of the things that you use every day that you might run out of, or wear out, and get a few extra to have as a backstock if you can. Things on my list include lip balm, shampoo and conditioner, coffee, my favorite salad dressing, laundry detergent, socks and underwear, and an extra pair of my favorite slippers. Take a look around your house and see what you would prioritize that might not be as easily available in the future. You can easily go overboard here, so be disciplined and just get a few things you know you will use that will make you feel comfortable.

Container garden: Even if you don't have much space, it's often possible to tuck a few veggie plants into a flowerpot or planting bed. Years ago, I bought a cherry tomato plant at the grocery store on a whim and planted it in an empty corner of our small yard. I did nothing else – no fertilizer or special care. It grew into a huge bush and produced hundreds of tomatoes!

Replace disposable items with reusable: This is one of my favorite suggestions because it's great to do in any circumstances. If you use reusable things, you never run out and you create less trash. This is not only better for our environment, but it is also important in a time of rationed fuel when garbage pick-up may not be as regular as we are accustomed to. Plus, it will save you money in the long run. Easy and inexpensive trades are:

- paper towels for cloth wash rags

- dryer sheets for wool dryer balls

- plastic wrap and sandwich bags for reusable glass containers or mason jars and lids

- paper napkins for cloth napkins

Jar vacuum sealer: This is a miracle tool that you need to know about in a time when food may be less available and spoilage is a greater concern. Most bacteria require oxygen to grow, and a jar vacuum sealer removes oxygen from your mason jar food containers, extending the life of your food, including leftovers. You will be amazed at what it can do for your avocados.

You can buy electric ones for around $25 (at the time I'm writing this), which I would recommend if you don't have agile, strong hands. If you've got a little hand strength, you can go full-prepper mode and get a manual brake bleeder, which you can use with a Food Saver jar kit. A brake bleeder is an automotive tool, but it works great as a manual vacuum pump. You attach the Food Saver jar adaptor to your mason jar (with lid on), put the brake bleeder hose into the hole at the top of the jar adaptor, and pump away. The lid of your mason jar will pop and you are sealed. There are how-to videos on YouTube demonstrating how to do this.

You'll want to get plenty of mason jars (I like wide mouth) and extra lids! There was a major lid shortage in 2020, so it's good to plan in advance, if you plan to do this, and have plenty of lids on hand. The lids are reusable unless you are canning with them.

Laundry drying rack: You can get an inexpensive, freestanding drying rack that folds up and stores neatly next to your washing machine or in a closet. In the event of an extended power outage, you might be glad to have a place to easily dry hand-washed items. You might find it's a useful way to take care of your delicate items in general.

Higher Cost Solutions

Home garden: If you have any space at all, a home garden is a wonderful idea. Not only is it a potential ongoing source of variety for your diet, but working in the garden grounds your energy and can be a fun way to pass the time. Be very mindful to choose the sunniest space you have available, choose things to plant that will work in your climate, and follow the seed packet planting instructions carefully. If you have the space for a garden but not the time or physical ability to manage it, you may be able to work out a trade or partnership with someone who has plenty of energy but no space to grow in.

Some suggestions for things to grow that are easy and high yield would be bush beans, kale, lettuce, beets, cherry tomatoes, and, if you have a lot of space, winter squash. Winter squash is usually harvested in the fall and is great for over the winter because it can be stored without refrigeration for many months.

Power station: If you can afford it, a power station is an amazing thing to have. When we have an outage, my portable power station is the first thing I grab. A power station looks like a car battery with a handle on the top. On the side, it has standard outlets where you can plug in a lamp, or whatever you like. I used mine to watch a DVD during our last outage. It gives you a comforting feeling of things being normal.

There are ones that are portable and lightweight but less efficient. There are other brands which use different technology which are heavier and less portable, but last much longer. You can purchase power stations with portable solar panels so that you can recharge them, or you can charge them from a wall outlet when the power is on, and just have it ready for when the power goes out. I charged mine and forgot all about it for 2 years. Then the power went out, and I dug it out of the garage to find that it had held 100% of the charge. Pretty awesome.

There are lots of different sizes and options, and many excellent reviews on YouTube to help you choose one that is right for you.

Bidet toilet seat: Remember the toilet paper crisis of 2020? You can get an inexpensive, basic, no-power bidet toilet seat that attaches to your existing toilet. It will cut down on or eliminate most of your TP usage. As of this writing, I found one for around $89, and I think there may be others that are less. One big pack of TP is currently around $35, so you'll make up the cost of the bidet in no time.

Food Dehydrator: This is a great way to extend the life of your food and save leftovers or extra produce. It isn't great at preserving minerals, but it will make food shelf-stable for long periods of time. Store your dehydrated food in reusable mason jars (be sure to buy extra lids!) and use the jar vacuum sealer I mentioned above.

Messages With Guidance for Preparing

ASCENSION EVENTS COMING SOON!
July 18, 2021

In this message, the Angels are candid about some of the hardships we may

face during the shift, and ask us to take some precautions for our safety. We are asked to have a way to purify our water, a backstock of food and a plan of escape if we are in an area that might flood.

They also reassure us and ask us not to be afraid. They tell us the shift is an amazing opportunity for us and for humanity because we will evolve into a state of caring and kindness toward ourselves, each other and the planet.

Channeled Message

We say welcome, we are beginning. We have for your perusal our thoughts about your ascension. Your beginning understanding of your arrival here. Within time passing soon arrives the events of which we foretold.

<blockquote>
You are warned to bring to mind your own safety, to have prepared some route of escape from waters high, some preparation of foodstuffs and water clear,
</blockquote>

of having methods by which you can reveal yourself in safety. These are all necessary to have, and we wish it were not so, but have them you must.

You are embarking on a grand canal, a passage through time, a transference of your knowledge and attitudes about the self into another dimension of reality. Into one in which you are freed from some heaviness that does require your own resolve to transfer on. To become more than this one expression done. To have the chance to be and feel your own being rising within this construct now. It is possible, coming soon.

You are facing some times of hardships dears, and must know we are present for all you will go through. We will rise within each heart that does remain to endure the challenge of what is left behind.

<blockquote>
You will find yourselves becoming more human, more kind and caring, more enlivened by each other's need and presence. This caring presence you become does enliven all beings here that remain.
</blockquote>

There is the thought, we must endure, face on to create anew what was behind, what we have lost but not in that shadow still. Create anew from the heart that does evolve, of caring kindness for self and planet does become universally felt.

We instruct you how to belong in this new great becoming, how to bring your own heart forward into being as a light as you can hold within. More light is necessary dears, more light must evolve within the self. More openness to your own becoming, less resistance to that which you are. Fight it not, receive it well. You are transforming as we call, call you onward through the canal of which we spoke.

This transference, energetic transformation on the surface of the planet does call you onward within. We bring the chance, the opportunity to rise within, and it is a voyage held open in this change, held asunder for yourselves to pass beyond where you have been, to take on new beliefs and means of being. It is opening soon, the canal within. The space you inhabit, your own mind will open to receive it, and it will carry you forward through to another place where you can habituate yourselves to become more of what you are. This passage happens soon. The opening does call. We cannot determine; as time does pass, it will unveil.

Be prepared physically, mentally, emotionally for what will come. Do understand it as opportunity, dears, as the chance to move forward beyond where you have been. Locked in, you have felt, among the tensions and angers of your time. These will be amiss, no longer relevant. You will feel the opening of one upon another, the times do blend, and you are lifted in between, allowed to pass unharmed, envoyed into this new reality and way of being.

Fear not what comes. It will pass and soon, in this lifetime, and sooner still than you imagine, dears. Be in preparation, but have in your mind the target still of that where you will evolve to. Be in mind of chance, of peace, of having all asunder brought into one harmonic choice. Transference of your own feelings into the collective, feeling how you're supported by them now, sensing your belonging as you have not done before now. It is happening in this lifetime; soon, as you are understanding. Be prepared in the light for what will become. In fear at times, we know it's passage. Do not alarm the self. All will be well. You will arrive, we see it now. It will become, as we have said.

WEATHER, GROWING FOOD AND RATIONING
This message hasn't been shared on YouTube

March 31, 2024

The Angels ask us to be prepared for changes in climate, both hotter and much cooler, We may want to think about growing foods that can thrive in warmer or potentially freezing temperatures. They say that life will go on in many ways, and we will still have an economy and the ability to travel, although not as much as we do today. There may be rationing of things like food and fuel.

Channeled Message

You have, and will, find yourselves needing to provide more durable crops for winter circumstances, which can grow in warmer and cooler conditions, for both shall arrive. There will be extensively hotter times, and potentially much cooler times, coming. Extremes of temperature are arriving, and you must be prepared for this in the circumstances of your growing, of your growing concerns. You must have the potential for both arriving - both. Be primarily concerned with the topic of freezing cold. Freezing cold temperatures can be arriving. Wetness, dampness, flooding, darkness can all come irregularly in the climate. It is sure to arrive, arrival comes soon, and you will find yourself needing to provide more flexibility and endurance in your planting of vegetables, and your ability to adapt to what is happening in real-time extremes of volatility is a primary concern.

We wish to stress not all things will be gone. Certain things are available. Availability will be found, but not all things can be found. There will still be an economy. Certain things will still be provided. You will find yourself not entirely in hardship. The world will go on. There will be meetings, there will be flights and cars, to a lesser degree. But all things are as in rationing. Rationed availability and limitation, binding upon what is found now versus later. It will be controlled.

The centralization of foodstuffs, the provision, as is deemed necessary to distribute with equality. There is concern for all, and this is developing among yourselves a sense of yourselves as the guardians of all persons. All peoples shall be concerned in the regulation of foodstuff, the provisions of what is necessary to be shared equally among all persons. This is helpful in the development of a collective consciousness that is centered upon equality and the needs of the many. Do understand us? That all persons are involved in this issue.

The farming culture shall change with the arrival of the climate changes. There shall become more regulation as is seen necessary to inhibit the development of further degradation of the living environment. But these shall be met with great opposition, as is occurring now in many places. This is a fervor among some persons, some people for there is starvation and disagreement about how to proceed, and therefore confusion creates dissipation in the availability and protection production of foodstuffs.

"We say make way, for the sun shines in all contexts. There is always light upon the Earth, and you are this. The substance of what you are makes way from and through this Earth. In this context, you are spinning your own freedom from the substance of what is drawn to you." – the Angels, November 18, 2023

Final Thoughts

In every message from the Angels, they always speak from the perspective of love. This is the perspective that will guide us through the events of these times. Even though the details of the unwinding may be daunting, the Angels say that "what is to transpire need not break the rhythm of your own hearts. It need not dim the light of your own joy. You can rise above what is."

We are meant to witness the experiences we have during the shift, allow our feelings about them, and then focus our attention on what is emerging from every loss. Where is this new world taking us? Let that be our guiding perspective that sees us through heavy times, because even in the midst of the hardest losses there will be hope. Our new world will be rising in midst of the chaos, like a phoenix from the ashes. The Angels tell us that "the one justifies the next. That in the experience of the turmoil there is yet more to be found of your own soul. There is the freedom of your own feelings. The sensation of your own heart being met by one another."

The shift in consciousness is already happening, and as we move into higher and higher frequencies, we will be able to create our own experience of reality from that higher perspective. This is what we can look forward to. Increasingly, we will have the "ability to remain within the freedom of your own exuding nature. And within the space of your own happiness, you create a world without friction."

Blessings!

Anne Tucker

Made in United States
Orlando, FL
28 November 2024

54284927R00173